Enoch F. Burr

Ad Fidem

Or, Parish evidences of the Bible

Enoch F. Burr

Ad Fidem
Or, Parish evidences of the Bible

ISBN/EAN: 9783337097929

Printed in Europe, USA, Canada, Australia, Japan

Cover: Foto ©Lupo / pixelio.de

More available books at **www.hansebooks.com**

AD FIDEM;

OR

PARISH EVIDENCES

OF THE BIBLE.

BY

REV. E. F. BURR, D. D.,

AUTHOR OF "ECCE CŒLUM" AND "PATER MUNDI," AND LECTURER ON THE SCIENTIFIC EVIDENCES OF RELIGION IN AMHERST COLLEGE.

BOSTON:
NOYES, HOLMES, AND COMPANY,
No. 117 WASHINGTON STREET.
1871.

Entered according to Act of Congress, in the year 1871, by
NOYES, HOLMES, AND COMPANY,
in the Office of the Librarian of Congress, at Washington.

RIVERSIDE, CAMBRIDGE:
STEREOTYPED AND PRINTED BY
H. O. HOUGHTON AND COMPANY.

"TO CHRIST AND HIS CHURCH."

ECCE CŒLUM;

OR,

PARISH ASTRONOMY.

ELEVENTH EDITION.

SUPPLEMENTARY EXTRACTS.

From the Theological Eclectic, [Edited by Professor Day, Schaff, etc.]

"The style is remarkably graphic and elastic, **and the matter is so skilfully grouped and lucidly stated as to be level to all classes of readers**. The writer has a rare **gift at popularizing science**, and his book deserves the **wide welcome it has received.**"

From the New York Observer.

"We have **never** yet seen a volume **on Astronomy that seemed** to us to explain more intelligently, to ordinary minds, **the visible** phenomena of the heavenly bodies."

From the Congregationalist.

"We advise **all** our readers who **have not yet read the** book entitled 'Ecce Cœlum,' **to embrace their** earliest opportunity to do so,—a book which certainly has **been** surpassed by nothing of this general line, for many years, if ever. There is a grandeur of conception—an easy grasp **of** great facts—a clear apprehension **of** deep and subtle relations—a power to see, and make others see, the nature and extent of the heavenly movements, such as are altogether wonderful. Many works **have been written** from time to time to **popularize astronomy—to bring its great** leading features **within the compass of unscientific minds.** But we do not know of a work in which this has been so finely done as in 'Ecce Cœlum.' Six lectures of about an hour each, tell the story, and the reader feels, all the while, as if he were upon a triumphal march. He is upborne and sustained by his guide, so that he has no sense of labor and weariness on the journey. The last chapter, on 'The Author of Nature,' is a most worthy and fitting close to the book. We wish it could be read by that great host of so-called scientific men, who are delving away in the mines of nature, with thoughts and purposes materialistic and half atheistic. They need the tonic of such Christian thinking as this."

From Hours at Home.

"This little book, from the pen of Rev. E. F. Burr, D.D., has already been noticed extensively and pronounced a 'remarkable book' by our best critics. The author first delivered the substance of it to his own people in familiar lectures. It presents a clear and succinct resume of the sublime teachings of astronomy, especially as related to natural religion. The theme is an inspiring one, and the author is master of his subject, and handles it with rare tact, and succeeds as few men have ever done in giving an intelligent view of the wonders of astronomy, according to the latest researches and discoveries. It is indeed an eloquent and masterly production."

From Harper's Monthly.

"The title page of 'Ecce Cœlum' is the poorest page in the book. We have seen nothing since the days of Dr. Chalmer's Astronomical Discourses equal in their kind to these six simple lectures. By an imagination which is truly contagious the writer lifts us above the earth and causes us to wander for a time among the stars. The most abstruse truths he succeeds in translating into popular forms. Science is with him less a study than a poem, less a poem than a form of devotion. The writer who can convert the Calculus into a fairy story, as Dr. Burr has done, may fairly hope that no theme can thwart the solving power of his imagination. An enthusiast in science, he is also an earnest Christian at heart. He makes no attempt to reconcile science and religion, but writes as with a charming ignorance that any one had ever been so absurdly irrational as to imagine that they were ever at variance."

From the Evangelist.

"We have had many inquiries in regard to the authorship of Ecce Cœlum,' the volume noticed somewhat at length two weeks since. To save writing a number of letters, we may say here, that the Country Pastor, who is the author of these six Lectures on 'Parish Astronomy,' is the Rev. E. F. Burr, D.D., of Lyme, Ct. The book is a 16mo of about two hundred pages, but in that small compass it comprises the results of long study, and will be found as instructive as it is eloquent. The grandest truths are made level to the plainest understanding. We took it up, expecting little from its humble pretensions, but soon found that it was all compact with scientific knowledge, yet glowing with religious faith, and were not surprised that Dr. Bushnell should say he 'had not been so fascinated by any book for a long time — *never* by a book on that subject '— and that it had given him 'a better idea of astronomy than he ever got before from all other sources.' We don't know if they have many such ministers ' lying around ' in the country parishes of Connecticut, but if so it must be a remarkable State.

"While the impression of this fascinating volume is fresh in mind," etc.

From Rev. G. W. Andrews, D.D., President of Marietta College.

"The author has succeeded admirably in his attempt to present the great facts of Astronomical Science in such form as to be intelligible to those who have not gone through with a thorough mathematical training, and to make them intensely interesting to all classes of readers. I cannot express more strongly the interest the volume excited than by saying that I read through at once. I can hardly remember when I have done the same with another work."

From Rev. Edwin Hall, D.D., Professor in Auburn Theological Seminary

"I received it last night, and have read it through with intense interest and delight. It is a worthy book on a mighty theme. I wish it might be in every household, and read by everybody. And I am sure it will be read with admiration and wonder long after the author shall have been gathered to his fathers."

From Rev. Prof. E. W. Hooker, D. D.

"The book is an admirable argument from the discoveries of modern Astronomers, for the existence of God; and indirectly for the truth of the Gospel. It is an honor to his kindred, to the

Church and the place of his birth, and, above all, to Him whose gospel he preaches."

From an Obituary of Rev. S. L. Pomroy, D.D., late Secretary of the A. B. C. F. M.

"He was a man of extensive information, a ripe scholar, and he retained his scholarly habits and tastes to the last. A few weeks since he read 'Ecce Cœlum' with great pleasure and satisfaction. When he returned it he remarked, 'I have read it all twice, parts of it three times, and have noted down certain passages.' He was specially delighted with the arrangement of the work — the grouping of the different system so as to give us something like a comprehensive idea of the grand whole."

From the Congregational Quarterly.

That a Connecticut Pastor should be able in six lectures to his people to shed more light on this profound subject — to make it more simple and yet more grand, amazing, and impressive — than many of the great masters who have written before him is a matter of surprise. Yet this seems to be the generally conceded opinion of the press. We hear but one testimony concerning Ecce Cœlum. Any intelligent reader of it can understand what before has been only a mystery. It is worthy of the widest circulation.

From the Lawrence American.

There is not a dry page in these six lectures; but the glories of the skies are presented in a most enchanting manner, vivid, popular, grand, and glowing. Young and old should read it.

From The Christian Union.

We can commend this book in the heartiest manner. It is one of the noblest examples of the moral uses of astronomy that have appeared since CHALMER'S astronomical sermons. Besides their intrinsic merit, these lectures show what may be done by a quiet pastor of a village church for the instruction of his people. Every preacher has not the equipment required for a course of scientific lectures: but "where there is a will there is a way," and much more might be done than is done in broadening a pastor's literary education and in raising the literary tastes of his people.

A REMARKABLE BOOK.

ECCE CŒLUM;

OR,

PARISH ASTRONOMY.

BY REV. E. F. BURR, D.D.

1 vol. 16mo, 198 pp. Price, $1.25. New Edition. Sen' prepaid by mail on receipt of price.

NOYES, HOLMES & CO.

117 WASHINGTON STREET, BOSTON.

The Publishers request special attention to the following unsolicited testimonials, which have been received from sources worthy of regard.

From Rev. W. A. Stearns, D.D., LL.D., President of Amherst College.

"I have read it with great profit and admiration. It is a grand production,—very clear and satisfactory, scientifically considered; very exalted and exalting in spirit and manner; and exhibiting a wealth of appropriate emotion and expression which surprises me. May the life and health of the author be spared to show still further that God *is* and that His works are great, sought out of them that have pleasure therein."

From Rev. Horace Bushnell, D.D.

"I have not been so much fascinated by any book for a long time — *never* by a book on that particular subject. It is popularised in the form, yet not evaporated in the substance,— it tingles with life all through,— and the wonder is, that, casting off so much of the paraphernalia of science, and descending, for the most part, to common language, it brings out, not so much, but so much *more* of the meaning. I have gotten a better idea of Astron-

with these views, large space has been given to the earlier topics of the book.

The author by no means professes to give all that he considers available arguments in favor of the Bible. He only offers such specimens as he has happened thus far to present to his own people. He knows that these are only a few out of many equally sound. But he also knows that these few are abundantly sufficient to put every true inquirer in the way of a rational faith.

The reader may expect to find throughout the work an air of great confidence. He is invited to attribute this, not to a professional habit, but to the sincere conviction of one who in a course of rational inquiry has been "brought out into a wealthy place." Not only was Diderot right when he said, "No better lessons than those of the Bible can I teach my child;" not only was Franklin right when he said with dying lips, "Young man, my advice to you is that you cultivate an acquaintance with and a firm belief in the Holy Scriptures — this is your certain interest;" but even Descartes and Newton were right when they said, "No sciences are better attested than is the Religion of the Bible — not even the mathematical." Nay, One still more illustrious than these great scientists was right when He said, "If they hear not Moses and the Prophets, neither will they be persuaded though one rose from the dead." Whoever will take the trouble to go as far as the metaphysics of the senses or of geometry, can find that even their ultimate principles are assailed by no smaller objections and defended by no greater proofs than attach to the Biblical Religion. And yet he would not be the wisest of men who should decline to believe in an external world, or should allow himself to suspect that he is following "cunningly devised fables" while following the triumphant demonstrations of Newton and La Place.

Lyme, Connecticut.

CONTENTS.

I.	Various Opinions	1
II.	General Assent to **Fundamentals**	19
III.	A **Sad** Exception	35
IV.	A **Great Offer**	55
V.	Will You Accept?	71
VI.	First Condition — A Sincere Wish for Light	87
VII.	Second Condition — Using Present Light	107
VIII.	**Third** Condition — Patient Direct Seeking	123
IX.	Presumptions	145
X.	Three Prophecies	187
XI.	An Incredible Imposture	205
XII.	Ancient Wonders	223
XIII.	Modern Signs	249
XIV.	Nearing the Curtain	267
XV.	The Curtain rising	291
XVI.	Christian **Dynamics**	315

Part First.

I.

VARIOUS OPINIONS.

I. Various Opinions.

1. THE FACT . . . .
2. THE STUMBLING . . . . .
3. WHY NOT? . . . . . .

VÁRIOUS OPINIONS.

MY attention is called to the great Conflict of Religious Opinions.

I see it. I acknowledge and proclaim it. It is in the religious field very much as it is in all other fields of thought. The views that prevail in this place you will find refused in that other place to which a few hours' travel will bring you; and a few hours more will bring you where discredit is cast on the views of both. The views which you hold you will find either not held at all, or held with variations by almost every person of your acquaintance. You can hardly make an assertion so trifling or so great but some one is ready to dispute or qualify it. You can hardly start a question which is not answered with some show of candor in as many different ways as the nature of the case allows. Have you found a position that seems as impregnable as very mathematics? Be sure some one will make an attempt to dislodge you. Have you fallen on a doctrine all of whose features seem bright with intuitive certainty? Be sure you will not have far to go in order to find a man who will question your axiom, and even pronounce oracularly that what to you is intuitively true is to him intuitively false. Is the case plainly one of such vast consequence to be decided rightly that it seems as if all the passions and prejudices of inquirers would be awed into a hearty desire to find the truth, and all men come together in a blessed uniformity of decision? Do not flatter yourselves with such an idea. Against any Scripture you quote an antagonist will quote another; and what you feel it important for all the world to believe, he will claim it important for all the world to disbelieve.

A wondrous confusion of tongues! Languages and dialects and provincialisms and personal brogues of opinions almost as many as individual men — what a stupendous Babel! Its summit is above the clouds, and its base covers all the lands.

Some evils of this state of things are very apparent. These conflicting opinions cannot all be true. The doctrine or the contradiction of the doctrine must be false. A large part of mankind — and indeed every person to some extent — is holding error on what is confessedly the most important of all subjects; and, so far as conduct agrees with theory, is kicking against the pricks of the constitution and course of Nature. Of course, much hurt and lameness follow. And then we have time-consuming controversy. We have the disturbance and alienation of feeling which dispute is apt to occasion. Every good cause suffers much from that want of union in effort which comes from the division of good men into sects and schools. Could these men see eye to eye, and at the same time truly, it would give an unprecedented impulse to the best interests of the world. A year would hold up in its exultant hands such purple fruitage as centuries of separate and too often conflicting action have not been able to ripen. The compact army marching as one man gains victories impossible to many times its number of chaotic soldiers, whatever their individual zeal and strength.

A sense of the many evils flowing from the huge conflict of religious opinion has led, at times, to great effort for its removal. The evils are great. Their thorns are such as men can readily feel. And so immense war has been made on religious dissent. The press and the pulpit and the rostrum have been earnestly invoked. Eloquent pens have labored day and night to scatter the persuasions and demonstrations which should convince their own and succeeding times. Eloquent voices have busily journeyed about for the purpose of charming society into such oneness of faith as suited their own particular views. In other times and countries men were wont to seek the same end by the argument of the sword. Until quite recently all parties have deemed it right to use the civil power to enforce religious unity; and, through painful ages, laws, prisons, exiles, and even scaffolds, were everywhere invoked to side with argument in the effort to secure the much coveted monotony of creed. Our honored fathers fell into the fault of their times. It was an act of uniformity which expelled them from their English homes, and it was by an act of uniformity that themselves expelled from American homes their dissenting neighbors. But discussion and violence, and what some have thought still more effective, a persevering letting alone, have alike failed of their end. Religious opinion takes about as many forms as ever. If old differences are continually dying out, new ones are continually coming to life. If people think more alike in fundamentals than once, they are perhaps further apart than ever on things of minor consequence, and the points of divergence are more numerous. The habit of speculation which the increased means of information and intellectual culture have made quite general, has increased many fold those nicer distinctions between views which are so unnatural to a rude and material age. So here we are, some crying one thing and some another, like the people of Ephesus; society very much of a Babel of confused and contradicting statements; as much so, for aught we can see, as if the learned had never disputed, the powerful never persecuted, and the prudent never allowed the bones of contention to rest.

But some one may ask, Why dwell on these disagreeable and, to many, stumbling facts? I answer, For the purpose of showing that these many have not the reason to be stumbled which they are apt to suppose. Does it follow from the fact that there are many different opinions in religion that you are at liberty to content yourself with no opinion at all? Does it follow that because there are so many different views plausibly supported you may adopt the one most agreeable to your wishes? The doubting, the disputation, the contradiction, that entangle all moral themes — do these show that nothing can be known with certainty on such matters, at least by men of ordinary talents and opportunities? Do they show the Scriptures unworthy of their reputation as the illuminators of mankind; worse still that God is unreal, or unmindful of the wants of men, or unjust, or unlikely to hold us responsible for any views we may hold? Far from it. It is an evil, and, in some respects, a perplexing fact that you see, doubtless; but it authorizes no such dreary conclusions. A variety of things at once mortifying and salutary may be inferred, but not one of those at once mortifying and pernicious things which would set us floating about on the dangerous sea of life without the rudder and compass of any fixed principle.

Notice that many of the so-called opinions on religious subjects are *unreal*. In cases not a few, men do not fairly believe what they affirm. This may seem to some a harsh statement; but not to most of those who have had some experience in the ways of the world, and have thought somewhat on that experience. Love of dispute for its own sake will lead some to challenge the positions which they hear.

Personal ill-will often leads men to oppose the sentiments of their neighbors. Motives of interest bring many to espouse a side which has no hold upon their judgments. No one doubts that this justly describes the state of things in the political world; its truth there is matter of proverb. What is there to prevent a like state of things in the religious world? Here, too, happen what, to say the least, is much less common elsewhere; namely, frequent mistakes by the mind as to what itself actually pronounces. It thinks itself to believe what it does not. By wishing to have a certain opinion and by trying to have it, we may finally come to think it a matter of actual possession, when in fact our judgments are still unconvinced. What is called conversion often brings out strange confessions. It often confesses to insincerities and self-impositions in former reasonings, of which at the time the man was all unconscious. He now sees that he had no true faith in the errors he thought himself to honestly espouse. And like discoveries are often made by events other than conversion. Dying, for example, detects to many a conscience what it seems to have done to that of Voltaire, beliefs in God and religion which have remained latent to all but a Divine eye for many years. No juggling is more wonderful than that which the mind is prone to play upon itself. If therefore any are stumbled by seeing so wide a variety of conflicting statements in matters of religion, let them abate somewhat from their stumbling by considering that this variety is far from being as great as it is apt to seem; that a large part of the so-called opinions of the day are too hollow and unsubstantial to deserve the name.

"But, after all the abatement on this account which reason will allow, there must still remain a very considerable honest conflict of opinion on the subject of religion." I grant it: but turn your attention to another fact of much consequence. It is that by far the largest part of this honest remainder relates to *non-essentials*. The things which must be understood in order to salvation and high virtue can scarcely exceed half a dozen particulars — though many other things would, in the believing, contribute to the symmetry and completeness of the character. There are many Christian sects, each at issue on some points with every other; each sect has many members, nearly every one of whom has shades and modifications of sentiment peculiar to himself; and yet the points in dispute between Congregationalist and Congregationalist, and between Congregationalist and Methodist or Baptist or Episcopalian or others, are such that each one of us may retain his own view and still repent and believe and set forth a most exemplary example. Through Christendom fundamental differences of creed are the exception. They are an almost inappreciable part of the whole sum of religious differences about us. What makes such outcry and strife of dispute is chiefly the mint, anise, and cummin of theology rather than its paschal lamb. That din of assertion and contradiction which stumbles some is for the most part made by skirmishing among the outposts of doctrine rather than by battles around its very citadel. Those outposts might all be lost and yet that citadel remain safe, though not undisfigured. It is a great satisfaction to feel this. It does much to lift from our spirits the shadows cast by those clouds of theological dispute which are always hurrying so noisily across our sky. Who cannot now see between the clouds great permanent spaces of cheerful blue vault?

"But, after one has subtracted from conflicting opinions on religious subjects all that are unreal, and all that relate to minor matters, there still remain some that bear on the very heart and marrow of religion." I grant it. If there is any important doctrinal ground in the world, it has been torn by the iron heel of controversy. Men can be found to differ as to whether man is responsible to the Supreme Being for his conduct. Some may be seen asserting and some denying the necessity of repentance and faith to salvation. Here we find some to affirm and there some to deny that we depend for regeneration on the Holy Spirit. On the one hand is a defender and on the other hand an opposer of a Divine incarnation and atonement. In the view of some God has opened for incorrigible sinners a future world of supreme sorrow; others maintain the contrary. In the view of some the Bible and all the Bible is the inspired Word of God; others maintain the contrary. In the view of some there is a God; others maintain the contrary of even this. True is it that such differences are of no secondary importance. There is nothing serious and mighty in the whole universe if they are not so. If there are any things on which it is useful and essential to be rightly settled in judgment, we undoubtedly have them here. Yet here there is division. What shall be said to this? To the man who feels tempted to stumble at this most sad and disastrous fact what shall be argued? I cannot deny that it is a fact in many points of view most afflicting and appalling; that famine, earthquake, pestilence, and war are not half so grievous and desolating. But still there is less to be made of it, as a stone of stumbling and rock of offense in certain directions, than some are apt to imagine. Does the existence of these conflicts of opinion show them to be necessary? Does the fact that some people call in question the Newtonian system of astronomy show that nothing can be certainly known respecting its truth? Men of sense in some things have been known to dispute the fundamental principles of Geometry; — does this show that uncertainty inevitably rests on all the conclusions of Euclid? Men of genius in some things have questioned the existence of matter; — does this show that no one is entitled to speak with confidence of outstanding forests, cities, mountains, stars? Men have advocated with appearance of sincerity an unmitigated despotism; — does this show that no one knows liberty to be a good thing? Men have argued with apparent conviction that our society of separate properties and homes were better resolved into one unqualified communism; — does this show that no one knows the doctrine to be an unqualified abomination? And when people come forward to attack Theism and Christianity and the leading Scripture doctrines, must I straightway conclude that the whole subject is involved in such doubt as ordinary men at least are unable to resolve? Must I qualify every doctrine of my creed with a *Perhaps*, because somebody can be found uninstructed enough or hardy enough to set battle in array against it? Among men of character who have carefully studied the subject of religion there is probably no more conflict of opinion on its fundamental principles than there is among those who have well studied the natural and exact sciences on what is fundamentally true in them. More turn their attention to the one subject than to the others, and so we are to expect more instances of dissent in the first case as well as more instances of agreement; but I am inclined to think that in both cases the ratio of dissent to agreement is substantially the same. As no man allows himself to be troubled about his mathematics, or other science, because he finds people to disparage, to misunderstand, and to reject even its more important features; so let no one allow himself to be troubled about his religion because men here and there make light of, misconceive, and deny even its gravest doctrines.

So far from showing it to be impossible to reach any decisive knowledge of the truth of these doctrines, the conflict of opinion respecting them does not even show that there is any *difficulty* in reaching that knowledge. What is easier to be known than that human bodies are before me, and that a hewed and jointed framework of timber surrounds me? Yet intelligent men exist who would question even that. Is it hard to perceive that the laws of nature and the facts of physical science are something more than the relations of ideas? Yet able men will contradict you even there. Are you puzzled to pronounce upon the merits of agrarianism and tyranny? And yet you need not go half round the world to find a plenty of logicians to advocate to you these patent absurdities. That there is a God, that Jesus Christ is His Divine Son, that the Scriptures are His infallible word, that men are held to awful account at His bar for all their conduct, that there is no salvation for the sinner except on account of an atoning Calvary and through an influential faith wrought by a Divine Spirit — all these may be among the plainest truths in the world though they are spoken against. There is nothing in the fact that they are contradicted by some intelligent men which shows that they are more than a single remove from the region of axioms. Some believe that they are quite intuitions to an honest and renewed heart; and there is nothing in the clashing of opinion around them to show that they are not intuitions to everybody.

But there is a consideration still more fitted to relieve our minds in view of the various conflicting opinions on the more important points of religion. I have said that these differences do not show that we are necessarily shut up on those points to uncertainty. I have said that they do not even show that clearness and even certainty are not easily attainable. I now go still further and say that, notwithstanding all the observed variance and disputation, the most fundamental questions of religion may be truly and satisfactorily decided by the *weaker* class of minds. It is not for the few talented who can pass by a glance to the depths of abstruse subjects that I make this claim, but for the many also who swell the ranks of mediocrity and inferiority, down almost to where the light of reason altogether vanishes. It is not for the man of leisure who can devote all his time to investigation that I claim it, but for those also who must get their daily bread by the daily sweat of their faces. All such may, by a certain way which the Bible points out, surely and speedily answer for themselves all the grand questions of religion. See, I pray you, how all these doubters and disputants may come to entire and swift unanimity! All they have to do is, after such measure of ability as they have, to set themselves honestly and carefully to break off all known sin, and to seek and pray for light and goodness at the hands of at least a possible God. This, according to the Bible, will soon bring discovery of God, faith in Jesus, a renewed character, and light on all main religious questions. For the Bible plainly teaches, profusely and throughout, 'that God will be found of those who seek Him; that they who do His will shall know of the doctrine of Jesus, whether it be of God; that He now commands all men everywhere to repent without postponement; that divine power has given to penitents all things that pertain to life and godliness through the power of Him who has called them to glory and virtue.' You see how unreservedly the Bible puts itself in our hands. The least such statements can mean is that all true Christians have sufficient light on chief points of religious doctrine; and that every man may become a true Christian without any considerable delay. Let men faithfully try the way. It engages to scatter all their principal perplexities. It engages to give them at least the beginning of a true faith. If it does not, then they know that the Bible speaks false; that Jesus is no God manifest in the flesh, made no atonement, is an impostor; even that a good God does not exist to reward them who diligently seek Him; that men are entitled to withhold faith from all the leading and peculiar Christian doctrines. So, in either case, the main questions are settled — according to the Bible in the one case, against the Bible in the other. Behold the supreme way of investigation! Behold a way the humblest and most hindered can take — a way for any of your friends, if unhappily they need it, out of the painful tossings of unbelief into the repose of positive faith! Do not fail to have them use this *Calculus* of religion.

Am I somewhat timid in saying this — lest some one should take advice, and seek relief by this experimental method, and then decide against the Bible and its fundamental teachings? Do not think it. I am just as brave in giving this method to you as the Bible is in giving it to me. It boldly stakes itself upon it. There is not a quaver of misgiving in its stately voice as it deliberately faces all horizons and says in all tongues, Try it! It knows what the result will be. And *I* know. Faithfully tried, this method will not only answer the main religious questions for doubters, but will answer them as the Bible answers them. They will find a personal God. They will find a written revelation from Him. They will find in man an undone race, and in Jesus of Nazareth a Divine Saviour. They will find repentance and faith linking sinners to the redeeming cross — a repentance and faith whose source is divine as well as human. I promise you that they will. I promise them speedy faith in all these things; not faith at its very ripest and royalist, perhaps, especially at the beginning; but genuine faith, faith sufficient for practical guidance, a faith so strong that one can reasonably base on it the conduct of a lifetime and the destinies of an eternity.

And, generally, let none of you be stumbled at the profuse religious dissent that you meet with in the course of your hearing and reading. This dissent is according to the way of the world. It does not show that nothing can be known in religious matters. It does not even show that one may not know to perfect certainty and with profoundest ease. Nay, it does not even show that such entire and easy certainty is not within reach of the narrowest and most hindered minds. Many of these so-called opinions are unreal; many relate to secondary matters; and those which relate to things primary and essential are matched by an equal variety in regard to the surest and easiest matters of observation and science, and can demonstrably be reduced to a unit by a plain practical method which the Christian Scriptures furnish. So do not be disturbed. You have no occasion. No man should be stumbled at such things who believes in his senses, in his consciousness, and in that glorious round of the natural and exact sciences which crowns so imperially the present age.

II.

GENERAL ASSENT
TO
FUNDAMENTALS.

II. GENERAL ASSENT TO FUNDAMENTALS.

1. THE FACT 21
2. EXPLAINED 23
3. NEGLECTED 26
4. ENFORCED 28
5. RELATED TO OURSELVES 31

GENERAL ASSENT TO FUNDAMENTALS.

CERTAIN religious doctrines command the general assent of those to whom they have been submitted; especially of well-informed, thoughtful, moral men. Belief in a Supreme Being indefinitely superior to man and worthy of worship, has been substantially universal in all known nations and ages. The same is true of a belief in the fallen state of human nature, in its responsibleness, in the Divine placability, and in a future state of rewards and punishments. Further, the Scriptures of the Old and New Testament are almost universally received as a divine message wherever they can properly be said to be known; especially among cultivated and well-living men who have gone into a formal examination of their claims. And there is also a substantial agreement among such men as to what are the main teachings of the Scriptures. Not one in ten thousand but will say that they teach an intense sinfulness of men, the necessity of regeneration by a Divine power, an atonement for sin in the sufferings of Jesus Christ, and one way of appropriating that atonement by repentance and faith. The unbelief on these points is a mere nothing compared with the belief. The handful of objectors is lost amid the crowds of affirming Christendom.

No such concord can be found on other moral subjects. Ask for the history of human opinion on main points of government. Inquire what has been thought about health and the treatment of disease. Follow, if you can, the course of speculation on the subject of education — its principles and practice. Let the inquiry be extended to such matters as art and literature and eloquence; and see what views men have held as to what is beautiful and excellent in these fields. You shall not find a main principle in any of them, which, through all known nations and ages, has commanded substantially unanimous assent, even among scholarly and candid investigators of the first class. What is the best form of government, and how to best administer it; what is health and how to best maintain and recover it — take note how variously questions like these have been, and still are, answered by the best and most competent men; and find, if you can, a single leading principle, not proved by direct sensation, on which virtually the whole world, so far as the case has been fairly submitted to them, are agreed. But the moment we pass over to the religious field we find ourselves breathing an essentially new air. It is one general concord as to main underlying principles. Is there a God? Yes — says a chorus that is essentially and to all intents and purposes unbroken from all sorts of times and countries and persons. Are men responsible in a future state of rewards and punishments? No doubt — answer all the points of the compass in such a flood of sound as quite drowns out of account any few notes of dissent that rise here and there. What about the Bible; is it God's infallible message? Most certainly — comes swiftly back upon us for answer from Grecists and Romanists and Protestants and Moslems even; from all the countries and times to which the Book has been fully submitted; from all civilized and enlightened lands; from substantially all those men of culture and character in these lands who have given the subject anything that deserves to be called an examination. So of the main doctrines which the Bible adds to the religion of Nature. When we ask, Was God manifest in the flesh, Is man in a ruined state, Did Christ die for him, Must he be renewed by a divine agency to repentance and faith in order to be saved from sin and wretchedness beyond the grave? then all the great Christian Denominations, and substantially all scholarly examiners of the Bible, exclaim with one voice, Such most certainly is the teaching of the Scriptures.

I am disposed to lay stress on this grand and unwonted consent of human nature, and especially of well-ordered and cultured and examining human nature, to the fundamental doctrines of religion. It seems to me very suggestive. Are these cardinal things so at one with the general reason of the world and with the special reason of fair-minded and actually investigating scholars — or does some Supreme so interest Himself to make them stand out like huge sunlit promontories to the gaze of all who will open faithful eyes upon them? Depend upon it, there is something here worth attention. Depend upon it, the unbeliever will do nothing unreasonable if he opens widely his eyes. What means this giant consent whose long arms so cleanly sweep into its motherly bosom all sections of mankind, and the rarest fruits of character and culture from all lands and times? Say that it is something to be pondered. Even say that it is something fitted most admirably to encourage belief and discourage disbelief. Of course the verdict of a single man on any topic is not worth as much as that of many men equally dowered and empowered in every pertinent direction. Much less is the verdict of the single man worth as much as that of many men of greatly superior powers and opportunities; say, if you please, of all such men. Had we some secular question to decide in view of such unequally competing opinions we should make short work of it. Suppose a man of only moderate faculty at languages, and who has been studying the Greek language for only a few months, is puzzling out the meaning of a Greek sentence. Whatever decision he may reach will be of no weight compared with that of the great body of ripe and accomplished Greek scholars — fully studying and at last agreeing in their judgment. And how much weight should any common inquirer into religious doctrine allow his own independent verdict as against such a combination of numbers, genius, knowledge, and character as through the long ages sustain the chief doctrines of religion? Here is the safest verdict for him to take, save that of his own personal experience. He may by actually embracing the practice of religion subject these doctrines to the supreme test of experience. He will reach what has long been known under the name of *experimental* acquaintance with the truth. He will, as it were, sensationize God, His written message, and other main things; will feel their truth by a sort of delicate instinct — a thing as much better than dry logical inference as full day is better for business than stumbling dawn. But he needs to be put up to this high method of experience. He must be crowded toward it by some fact that impressively suggests the probability that the main facts assumed in a religious course are all real. This is done by the magnificent agreement that exists among men in relation to them. It says, Are all these persons mistaken? How happens it that mankind agree so unwontedly in accepting doctrines intrinsically disagreeable? How happens it that among competent, cultured, and well-deported men really examining these doctrines the verdict is substantially all one way? And as it queries I see its eye light up with a profound significance. I see its great hand beckoning toward the Religion which comes so splendidly recommended. Never was there such quantity and quality of certificate! Never such a profusion and glory of autographs on the back of any document! One sees endorsed and engrossed on some of the chief religious doctrines the great name of Mankind; on others the proud glittering names of all present and past civilized and enlightened nations under whose notice they have fully come; on others still, and indeed on all, virtually the sum total of the names that illuminate history, that grace the annals of learning and science and genius, that tell of extraordinary endowments or attainments or worth — just so far as they have submitted these doctrines to any suitable examination.

I say suitable examination. For I have a secret to tell you; yet not altogether a secret. Is not yon able and scholarly man an unbeliever? So it appears: but then you are to understand that this able man has never *examined* the Christian Evidences. I declare to you that he has never really applied himself to find out the facts in this case. You know that one may go through the form of investigation without having anything of the reality. But really, ten to one, this man has not undertaken even the form. A thousand to one, he has never spent on this Bible an hour of honest probing inquiry. He has investigated other things — the botany, the astronomy, the politics, the finance — and is, undoubtedly, in these matters a sagacious and well-informed man. But do not on this account think that he has well investigated religion also. Nothing of the sort. His thoughts have floated about the subject, more or less; he has, in a loose, hap-hazard way, heard and read more or less about it; but as to his having examined it in the manner of a candid scholar and with a care suited to its importance, he has done no such thing. He knows he has not. Put it to him — he knows he has not. The most he has done has been to casually touch the subject here and there; become acquainted with a few difficulties such as embarrass every subject with which man has to do; and, in sympathy with them, make a few points after the manner of an advocate. This is all. Witness a not inconsiderable experience and observation of my own. Witness, I think I may confidently say, the experience and observation of as many among you as have had any experience and observation at all in such matters. And together we will affirm that the great concord of which I have spoken, and to which I have called attention as a most suggestive and encouraging fact to the believer, is not at all discredited nor impaired by the cases of these able and scholarly unbelievers who somehow never turn their ability and scholarship in any reasonable and sufficient way toward religion.

Now these great principles to which men so testify as with one voice are evidently those which are to be chiefly insisted on by those believing in them. The ministers of religion should lay their chief stress here. Here should chief stress be laid by religious authors, and by all in fact who talk or think on religious subjects. It may be safely claimed in behalf of the evangelical ministry, that, as a body, they are in the habit of acting on this principle. In their preaching, they do dwell longest, most frequently, and most emphatically on these great and comparatively unchallenged fundamentals. They touch on almost all profitable topics. They have their words and even sermons on secondary points. But their strength is laid out on such main doctrines as we have been considering. It is not so among religious authors. There are probably many more books on the secondary matters which are in dispute between Christians than there are for the illustration and enforcement of those primary matters in which all agree. But it is in conversation and lectures and the transient literature of newspapers and pamphlets that the true principle is most strikingly violated. Here difference and contention rule the day. It is the doctrines on which capable and good men divide, rather than those on which they unite, which attract attention. The air is filled with the uproar of discordant sentiments, with the clash of buffeting and rebuffeting words — mostly on matters comparatively trifling. And when men, not practical believers, turn their attention to religion, they are very apt to follow this example and notice the topics of dissension rather than the topics of agreement. They call attention to how many creeds and Denominations there are. They mention the many disputing schools of theology. They instance, perhaps, scores of points on which not only different nations and times join issue, but also Christians. And sometimes they tell you the whole matter is confusion confounded. Nothing but war, war of breath and of types, listen and look where they will! So they infer severe things of religion; as if nothing can be certainly or probably known about it, and as if the thin foam of the sea is the sea itself. Is this as it should be? Why do not these men give most notice to those great primary matters which command almost universal assent? Instead of noting exclusively or chiefly the turmoil on the surface of the sea, is it not their duty to note most the profound quiet that reigns everywhere below in the clear gem-haunted depths? Yes; it is here men should chiefly look. Here they will find first things. These splendid, illustrious, deep-lying affirmations, over which the general assent of mankind is breathing its peaceful greetings, are comparatively everything. Our stumbled men should look through the contentious waves and spume of the surface to where, at the bottom, in clear water and unvexed repose, not sleep, but live and glow and burn the foundation-pearl and ruby and sapphire truths of religion. When they see the world torn with conflicting opinions, and even Christians differing and disputing, let them remember that this is only a partial view of the case; that there is a world of unity as well as of diversity, a world of consent as well as of dissent; and that those particulars of religious faith in which examining mankind, and especially the cultured and virtuous part of it, agree, are the cardinals and princes and kings of them all. Here is the true Ecumenical. Here is the real Concord of the Ages. Here is the very Choir whose members are kings, whose cathedral is the world, and whose anthem is the voice of many waters.

I join my voice to the great Concert of Faith. It is the voice of my instinct, of my need, of my heart, of my reason, as well as of my traditions. It came to my childhood from the fathers. From childhood onward it commended itself to my ear by certain delicate cadences and idioms of truth, better felt than expressed; by certain nameless proprieties and adaptations and verisimilitudes, which, like the summer dews, will not bear exposure but are none the less real for that; by certain subtle myriad harmonies with the Nature which I saw without me and the Nature which I felt within me, and of which I became aware as men become aware of a healthy atmosphere before it has been analyzed, or as some animals become aware of the presence of the food that is suited to them before they have tasted it. At a later period I tested it after the manner of the scholar. And I am glad to tell you my result. That voice of the fathers is a true voice. That voice of the fathers is a grand true voice. I freely adopt it as my own. I send it forth to you with full lungs. I declare to you that the ancient Jehovah is real. I declare to you that Jesus is His messenger Son. I declare to you that the Bible is His inspired Word; and that the system of belief known as the evangelical is a true summary of that Word. It is but a small contribution that I make to that sea of sound that dashes up from so many ages and nations, but it is a pleasure to make it. I make it with all my heart. I round out my voice and send it forth upon you to match the loudest of those choiring testimonies. Would that I could orb it out to embrace the whole world and distant ages!

I desire to believe that all of you who hear me have similar views and feelings. I feel that some of you have. In the great concert of faith you are prepared to join with voices as decisive and superb as any you can hear swelling forth from the lips of living men, or from the tombs of the faithful dead. Not that you have formally examined the Evidences after the manner of the schools. You know by a shorter argument. You know as men know the food, by trying it; as men know the sunlight, by seeing and enjoying with it. You silently feel in this Biblical Religion the natural counterpart to human nature and need. You almost unconsciously take into account the suggestive analogies that unite it at almost every point with the general system of the world, and divine what it would do for mankind if cordially and universally embraced. And so you firmly believe. Most warmly do I congratulate you. You have the repose of settled convictions.

You have the inspiration of immortal hopes. And your quiet present, with the rainbow on its horizon, is held in common with a great and goodly company. You have with you the wisest and best of mankind. With you are the conscientious livers. With you are the praying people. With you are the great examples of love and pity and helpfulness. With you are the lives heroic with self-denial, and the deaths triumphant with hope. With you are the exact students and scientists, just so far as they can be moved to turn learning and science in the direction of the Evidences. With you are the purest pleasures, the most salutary restraints and the best promptings. With you are all the healthy ages, all the healthy peoples, and all the healthy traditions. And with you are those who have been anointed with *sainthood* — a crystal elixir, scented as spring, whose drops, as they fall from golden cruse on transfigured heads, show in their clear deeps the image of God, and cast a rainbow of promise far away on the great To-Come.

So much I can say of some of you. If there are any of whom I cannot say it, or must say it with abated and impoverished language; if some of you cannot be parties to this great consent, or are backward in joining it, or cannot join it with that graceful freeness and momentum which you could desire, I am sorry for you. It is a great trouble. And I know how the trouble began. The fathers taught you as they did me. The same subtle ministries which drew my childhood faithward drew yours also. But your natural tastes ran against the Religion, you grew more and more reluctant to practice it, and you gradually allowed yourselves to hear many conflicting opinions without investigating any. This brought up the fogs upon you like an east wind. The things we do not like we are willing to have become doubtful, and what we are willing to have doubtful readily becomes so when we resign ourselves with uncritical ears to all manner of cavils and objections. You probably have heard unbelieving speakers. You probably have read unbelieving books and journals. You have heard and read without examining. This is how you gradually came to stand apart from the great consent. Here is the secret of the no-faith, or the weak faith, or the faith less pronounced than you could desire; and it gives a hint of the manner in which you must, if ever, find your way back to due faith. Among other things, you will have to take heed what you hear; and become slow to open your ears to everything men can be bold enough to speak to you, and your eyes to everything men can be bold enough to print for you. You will have to assure yourselves that it is not necessary for you to taste poisons freely and always in order to know them to be poisons, or to try on yourselves the points of the various weapons of death in order to know that they will kill. There is a better way.

III.
A SAD EXCEPTION.

III. A Sad Exception.

1. ILLUSTRATIONS 37
2. DOUBT ON FUNDAMENTALS 41
3. DOING NOTHING 42
4. DEPLORABLE 44

A SAD EXCEPTION.

WHEN we see a ship that has just finished its voyage lying all reposefully at anchor — the masts bare, the ropes and sails stored away, the sailors reclining at their ease along the decks — the sight does not strike us unfavorably. That ship has earned the right to rest. It has done its work; it has been for months battling with the winds and waves of the ocean on its appointed route of voyages; it has fought its way faithfully through to port with its cargo; and now it is every way fitting and graceful and honorable that the good ship should lie for a while at its ease in the quiet and sunny roadstead.

After the well-fought campaign, who blames the tired army that has gone into winter-quarters? There, day after day, flap the banners idly against the rooted flag-staffs; there, day after day, the white tents and the bronzed men lie along the same droning fields — eating, drinking, sleeping, talking, basking, resting; for weeks together those soldiers perform not a drill and fire not a musket. I say, who blames them? In their circumstances repose is becoming. They have been marching and watching and fighting and conquering for many months; they have faithfully and gloriously done the work they were set to do; and now they have a right to repose, and the country does not object to hear that all is quiet on the Potomac.

If during all his youth and maturity a man has exerted himself with spirit in some honorable and useful calling, duly taxing body and mind to fill to the best advantage the sphere in society assigned him, and now that he is old unbraces himself somewhat from the strife of life and betakes himself to the quiet arm-chair of rest and contemplation — are we disgusted, do we feel authorized to utter a single word of remonstrance? Far from it. It is all right, suitable, graceful, necessary, to unbend at the falling of the evening. From sunrise till now he has fulfilled Nature's law, and strenuously wrought; now that the shadows are settling on the fields it is his privilege to lay aside his tools, and enter his house, and sit down to rest. Let him take a Sabbath, as the Scriptural God is said to have done when He had finished His creating.

Repose after achievement — when the thing to be done is finished, or has been carried as far as the jaded powers will permit — will be justified on all hands. But what shall I say of repose before achievement — before the work is half done, before anything has been done, and while the laboring powers are altogether vigorous and even fresh?

We do not apply fair-sounding terms to that. No healthily constituted mind would think of calling such inaction fitting, graceful, honorable. Men wonder at the well-appointed ship that stays idly rocking in the harbor, season after season, without having made a single voyage. They wonder at the well-appointed army that, season after season, hugs the same quiet camp-ground without having seen a day of that actual service for the sake of which it was mustered. They wonder at the able-bodied and able-minded person who has yet his place to make in the world, but who lounges out his youth and lounges out his manhood without an attempt to turn himself to some account. — Is it far advanced day; and yet not a stroke of work done in the needy field, for my needy family, for my needy self; nothing but reclining, drowsing, basking in the sun, while other men in my circumstances have been hours abroad striving out a living; nothing but resting before work as wearied men are honorably wont to do after work? If I am without hands, if I am sick, if I am imprisoned, none shall blame me. Otherwise, next to none will justify me. It is idle, it is discreditable, it is matter for shame — to rest before doing anything. For rest after work none blush, nor have occasion to blush. It is the law of Nature. It as much belongs to the structure and scope of the scheme under which we live as does the coming of evening after day. But resting before working — who will venture to stand up for that? It shall be scouted. Hard things shall be said of it. No man shall do himself credit by practicing it or defending it.

Apply these illustrations to matters that most nearly concern us. To settle the main religious questions correctly and to act accordingly, is as much our human business as it is the business of a ship to make voyages, or of an army to fight battles. It is what we are made for, if we are made for anything. Nothing we do in this world is of any account in comparison with this, and only as it bears on this. It is an insult to the good sense of a man to suppose that he does not see this as soon as it is stated to him. It is an insult to the prudence of a man to suppose that he allows such a fact to slip out of his memory, or to remain uninfluential on his conduct.

Some persons refuse to commit such an imprudence. Finding themselves, somehow, without settled religious convictions on chief matters, they refuse to content themselves in such a state. They set themselves vigorously to work. They study to know the "place where light dwelleth." They inquire of all points of the compass. They labor at honesty of heart, labor at correct life, labor at prayer, labor along the lines of Nature, to see if God and Christ and a Written Revelation can be clearly and brightly known. Against natural sluggishness, against example, against the snares of pleasure and business and habit, they put themselves into harness and fight. Thus the voyaging ship buffets, in the way of its mission, the waves and winds of ocean: and thus, in the way of its mission, the army goes marching and sieging and battling. And, as the one after its voyaging is done rides quietly in port without blame and even with honor; and, as the other when its campaigning is done settles down properly and creditably in the profound repose of its winter-camp; so, if these men shall fairly win their way into clear and influential faith in the Biblical Religion, then it is a fitting and fair thing, to be censured by nobody, that they should dismiss their cares and struggles, and, as it were, ride peacefully in the secure port they have gained. They have done their work. The imperative examination is behind them. It is beautiful and fitting that a Sabbath should follow their working days. All the proprieties vote them a rest. The soul loosens its girdle, smooths out the care-wrinkles from its features, stretches itself at its ease in sheltered nook and warm sunshine of hopes and comforts and pleasant thoughts, perhaps quietly sings an accompaniment to its cheerful repose; and it is all right, suitable, just what was to have been expected and desired, just the thing to pronounce benedictions upon.

But then there is another class who insist on resting before working. As yet the great questions are unanswered by them. They are still in doubt over the Bible, over a Saviour, over a God even.

In their minds one giant interrogation point stands behind the whole Biblical theology. And yet they are doing nothing — never have been doing anything. They are riding at anchor. Sails are all laid away. Ship-forces are lying at their ease about the decks. Holiday sounds of song and light-hearted converse and conviviality occasionally float abroad from them. One would think they have nothing to do. Where are the anxious looks? Where is the eye of grave and vigilant resolution? Where are the solitary meditations, the careful readings, the anxious counsel-takings with wise and good men, the fervent prayers to the possible Light? Where are the contests with sluggishness, with trifles and affairs, with the strong example of a trifling and delaying world? Nothing of the sort is to be seen. Are they without the requisite faculties for thoroughly examining the Evidences? If so, we cannot blame them — we deplore them. Are they irresistibly kept from the use of faculties in themselves sufficient by the hamperings of circumstances? If so, we cannot blame their guilt; we can only lament their misfortune. But neither trouble exists. They have the same powers and circumstances as multitudes who have striven their way into great faith; nay, into faith of the most magnificent pattern. And yet here they are, dreamily lying at anchor, reposing at random as if in winter-quarters — perhaps shaking the air with holiday cheerfulness and merriment — life's great work still unbegun and all the powers for a sacred investigation still fresh within them. They are resting before they have done anything. They are reposing before achievement, instead of after. What shall we say to repose of this kind?

Let us say that it is unseasonable.

Repose is not to be objected to — only it must not be misplaced. Doing nothing when there is no need of rest, but, on the contrary, great need of prompt and vigorous labor, is vastly out of season. It is a discord. It mars the situation. It is an offense against symmetry and the essential nature of things. Have you really struggled so hard at the Evidences that there is no longer any struggling faculty left in you? You will hardly say this, my friend; for you will remember that your prayers, if real, have always been of the briefest and feeblest, your religious meditations only occasional and momentary, your actual efforts to test the Religion whose shadow covers half the world, a mere nothing. You and I both know it equally well — you have never taken any pains at this point at all proportioned to its consequence. And the time is urgent. Your great life-work is still entirely before you; and how much time you will have to do it in no tongue can tell. The Scripture, which, to say the least, has many looks of the true and divine about it, insists on your pushing your inquiries now. Men, experienced and enlightened in such matters, call to you and insist upon now. What observation of others has taught you, what experience with your own heart has taught you, is all against the plan of resting now and working by and by. You confess to your own hearts — how well do I know it — that, of all investigations, this of the Evidences deserves the first place. Everything seems to say, Attend at once to the great unsettled business; Up, weigh anchor and spread sails for the science of Religion; Up, break camp and march, through conflicts, if need be, to the repose of settled faith!

Let us say that it is dangerous.

It is, perhaps, as common for men to incur worldly disasters by not acting at all as by acting wrongly. Ignorance seems to have quite as many victims as error. Many a battle has been lost while commanders have doubted and hesitated — lost just as conclusively and fearfully as if by one atrocious error they had confidently plunged their armies into battle against all the principles of military science. Many a fortune has been sunk while the owner has leisurely hesitated over a safer investment — sunk just as totally and ruinously as if it had been embarked without misgiving in some frantic speculation. — See you this man in a flaming building! If he doubts the reality of the fire, and makes no examination to test the truth of those loud cries of alarm which are ringing without, and keeps his seat, though with misgiving; the raging element will soon cut off all avenues of escape, and consume him as mercilessly as if he had been madman enough to believe most firmly that he was in some gay banqueting hall, and that the fitful light which glared in at the windows was but from a hundred glancing festival lamps, and the din of firemen and the flames but from the mazy tread and music of the merry dancers. — See you this ship riding negligently in the outer circles of a mighty whirlpool! If the master doubts the Charybdis, and will not examine, but goes on allowing his ship to float about at its own idle will; the grasping vortex will soon fasten him in inexorable embrace, and, hurrying him round and round in swifter and swifter circles, will finally engulf him in its boiling center as mercilessly as if he had been insane enough to believe himself in safest waters, and the roar of the whirling currents but the hoarse joy of the kind sea-gods bearing him in their own fantastic way into his wished-for haven. According to the Scripture, you are this ship, O men of little or no faith, and yet floating about at your careless ease as if in some Golden Horn! According to the widely credited Scripture, all you have to do is to remain for a little in your present doubting and inactive state, and you will come to wreck as surely as if you had sailed for it with all sails spread and with aiming rudder.

Prudence does not object to repose as such; but it does object to repose on the brink of a precipice; does object to careless inaction while it is yet in doubt whether eternity is provided for. It may be there, it may be here — that astounding precipice which has no bottom: we may reach it to-morrow, we may reach it to-day; who knows, the fog about us is so thick, whether there is a single yard between us and it! But this we know, that a plausible Bible with a noble following, affirms that whoever goes plunging from that brink without a true faith had better never have been born. That fall shall take his life away. Is that a fate to be lightly risked, O thou lover of thine ease? Is Col de Viso a summit to throw one's self carelessly about upon in the dense fog, O madman of a traveler? Look down that depth and shudder! Look down that depth and beware! The situation is too dangerous for a careless and comfortable stupidity or light-headiness. Till you are safe be vigilant and laborious. When the crisis is passed, when you have no longer beneath you thousands of fathoms of sheer descent into which a single misstep may plunge you, then you may put yourself at your ease; but now — I am surprised at you! Was ever such unaccountable behavior on such dizzy and dusky brinks! Yes, there is one behavior that matches and surpasses it. It is that of the man who is careless and drowsy on possible Eternity-Brinks. By diligent effort what may he not gain — by a day's inaction what may he not lose! Who through that thick haze can see a day, or even an hour, or even a minute, in advance? Now is the time for anxiety, now is the time for careful stepping, now is the time to send voice of prayer for an extricating Arm among and across the eternities of joy and sorrow, which, he is told, are eagerly competing at his feet for the possession of him. When his efforts have proved successful, and light has broken in on his doubt; then let him praise and obey the God whom he has discovered, and ride at anchor; then let him praise and follow the Saviour whom he has reached, and spread out his tired forces in the repose of their winter-quarters. Now repose is safe. Till now it has been the hight of venturesome insanity.

Let us say that it is irrational.

Reason does not object to repose — but it does object to repose before anything has been done; does object to a careless sluggishness for which no good reason can be assigned. If the man were only able to say that he could not examine; if he were only able to say that the Biblical Religion is not worth examining; if he were only able to say that some future day would be better for the examination than the present; if he were only able to say that success would be no more favored by care and struggle than by careless inaction — then, undoubtedly, reason would say, Remain at your ease, Ride dreamily at your anchor still, Refuse to break up the easy negligence and comfort of your winter-quarters. But what man lacking faith can justify his supineness on any such ground? Not one, I verily believe; not one, even to himself. Compelled!— he knows better. Not worth the pains!— he knows better. To-morrow better than to-day!— he knows better. The chances no better for energy than for indolence!— he knows better. He knows more in such matters than he even gives himself credit for. Profoundly in his heart he knows that no good reason can possibly be given for droning away what may be his probation and chances for a happy immortality. No such reason was ever supposed to exist. What says our better judgment in such a case to the ship that sways idly at its anchor when, it may be, the kingdom of heaven is yet to be sailed for; to the army that sleeps and saunters and sings away the spring and summer in perpetual camp when, it may be, eternal life is yet to be campaigned for? It darts the word *irrational* at it like a javelin. It disowns all friendly relationship to such an unreasonable and hazardous repose. It rebukes it in the name of that Supreme Reason of which it tremblingly conceives — it rebukes it in the name of what men call science; in the name of that instinctive science which men call common sense.

It seems doubly irrational for men to carelessly allow themselves in dimness and uncertainty of religious views while they are, to a man, paying great attention to clear up other matters confessedly far less important. Why, yonder is a farmer who is taking vastly more pains to get a clear notion of the state of the market than he is to satisfy himself whether he has any God. Why, there is a tradesman who is putting forth more real effort to understand well a small invoice of goods than he ever used to understand whether Jesus was true Christ. Why, here is a scholar who sets himself with more faithfulness and heart to investigate a point of grammar, which most men cannot see at all, than he ever gave to inquiring whether the Bible is a Divine Book. Not a man of all those who make no effort to clear up these great matters to their doubting minds but is often found making great effort to enlighten his mind on subjects of far less consequence. You cannot but feel that this conduct is exceedingly unreasonable. No intelligent man can justify himself to his own judgment in making such a distinction as this between things secular and religious.

Let us say that it is unhappy.

We call it living at ease, but it is really living at misery. The doing nothing is really suffering much. Intelligent people cannot be in a state of inactive indecision in regard to questions of such enormous magnitude as the main religious, without falling prey to a subtle and omnipresent anxiety. They are haunted by fears of what may lurk behind that unlifted veil. — Behold that man at the junction of two roads! One is right and the other wrong, but which is right he cannot tell. Sometimes he thinks it this, sometimes that — sometimes he pro-

4

ceeds for a few moments in one direction, then he retraces his steps and proceeds for a few moments in the other. What shall he do? His face is a picture of indecision, of painful indecision — for is not the night coming on, and are there not alarming rumors abroad as to what that night contains? How can he be otherwise than anxious? Even were no element of danger supposed to exist in the case, such an unsettled state of mind is itself no small discomfort. To be like the ball beaten to and fro between two battledoors, or like the vane which trembles now to this point and now to that as the uncertain wind chances to blow, is necessarily a wearing uneasiness to natures built like ours. But danger is announced. Great danger is proclaimed. The Scriptures protest that faithless men are ruined men. The air is thick both with the signs of night and with rumors that the night will be fatal to all but the believing followers of Jesus. The man is conscious of never having done his duty by the Evidences; is conscious of not doing it now. He is riding at anchor when he should be sailing for light with all sails spread, and with wheel most bravely and watchfully handled. How can he feel quite safe? He does not. It is contrary to nature. It is contrary to your experience, my hearers — such of you as are so unfortunate as to have little or no faith, and no effort to have it. Do I not know your history just as well as if you had risen in your place and told it forth to me? It is a perpetual chafing. You are in a subtle ache and worry from morning to night. Beneath your smiles, beneath your cheerful and jocund words and port, lurks an apprehension, sometimes weak and sometimes strong, as to what the future may bring the neglectful unbeliever: and when you are specially thoughtful that apprehension swells into a great fear gnawing voraciously at the seat of life. No matter who denies it, you know that all these unbelievers so drowsily riding at anchor when they should be sailing, sailing with might and main toward the light, are like "the troubled sea that cannot rest." Have I not seen that sea wrinkling and wrinkling, waving and waving, tossing and tossing, as ever the night drew on — in growing sign of the great billows which the storm is preparing to lift?

Let us say that it is criminal.

If it be true that such conduct is unseasonable, unhappy, irrational, and dangerous, then the man who allows himself in it is a guilty man. What is reason good for, if not to try such questions as religion concerns itself with? Have we a right to expend all our inquisitiveness on least things? Are we at liberty to take our souls in our hands, and saunter along with half-shut eyes, where, at least, are glimmers of something like slippery ways and abysses which cannot be sounded? Oh, can we strain every faculty to solve the little riddles which science and business and pleasure offer, and still remain innocent when we refuse to put our thoughts faithfully to the mightiest problems of existence? It ought not to be hard to convict every man, with little or no faith and yet making no worthy effort for light, at the bar of his conscience of failing greatly in his duty to himself, to truth, and to the society which his example at once solicits and attacks. It is not hard. He stands self-convicted before a single word of reproof from without reaches him. He rides at anchor in defiance of his own conscience and of the sonorous proclamations of his own better judgment. While men bearing the names of prophets and apostles and Son of God are protesting — while a Christian land is raining objection from its whole sky — while libraries of helps to inquiry, the accumulation of ages and the legacy of unquestioned wise and good, are beckoning and saying, Up and inquire — while the very sun shines remonstrances with all his swarming rays as he hastens from rising to setting to open myriad graves and measure out our scanty days — from inmost self comes up a voice that refuses to be silenced, and says Amen to all the crowding remonstrances from without. Will he still wretchedly drowse? Will he allow day to melt into day, and year into year, and the end to draw nigh; and still do nothing? Will he still ride at anchor — just so unseasonably, unhappily, irrationally, dangerously, and contrary to all the habit and wisdom of his secular life? Ah, guilty man! How like to truth is the Christian philosophy of unbelief, Every one that doeth evil hateth the light, neither cometh to the light lest his deeds should be reproved. Shall I translate? Want of faith is due to sinning. Our minds are dark because they are guilty.

I know of no condition worse than that of the man who has little or no light on the supreme religious questions, and who at the same time is making no effort to come to the light. Better be without every outward possession. He is far more an object for pity than those on whom the tender-hearted are most apt to shed their tears and helps. If you have any tears to spare, O friends, shed them not on him who wants the daily bread and comfortable clothing, nor on him whom cureless disease has stretched in weakness and pain, nor on him who has been stript of kindred and friends till he looks the single forlorn tree of a desert plain. Rather reserve them for him who knows not whether he has a Revelation, or a Saviour, or a God — whether he has an immortal soul, a Divine Message to instruct it, a Divine Friend to redeem it, a Divine Spirit to renew it, and a Divine Heaven of glorious virtue and reward to be had after his brief day here is set. I say, reserve your tears for *him*. Beneath the heavens I know not so fit an object. He is such a Sad Exception to believing Christendom! -

IV.
A GREAT OFFER.

IV. A GREAT OFFER.

1. NATURE 57
2. APPLICATIONS 59
3. IMPLICATIONS 61
4. CONDITIONS 69

A GREAT OFFER.

GOOD AND UPRIGHT IS THE LORD; THEREFORE WILL HE TEACH SINNERS IN THE WAY.

BEHOLD a great offer made by the Scriptures to all whom it may concern! It at least amounts to this — if a man will only comply with certain reasonable conditions, God, in virtue of His goodness, will surely show him the course to be taken on all the graver matters of religion.

One desires to know clearly whether there is an Infinite God. The Scripture comes to that man and says, "God is good; and He has made provision to reveal Himself to you, if you will place yourself in a certain light and attitude." Another desires to know whether the Christian Religion is true. The Scripture comes to that man and says, "God is good; and He will surely show you that Jesus brings a divine message, if you will only betake yourself to a certain point of view." Still another desires to know whether certain great doctrines are really taught in the message; whether, for example, it teaches the desperate wickedness of all men in their natural condition, their exposure to ruin on account of that wickedness, a complete atonement freely offered to all, that atonement made personal and reformatory by repentance and faith in Jesus wrought in the heart by the Holy Ghost. The Scripture comes to that man and says, "God is good; and He will doubtless show you whether such great meanings as these are fairly written out in His Word, if you will trouble yourself to get into the state and circumstances suitable for such a disclosure." Still another desires to know how to apply the general maxims of duty furnished in the Bible to the finding of his own peculiar duties, especially of those great courses of duty which return with every day and spread themselves over a lifetime. The Scripture comes to that man and says, "God is good; and surely He will discover to you the sphere of duty to which you properly belong, and set up for you finger-posts of direction toward all its leading highways, if you will only fulfill certain reasonable preliminaries." And another still desires a knowledge even more distant and arduous, if possible, than either of these: desires to know how to bring his perverse nature to do the duty which he has discovered, how to keep the grace he has attained, how to master temptations, how to guard successfully against the main weaknesses and treacheries of his evil heart. The Scripture comes to that man also and says, "God is good; and He will surely teach you how to do the main practice as well as how to believe the main theory of religion; how to guide your bark according to compass and chart and star, after you have learned from them what course is desirable; only do you put yourself in communication with the teaching power after such suitable modes as God may choose to appoint you." In a word, whatever questions of the more important class in religion press on our attention, we are bidden to see in the goodness of God an assurance that He will help us to a solution of them, provided we are just to ourselves.

If any of you are perplexed and painfully tossed by unsettled questions of this nature, let me commend to you the gospel which lies enfolded in this offer. Here is comfort for you. Here is light ready to shine in on your darkness from afar. Only draw aside the heavy curtains, open the close-fitting shutters, and look upward. Perhaps at first it is only the silvery starlight which streams faintly into your eyes; but still wait and look. In time, the moon, crescent or full, shall mount your horizon and walk in brightness; bathing the night in its soft, pale flood; and revealing in dusky outline the mountain, the river, the forest, and all large features of the landscape. Still wait and look; and at last the day shall dawn, and the sun rise, and all the objects with which human life and labor are chiefly concerned stand out so distinctly in the golden beams that you can go forth to your duties among them with assured and rapid step. So says the offer. *Good and upright is the* **Lord;** *therefore will He teach sinners in the way.*

This offer implies several things. Let me interpret them to you in the light of the whole Bible.

First, it is very important that men understand their main path in religion.

I mean that the Scriptures teach so. There is abundant teaching to the contrary in the world; and you have only to open your ears, to hear from many quarters and in many shapes the sentiment that we need not perplex ourselves with religious matters of any kind; that neither our own private interests nor those of society at large, are any the more likely to suffer from our living along in careless neglect of all questions that may be started in respect to our religious relations. It has even been claimed that religious doubt is philosophy and the highest dignity of man. No trace of such views can be found in the Scriptures. With them our course as moral and religious beings is the most important, beyond comparison, of all the courses we pursue. Everything, according to them, hinges on our success in mainly finding and following a certain path. Certainly it was not from the Bible that men took the maxim that it matters not what a man believes if his conduct is right. The doctrine of the Bible is that the conduct cannot be right while the belief is fundamentally wrong; and that God insists on a leading soundness of religious opinions with as much firmness and penalty as He does on anything. Not inattention but inquiry, not ignorance but knowledge, not doubt but faith, is demanded under stress of all wondrous liabilities both of sorrow and of joy.

IMPLICATIONS. 61

We must believe in God; we must believe in Jesus Christ; we must believe in the Bible as the inspired record of His religion; we must know the Scripture way of salvation, with a variety of doctrines involved in it and essential to its practical power; we must know main points of duty and the art of self-government so as to fulfill them, or we perish. So the Scripture teaches, not once nor twice, but throughout; it is stated or assumed everywhere; it is ingrained into warp and woof of the Record, and we cannot by any skill pick out the disagreeable pattern without resolving the whole texture into shreds.

Their path in religion — what they are to believe and what they are to do in that field — is something, secondly, which men will never sufficiently learn of themselves.

I mean that so the Scripture teaches. We may set ourselves down to some worldly art or science, and acquire as much knowledge about it as will amply suffice for the wants of our position; and all, it may be, by the unassisted action of our own intelligent powers. With skillful human teachers at our side, we are able to do the same thing with greater ease and rapidity. By these merely human faculties, our own and those of other men, we may learn the geography or the geology or the astronomy to any extent which our post in life may require — at least we are not informed that any supernatural assistance is necessarily involved in such an achievement. And we are not authorized to say that there are not many things in religious science and in the art of living righteously, to know which only the common powers of men are required. But there is this peculiarity about the sphere of religious knowledge — if we are to credit the Scriptures — that no man will ever explore it sufficiently for his necessity by mere force of such powers as belong to men. He can and will know very many things here as elsewhere by simply asking his own thoughts and those of his fellows. But he will never in this way come to know his path in religion sufficiently well to secure the general safety and success of his journey. He may possess a profound understanding. He may be equipped with the finest helps of culture and leisure. A written Revelation may spread out its abiding pages side by side with the parables of Nature for his unlimited study. Books of the wise and good, living voices eloquently and sagely discoursing their own sure knowledge and experience, may gather about him with their treasures and do their best to communicate the abundant hoards. But it will be in vain. He cannot be enriched in this way. After all he is but a fairly chiseled and polished statue around which its friends may twine a few flowers and hang a few fruits, but which has no power to snuff the sweetness of the vase of precious aromatics which one beseechingly and patiently holds under its marble nostrils, or to taste the sweetness of the jeweled goblet of milk and honey which another presses to its marble lips. The stiff stone must become flesh and blood. The classic form must have a soul created under its ribs of death. Not till this is done can it really appropriate and use the luxuries offered it. And yet, perhaps, we ought not to compare any man with perfectly helpless stone, though hewn into the shape of an Apollo. Rather let that strong and cultured mind, to which all choice circumstances are endeavoring to minister the various particulars of fundamental religious knowledge, be the giant Patagonian, practiced in the conflicts of the chase and battle, around whom in his native wilds gather the missionaries of civilization, with hands loaded with the best wares of the best countries. They hold up to his acceptance strong and rich textures, and tell him how they will protect him from summer's heat and winter's cold. They put under his eye the seeds and implements of agriculture, and tell him how they may make his fields smile with plenty. Here are epitomes of all the useful arts; here are handicrafts, sciences, accomplishments without number; and they tell him how with these to fill his wilderness with gardens and palaces. And what comes of all these proffers and explanations? He takes a few nails to point his arrows and turns away. He has no patience, if faculty, to master the strange ideas. He has no taste for new modes of life. Nature and habit and tradition, all conspire to blind him to the nature and value of the blessings pressed upon him, and to send him back to the almost unmitigated wretchedness of his hovel and his desert. Just so, according to the Bible, there is a native wildness in every man, opposing the richest offers of religious truth; and as long as he has only men like himself to come around him and recommend to him, however earnestly and eloquently, the great fundamentals of sacred doctrine, they are sure to be misapprehended and rejected. He will receive some things, perhaps, but he will refuse more and greater. He will fail to grasp the proffered solutions to life's greatest questions. His true course as a moral and religious being will fail to be substantially apprehended. If there is any man whose views on all leading questions of religion are correct, it is surely not his own depth of understanding and skill at argument, nor the wise instructions of human teachers, living or dead, to which he owes the blessing. As says the Scripture, The natural man receiveth not the things of the Spirit of God, for they are foolishness to him; neither can he know them because they are spiritually discerned.

But, thirdly, what man certainly never will know by any merely human teaching he can know by a Divine.

I mean that so the Scripture teaches. The God of the Bible is both omniscient and almighty. He can reveal Himself to the man who has no God. He can reveal Jesus Christ to the man who has no

Saviour. He can so write His name on the Scriptures before the infidel that he can be infidel no longer. The plan of salvation, and all its great depending doctrines, He can make clear as noonday to the dullest mind. The sphere of duty belonging to each person, the great courses of religious practice into which our affections and energies should pour themselves, are all known to the Infinite, and He can easily place them before the mind in so strong a light that ignorance shall not be possible. How well can He who knows all things and made all men bring truth home to error-stricken souls through a hundred avenues! How mightily could He, should He once set himself to do it, argue down all the difficulties of weakness, and all the objections and cavils of unbelief! What darkness could abide such beams as He could rain into it in whom is no darkness at all — what heresy hold its ground against the light of His countenance! Men born blind and living in blindness to old age; men with eyes swathed in hundred folds of traditional prejudice, and immured in windowless dungeons of error by sin and miseducation — no doubt the Mighty One could find out some method of bringing the bright day home to the most hapless of them all. Man cannot do it for himself, man cannot do it for his fellow, but the God of the Bible is one so grandly equipped with knowledge and power that He can do it for all men and against all hindrances.

And, fourthly, it is equally true that the God who can thus teach sinners the way, can consistently teach it, under certain conditions.

I mean that so the Scripture teaches. We are told that there are very many things which God can do which He cannot do righteously. But we are also told that the discovery to benighted men of their main path in religion is not one of these things. God is left at full liberty by the circumstances of His government to teach us what we so much need to know; only we must assume certain positions suitable for receiving the blessing. Only we meet the condition, and the way is open for God to pluck hand out of bosom in our behalf, and put to flight the ruler of the darkness of this world — whether he dwell in us in the form of atheism, or deism, or heresy, or ignorance of leading duties and of the mode of compelling our deceitful and resisting nature into a permanent performance of them. He will be hampered by no necessity of general laws. The nature of free moral agents will not veto His activity. The conflict of the greater good with the less will not compel Him to leave us to our darkness. It will harmonize perfectly with all great interests of His government to turn our doubts into faith, our errors into truth our byways into highways that lead straightly to the City. Fulfill certain reasonable conditions, O ye who are perplexed with the great problems of life and are beaten about by many a wind of doctrine — and surely then the way of the Lord is prepared so that He can come to you through the night and over the water. O ye who find the Gospel a sealed book, to whom all chapters are parables and all doctrines mysteries — only be just to yourselves, and God can consistently come to your help with the sun in His right hand. And ye who see not the evil of sin, nor the preciousness of Christ, nor the danger of the impenitent soul; ye who see not the wisdom of the Gospel, nor the justice of Providence; ye who know not what manner of spirit ye are of, whether earthly or heavenly; ye who think yourselves inquiring after duty and unable to find it; ye whom the craftiness of a heart mysteriously wicked is so continually circumventing and assaulting into sin, and to whom no methods of successful resistance present themselves save in most doubtful outline — be of good courage and do your part, and there will no longer be any incompatibility between your relief and the interests of the Divine Kingdom. Above all, O ye whose trouble is greatest of all — since ye are they who scarcely know what to believe, though it be a Bible or a Saviour or even a God that asks for faith — to you, most hapless of all, I specially say in behalf of the Bible that spares not its promises, Be of good courage, and do a certain reasonable part that belongs to you, and a way shall be prepared for you through the deep; even though, in order to prepare it, the Omnipotent must smite the waters with His own purple mantle.

If men are naturally ignorant of their path in religion; if it is of incalculable importance to them to know it; if they certainly never will know it merely through themselves and human power; if nevertheless God can teach it to them, and do it without violating the proprieties of His position, provided they will supply certain reasonable circumstances under which the great instruction may proceed; then it follows from the goodness of God — I speak simply as an interpreter of the Scriptures — that when these circumstances are supplied He will come forth from the hiding-places of His bright strength, to quicken our dull understandings, resolve our problems, give us chart and compass for a wise sailing over life's main. He is more earnest for us to know the way than we can be. He loves our safety, our peace of mind, our usefulness, our abundant entrance into the everlasting kingdom infinitely more than we can do. So, as soon as we have cast up the highway and gathered out the stones, He will begin to travel toward us in the greatness of His strength — the dark growing whiter and whiter with every dazzling though distant step of the King whose twin names are Light and Love — and at last, in the time He sees best for us, He will arrive, bringing with Him the day. Then the cloud will be gone from the main theory and practice of religion.

The dusky mantle which muffled the Evidences so heavily will interpose its envious folds no longer. The inspiration, the atonement, the probation, the plan of salvation — all the facts and doctrines with which our leading interests as moral beings are bound up — will uncover their faces and fix upon us starry eyes. So I read the promise. And I am sure that I read it correctly. It is stated and implied too generously to allow of mistake.

But what are the *conditions* of the Offer? I come to utter them. I utter them to you distinctly, emphatically, and joyfully; as being the full Scripture way to main light, whether on the theory or the practice of religion.

1. We must sincerely desire the light.
2. We must use the light we already have.
3. We must patiently seek light in the double way of prayer and rational inquiry.

These are the Biblical conditions of a plain path. I will not now cite particular passages in proof. Let me rather bring you the testimony of a long familiarity with the Scriptures. Let me appeal to your general sense of their scope and spirit. Let me appeal to all you careless and doubting readers of them — when you have ceased to be careless, and when God's ostensible message to men has been as faithfully examined as its pretensions merit. Be assured you have before you the great Bible secret of How to believe.

Try it, and see whether it is good for anything —

all ye who in any degree or from any cause are deficient in faith. Here is a decisive opportunity for settling all the great questions that trouble you. The Scriptures have committed themselves. See whether they will be as good as their word. See whether a God, a Jesus, and a Bible will brighten on your sight as you honestly desire, and patiently pray, and conscientiously do, and faithfully examine. I am a seer. I take it upon me to predict what the result will be. And I stand here, with voice as steady and assured as ever went forth convincingly over assembly, to foretell, not merely a result to your inquiry, not merely settled convictions one way or another, but a result and convictions on the side of the Biblical Religion — a result about as ample and brilliant as you may choose to have. Make trial. I declare to you that there never was a person who fulfilled those Three Conditions but came at last to know all things pertaining to life and godliness through the power of Him who has called us to glory and virtue. I declare to you that never, as long as the world stands, will any religiously benighted soul thus patiently desire and pray and labor for the break of day, without at last seeing the eyelids of the morn unsealed, and the painfully dusky east gradually redden into the sun.

V.
WILL YOU ACCEPT?

V. WILL YOU ACCEPT?

1. RESUMÉ 73
2. WILL YOU ACCEPT? 78
3. PRAY DO 79
4. I WILL 85

WILL YOU ACCEPT?

WHAT IS TRUTH? We are told that Pilate put this question to Jesus. It was the natural expression of doubt as to what could be considered true in religion. "You speak of truth. And you say, To this end was I born, and for this cause came I into the world, that I should bear witness to the truth: every one that is of the truth heareth my voice. What *is* truth? I was born to the religious opinions of Pagan Rome. I have been educated in the schools of the Greeks, with their many conflicting religious speculations. I now govern a people having views on such subjects differing from all others. You are a new teacher of religion, and tell of the new system of truth which you came to unfold. Among these many mutually conflicting systems which is the true?"

This inquiry has an air of investigation. It is just such as a sincere man always proposes to himself when he sits down to the solution of some high problem. Pilate did well in making it. He would have done still better if he had coupled with it the candid investigation of which it was the fitting herald, and that special plan of investigation of which Jesus could have told him. I undertake to say that this would have solved his doubts. He would have come to see, in the Hebrew Jehovah, the one living and true God. He would have come to see, in the persecuted Jesus, God's messenger and Son. He would have come to see, in the sacred writings of the Jews, God's own message. He would have come to see that diversity of religions no more proves that there is no ascertainable true religion than does diversity of bodily condition that there is no attainable condition of health, or diversity of character that there is no attainable upright character, or diversity of coins that there is no attainable genuine coin. His new convictions might have issued in conduct to match. And then, instead of becoming infamous for all time as the executioner of Jesus, and dying in extreme anguish the death of a suicide, he would have taken his place among Christian Constantines, and have died in due course of nature with pale face beaming with joyful expectations of possessing a government more extensive than ever belonged to Roman Procurator, and a throne more imperial than ever held Roman Cæsar.

We have great cause to think there are some in our Christian congregations who hold somewhat the attitude of Pilate. They have yet to settle what truth is. They do not allow themselves to be called atheists or infidels; yet they are in doubt. How else can we account for the fact that there are so many among us, who, notwithstanding all the pressure brought to bear upon them, neglect the

Biblical Religion as a practice? It is hard to see how they can venture to trifle with and disobey that Religion as they do, if they have proper faith in it. The fact seems to be that they are, perhaps almost unconsciously, halting between two opinions. They are not yet grounded in a clear intellectual faith. Have I such before me to-day? I protest to them that it is of the utmost consequence that they do what Pilate did — ask what is truth, and ask it of Christ. I protest to them that it is of the utmost consequence that they do what Pilate did not do — couple this inquiry with that Biblical Plan of Investigation which will surely enable them to answer it. I have stated what that Plan is. Is it understood and remembered? Let me paraphrase it to you as follows.

Want of faith will not supply itself. If there is a vacuum in the atmosphere the subtle air will at once set itself in motion from all sides to fill the vacancy. That element has a natural bent to go wherever its presence is needed. It is so to some extent with natural light. You have to take pains to keep out of a room the light of a bright day. You must close the doors, you must drop the curtains, you must bring the carefully matched shutters together. But faith does not rush in upon vacant minds in this instinctive and assailing manner. Whether it have respect to God, or Christ, or the Scriptures — you must not expect it to set in upon you by a sort of natural gravitation; as stones fall to the ground, and as rivers run toward the sea. Nor will God, in an independent way and in the exercise of an almightiness that cares not for your coöperation, put the blessing to which you are indifferent within you; as men freight the deep holds of ships and vaults of banks with precious wares and metals — the one party choosing and struggling to make the deposit, and the other passively receiving it. This is not God's way. Great as is the blessing, vastly as He desires to communicate it at once and universally, He cannot be counted on to do it after this mode. He requires of you a positive effort at seeking and obtaining. You must set yourselves to work, in certain specified ways, to get light. If a man wants the treasures of the mine, let him explore and excavate and wash and refine; if he wants the harvests of the soil, let him plough and plant and till and reap; if he wants the valuable things of the sea, let him prepare his boats and his nets, and go watchfully tossing and dragging along the wave. Once in a great while God will send ravens to feed an Elijah; but were men to wait for that method of supply the great majority of them would starve. So will the men who wait to receive faith aside from their own exertions. God will keep to the analogy of Nature. He will keep to the declarations of His Word. "My son, if thou apply thy heart to understanding, yea, if thou seekest her as silver, and searchest for her as for hid treasures, then shalt thou understand the fear of the Lord, and find the knowledge of God." "Then shall ye find me when ye shall seek me with all your heart." All defective notions of the Supreme Being, all want or weakness of faith toward any part of the Biblical Religion, must look for correction in this way. It is the traveled road. It is the one used from the beginning. It is the one that will be used to the ending. All along and for all, it is the appointment of God that men " seek after Him if haply they may find Him : " by nourishing a sincere wish to know the truth ; by prayer that God will reveal Himself and His — crying after knowledge, and lifting up the voice for understanding — by carefully following conscience, so that the faithful steward of five talents may have ten, and the doer of the will know of the doctrine ; by wakefully studying, as men do other important subjects on which they wish to be informed. Is a man sensibly or doubtfully without faith in the inspiration of the Scriptures? Let him not wait for what will turn up, but let him put on the harness of strenuous endeavor. Worse still, is a man without faith in Christianity? Let him not wait for the clouds to clear away of themselves, but let him besom them away with sincerity and prayer and thought and good-living, well wrought at. And worst of all, is a man without even an intellectual faith in God? Alas, alas, and thrice alas, for this great misfortune and sin! But let him not expect to emerge from this dreary night by lying indolently on the bosom of Providence and natural law — as men sleep through the dark hours into day — but let him inquire after God; in the spangled heavens, along the verdant and peopled earth, in the depths of his own wondrous soul and still more wondrous Bible; praying, observing, reflecting, doing, with no stint of pains. For this is the one Scripture Way, by which it offers to stand or fall.

My hearers, who of you is qualified to say that this Way is not reasonable? Is it plain that God would not be entitled to choose His own way of revealing Himself and His; especially if He only proposes to hold men responsible according to the light they do or may possess, and especially if He guarantees that His way shall prove triumphantly successful? You have heard the strong promises — He that seeks shall find; To him that knocketh it shall be opened. Who does not know that these are but samples of the clear-voiced and courageous engagements that sound out from both Dispensations and from all parts of the Bible? Do as the Bible says, and then — if there is any faith to be put in grave and earnest assurances — God and His Son and His message shall come as near to you as any miracle could bring them. I confess to thinking this offer most reasonable and even liberal. I confess to feeling it a great favor that the Bible does so courageously commit itself: enabling me to tell you that on this its chosen line of investigation success is altogether certain, as it is not in any worldly inquiry to which man ever put thought. I confess to feeling very joyful for that audacious offer by which the Biblical Religion puts itself in your power: enabling me to tell you of victory mortgaged to you from the outset of your inquiries; of the prize you desire so securely anchored for you at the end of the course appointed for your sailing that no stormy violence can tear it away.

Bethink yourselves that it is no small thing that there is a moral discipline in the use of this way of getting light! Your success is conditioned on and proportioned to your honesty of heart, your love of the truth, your conscientious living, your faithfulness and patience of seeking labor. You are being fitted to make a good use of the light by the very process you take to get it. You will value it more highly for the pains laid out upon it. You will, with your disciplined watchfulness and muscle, grasp it all the more firmly and hold it against attack all the more triumphantly. And will it not nourish you as it could not do without the healthy labor which precedes its acquisition, and which tones up the system to a preparation for the marrow and fatness of this imperial diet? You must work for your daily bread. This work gives you an appetite; it puts the body into a condition to be nourished by the food it gathers; by it the whole system is strung to relish, retain, and assimilate the viands which it needs and with which it cannot dispense. Who shall say that the Bible plan of feeding the soul of man with religious knowledge does not gather about it similar advantages? For one I believe in the supreme reasonableness and noble liberality of this plan. Better than to be mere vessels — passive recipients of ideas and favors thrust into us by some miracle and almighty force! But why does not God so lighten on my astonished vision, or at least so record Himself by sudden invisible influences on the tablets of my understanding and heart, that I shall at once know Him whom to know is life eternal? Who knows this to be consistently possible? At all events you are called on to try what may prove a more excellent way — a way in which you shall surely reach your object, and reach it with a precious preparation for making the most of it.

Hear a Scripture narrative. Israel had fallen asleep. They had ceased to take pains to retain and improve their acquaintance with God. They forsook His synagogues, they read not His Word, they restrained prayer before Him, they made no account of His commandments. The consequence was that the idea of God faded from their minds. They knew little of Him and cared less. And when their attention was summoned to this state of facts, they were indisposed to improve that state in God's way. For aught I know they would have been willing to see some wonderful fire-works of Divine manifestation, could such have been brought to their door and paraded before them. For aught I know they would have made no objection to God's putting faith and reverence and piety into them, provided it could have been done without any trouble to themselves. But they were not willing to seek and inquire after the God of their fathers. They were not willing to pray after Him, and look after Him through His wonderful works, and study Him out in the hights and depths of the inspired Word, and work out a powerful conception of Him by conscientious living. They would not do so toilsome a thing, even to reach so magnificent a thing as the knowledge of God. For this God was incensed. For this He sent His judgments upon them. Witness many an Old Testament writer!

What does this mean? It means that if men decline His plan for giving religious knowledge, they must expect that God will indignantly refuse that knowledge to them. A sad refusal! Yet I cannot see that it would be unreasonable. So let the warning be taken. It shakes menacing finger at these distant times where men are hunting the world, and the worlds, through for all things rich and strange and fair — the lands of eternal ice, the glowing equinoxes, the profundities of the seas and the profundities of the skies — and do it with the zeal of enthusiasts. Why not explore for God and a Saviour as well? Is there a greater treasure? Is there a nobler and more rewarding acquisition? Shall men travel the great world around seeking for gain, and not go a little way, or a great way, seeking for God? He that postpones his God to all things else should hear the Scripture toll in his ear like a bell: "I will also stretch out my hand on Judah, and on them that have turned back from the Lord, and those that have not sought the Lord nor inquired for Him." Toll on, O tocsin Zephaniah, now for the Gentile as anciently for the Jew! Perhaps these gold-hunters, these pleasure-hunters, these reputation-hunters will take note of the retributions that warn in that doleful music. He that hath ears to hear, let him hear!

Will you not accept the Biblical Offer and Method of investigation — ye men of less faith than you could desire, of weak faith, of no faith at all! Will you not test this Scripture way to faith to the utmost, and do it at once? You cannot reasonably complain of darkness if you refuse. Here is a method offered you, having great aspects of reasonableness; you can try it without risk; you incur great risk if you do not try it; there are many unimpeachable witnesses to assure you that they have tried it successfully; it is really this method or none. Will you not then promptly and earnestly make trial? Consider what a sad thing it is to be without settled religious convictions; especially to be riding at anchor with all the Great Religious Questions unanswered. These are the questions of the hour to you. How unreasonable, dangerous, uncomfortable, irrational, and guilty to go into winter-quarters with these all unconquered and even unattempted! Make one good, honest, sufficient effort to get out of your darkness. Try the offered way out — a way which from the nature of the case must be decisive. You will either settle that the Biblical Religion is true, or you will settle that it is untrue. And probably very soon. But if it were necessary to exhaust years in the investigation — if it were necessary to toil at it till the eye is blear and the cheek cadaverous — if it were necessary to grapple your intellects on the arduous theme till they bow and tremble almost to dislocation under the mighty strain, still it would be time and toil wisely laid out.

You profess to want to know the truth. Then take this safe, reasonable, and long-tested Scriptural Method. By means of this theological calculus give the theology a suitable examination. This is the least that can be asked of you. And you know profoundly that it is a most reasonable asking. I ask it not for the sake of the great Biblical Religion that has weathered so many storms and centuries. She needs it not. She will flourish strong and fair and immortal whatever you may do. I ask for her a candid hearing, after her own way, for *your* sakes. Your highest interests are involved. Do not let indolence or business of this vanishing world stand in the way of this First Thing being done. *Business* — it would seem as if men thought there were infinite apologies for all manner of neglects in the mere suggestion of that word! Let me say in your ear what you already know — *there is but one business.* It is that of getting light on the Great Religious Questions, and acting accordingly. Like rational beings, put everything second to that, without demur. If you must reject the Religion, let it be on the basis of a manly examination. This Religion may be true. If true, it is of immense importance that you positively believe it. All doubt can be dispelled by a certain investigation. You have no right to expect that it will be dispelled in any other way. To neglect it under such circumstances is highly criminal. To neglect it is contrary to all the prudential maxims which are wont to govern you in all important secular affairs. If the loss of a thousand dollars were possibly involved in your failing to clear up some imperfectly understood matter of business of no great difficulty, with what promptness would you set yourselves to the labor of elucidation! If the loss of life or health were very possibly involved in your failing to clear up some obscure point in physiology of no great difficulty, with what energetic promptness would you set yourselves to the task of dissipating that obscurity! But the loss of an estate greater than you ever imagined, the loss of a health and life more precious than ever asked help at the gates of medical science, is very possibly, to say the least, involved in your neglecting to give the Evidences of Religion that suitable examination to which I earnestly invite you. Why not be as judicious for the soul as you are for the body? Why not be as prudent for eternity as you are for time? Why not do as Pilate did — ask what is truth, and ask it of Christ? Why not do what Pilate unfortunately did not do — take to yourselves a sincere wish to know the truth, break off obscuring and misleading sin as far as known, ask for light at the hands of the possible Great Supernatural, and seek that light also in the use of the natural means of light which abound on every hand?

Methinks I hear you say — "I will accept the Scripture Offer. I will try this boldly promising Bible Way to faith."

VI.

FIRST CONDITION—
A SINCERE WISH FOR LIGHT.

VI. First Condition — A Sincere Wish for Light.

1. Logical Value 89
2. Doubtful Existence 92
3. Tests 94
4. Well? 105

FIRST CONDITION — A SINCERE WISH FOR LIGHT.

YOU are wanting in faith. You have concluded to try the reasonable **Bible Way** of meeting that want. Then ask, Do I meet the first condition of that Way — *have I a sincere desire to know the truth?*

According to the Scriptures, our business with religion as intellectual beings includes the following particulars. First, we must perceive that there is a God. Next, we must perceive that the Christian Scriptures are His message to men. Then, we must grasp the true meaning of this Divine Book — its various statements of facts, doctrines, and duties. And lastly, all these particulars of knowledge should be matters of clear, distinct, and vivid conception; lying in the mind, as nearly as possible, as the facts themselves lie in nature — with the same hues, proportions, and bearings.

Now, from first to last in this intellectual dealing with religion — from the point occupied by the atheist, to that occupied by the Christian who is conscious that with all his faith and knowledge there is a certain want of vividness and life-likeness in his views of religious facts — I say, from first to last in this intellectual process, there is one thing more important to success than any and all things else. This is A SIMPLE DESIRE TO KNOW THE TRUTH. It is an excellent thing to have a mind naturally sharp, comprehensive, and logical — able to make nice distinctions, to take in at a glance a wide variety of facts, to march swiftly and in an orderly way along the highways of thought. It is an excellent thing to have the mind well trained in the discipline and culture of the schools, and furnished with the treasures of learning and science. It is an excellent thing to have leisure for study, copious libraries, and wise living companions and counselors. Still, these things, the best of them and all of them, are by no means sure to bring our minds to the more important religious truths. With great faculties, great education, and great circumstantial facilities — nay, with the very greatest — it is possible for us to come to mistake the Scriptures on main points, to disbelieve them, and even to disbelieve a God. But, according to the Scriptures, with a sincere desire to know the truth, such a result cannot happen. All those humble, illiterate, labor-pressed men, of whom the world is full, need the great truths of religion as much as others; and so we are given to understand by the whole spirit of Scripture that, as soon as we are honestly disposed to see things as they are, our minds will begin to gravitate and move toward the truth. At last they will reach it. God will come to the help of our honesty. The hidden mechanism of our natures will all unconsciously work us along toward the light, to which they have acquired a mysterious affinity. Certain flowers point always their painted petals at the sun, and move with him in his daily arc from east to west — they know not how, they make no conscious effort; but there is a certain something, deep within the life of the plant, that draws it with the force of a natural law toward the pleasant light and warmth by which it must live and grow. So instinctively do our minds bend toward the great facts of religion, when once they have become possessed of a truth-desiring spirit. At the very least, we do assuredly gather from the whole tenor of the Bible, that, between Nature and the Supernatural, it is provided that all who want to know the truth on leading religious matters shall in some way come into possession of it — not at once, perhaps; not without pains and perseverance, perhaps; but surely at some time and after some way, ministered primarily by a sincere regard to the truth. The unrealizing Christian shall have his truth seem life-like to him; the heretic shall lay hold on orthodoxy; the unbeliever shall gain faith; the atheist shall find a God. The best ground for cheerful expectation has that man who, amid present obscurity on religious points of great importance, can yet see that his heart has sincere aspirations after light, and would honestly welcome its coming.

But at this point a difficulty arises. It is not

always an easy matter to see whether we have a sincere wish to know the truth. The heart is desperately deceitful. Many a man has really hated the truth when he thought he loved it; and, on the other hand, not a few have loved it very considerably when they thought they did not love it at all. The best heart that ever beat in bosom often practices strange deceptions on its owner. Willing to be told his faults? Oh, certainly he is, and will even be glad and thankful to be told. But, when the telling is done, he is mortified to find he has misunderstood himself. He really did not want to know the truth. Willing to allow full weight to the opposing argument — desirous to be convinced by it if sound? Oh, to be sure he is: let him not be suspected of so much unfairness of mind. But the friend who stands by and watches the process of the disputation knows better. The good man has fallen into one of his bad states, and is really unwilling to see truth on the side of his opponent. Almost every turn in the argument shows it. And yet he maintains, and really thinks, that he sincerely wishes to know things as they are. Hence you see it is often no easy matter to decide what is our real feeling toward the truth. You can tell at once and beyond dispute whether you have a rose in your bosom, or a gold eagle in your purse, or a harp in your house. You look and are convinced. You grasp the instrument and strike its strings and hold it up to your neighbor, and he is convinced. But as to the existence of a small, weakly affection away down at the bottom of a heart deceitful above all things, here you have a problem that will not get safely resolved by a glance. If a man desires the truth to a passion, if the feeling has become fairly epic and heroic in its measure, then of course there will be no difficulty. But this is not often the case. The soil is seldom so fat with gold that one simple delve of the owner's spade shows him its riches: he has to take the opinion of the geologist, and send off to the laboratory specimens which after all may prove to be without a single atom of the yellow metal. In most bosoms where it exists, this desire for the truth exists in such a mixed state and scanty measure that close inquiry must be made and searching tests applied before the reality of the treasure can be considered established. I propose to mention some of the tests which must be resorted to in such cases.

At the outset let us note carefully the precise matter to be tested. It is not the existence of an honest desire on your part to know the truth at some time between this and your last moment in the world. All of you, probably, can settle that point very promptly without any tests. But the true point is, Do you honestly desire to have the truth now— on and from this very instant to see the facts of these great religious questions in their true colors? Whatever the obscure and perplexing topics of your religious thought may be, have you a wish for a present clearing up of the exact facts in the case, however much it may disappoint your partialities and convenience? — Further, the question to be answered does not relate to the existence of an occasional honest wish for the truth, as an immediate possession even; it points at what is habitual, and a part of the standing furniture of the heart. Who among you does not have his moments when he sincerely would like to have all the dark matters in his theology opened to him, just as they are, and at once! But it is not such a desire I have been speaking of as sure to bring in sooner or later a clear solution of all the fundamental questions of religion. It is one of which the soul is the home — not the inn where it passes the night and is up and away with the first blush of dawn — as well as one whose burden is to-day and not to-morrow; to-morrow, that is always coming and never arriving.

Now, what tests may you have of your possessing this important state of mind? I answer.

1. *If you have it, you are not in the habit of requiring demonstration as the condition of assent to any religious doctrine.*

Perhaps you think there may be persons for whom this would be no fair test. Their attention has not been properly called to the nature of moral argument. They have not reflected on the degree and kind of evidence they are obliged to act on and are accustomed to act on uncomplainingly, in all secular matters, even those of the highest importance. They have not been awake to the fact that it is as absurd to ask for mathematics in theology as it would be to ask that matter and quantity should change their natures. There may be something in this, though I think not. But this I may unhesitatingly say, that if, after their attention has been distinctly called to the nature of moral evidence, these persons persist in demanding that such points as the being of a God, the Divine mission of Jesus, and the truth of the Scriptures, shall be proved as men prove that the three angles of a triangle are equal to two right angles, or that two and three are five, it is very certain they have no real desire to know the truth, at least at present. Men who are not willing to know the truth probably, at least until something better can be reached, are not willing to know it at all. Men who, with their eyes open, mark off a given field of moral questions and arbitrarily declare that within it they will accept no evidence save the demonstrative, while on other fields of the same nature they are accepting probabilities a hundred times a day, and believing, and even knowing as it seems to them, on the basis of these probabilities — such men, I say, cannot flatter themselves that they really want to know the truth which they test by such a singular and impossible standard. Is not this fair reasoning? Notice how men treat evidence in matters other than religious. In these matters what one wants to recognize as truth he seldom finds any difficulty in taking probable evidence for, as incontestably reasonable. He does it instinctively and unhesitatingly. But the moment he falls in with a statement he is reluctant to accept, then our logician becomes more difficult. The sort of evidence that was good enough before suddenly becomes unsatisfactory. He must have something better to convince him. He raises his standard. And, if his aversion to the point to be proved is considerable, you may see him push that standard up so high among the clouds that nothing but winged geometry can reach it. This is well understood. Every one knows why it is that his neighbors sometimes demand in worldly affairs such enormous and impossible evidence. He knows that the reason lies in their unwillingness to find the truth lying in certain directions. And this is really why men are so unreasonably exacting of evidence on questions of religion. They will have demonstration or nothing. And yet perhaps they think they would be glad to know the truth, whatever it may be. They are mistaken. Their wishes, instead of being for knowledge, are against it, at least as a present possession. They may desire it for to-morrow but not for to-day.

2. *If you have an honest desire to know the truth, you are willing to pray for the knowledge to Almighty God with some degree of care and perseverance.*

Here is another test equally applicable to all minds perplexed on religious subjects, including such as hesitate on the being of a God.

Take the strongest case — that of the man who doubts whether there is a God to pray to. This man who fails to see that a God is, also fails to see that He is not. He cannot deny that Almighty God is possible. A reverent, sincere prayer to this possible Being, simply as a grand possibility, certainly will do no harm and may be useful. For, if He exists, this Sun can very easily do more to throw light on our darkness than a whole firmament of twinkling philosophers and philosophies. And how much trouble is it to say, even several times a day, " O God, the possible God, help me to light!" A few seconds of time, a few breaths of voice or thought, absolutely no labor nor sacrifice — who that has any real desire at all to find his way to clear views in religion but is willing to try this easy plan of securing help! Suppose he should do it for a year or years, what would the labor and trouble amount to! To just nothing at all. Hence I say, If, when this state of the case is properly laid before him, he is not willing to go with some attent and perseverance of prayer to possible Almighty God for help, he cannot be considered as being really desirous of help. He deceives himself if he thinks he is. It may be that he desires to have the truth at some time between now and never; but as to wishing to have it now, the thing is absurd. Much more absurd is it to suppose that a man who really believes in the prayer answering God of the Scriptures, but who does not know what to believe on other important matters, and yet honestly desires to know — much more absurd is it to suppose that such a man would, after the matter has been properly laid before him, stoutly refuse to breathe a brief whisper or a series of brief whispers, vocal or mental, up into a merciful heaven for light; that heaven which keeps the key of all mysteries, and, when it chooses, can shoot back with supreme ease the ancient and massive bolts on which genius and industry might wrench for ages in vain. So, man of doubt or dim views, will you not apply this test to yourself? Whatever your special darkness is, are you willing to pray to God perseveringly for light? Has it been your practice to do so; or, your attention having now been drawn specially to this method of help, will you make it your practice hereafter? If you cannot answer affirmatively, consider that in respect to honest desire to know the truth you have been weighed in the balance and are found wanting.

3. *If you have an honest desire to know the truth, you are not altogether without some direct, personal effort to investigate that truth.*

When a man has lost his way and desires to find it at once, what does he? For, certainly, he does something. His mind takes on wakefulness. His eye looks for guide-boards, and notes the bearing of roads. Instinctively he watches for some familiar object or phase of the landscape which shall serve as a clew of guidance. If he meets a person who may give him information he takes the trouble to question him. Remembering that he has in his pocket what professes to be a guide-book for that part of the country, he takes the trouble to examine it. Of course the thoroughness and eagerness with which all this is done depends on the degree of concern he feels at being lost; but if he feels concern in any degree he shows it instinctively in some of these active measures. Should he saunter smilingly along without an effort to compare roads, or to lift his eyes to spell out faded directions at corners, or to ask the persons he meets, or to study the map within reach of his hand, men would say that he either is insane, or has no real desire to recover his way, at least just yet. So, whatever desire a man has, it at once sets him to looking after the appropriate natural means of gratifying it; and if he finds such means accessible and capable of being used, with little or no expense of time and labor, he is sure to be found working them; feebly, if the moving desire is feeble; strongly, if the desire is strong. Thus if a man sincerely wants to have your interests promoted, and if there are many opportunities and means of promoting them open to him and continually occurring, some of which can be used without any appreciable trouble to himself, why, he is certainly doing more or less in your behalf. He does not content himself with praying for you. He does not refuse to lift a finger or turn a corner in the natural way of helping you. Should a professed friend of yours do so, you would turn your back on his professions of regard as altogether hollow and worthless.

Now human nature necessarily acts just so under the influence of a desire to know truth in religion. There are natural means and opportunities, recognized as such by us all, looking toward the clearing up of religious problems. And some of these are exceedingly simple and easy, so simple and easy that their use would be no real tax on the time or strength or patience of any. How many persons within your reach who credibly profess to have studied the points on which you are in the dark, and to have come to clear views! Would it be any trouble worth mentioning to confer now and then with such persons as they cross your path? How many books and essays, lying about on all sides, and written expressly to throw light on these very points of your perplexity — how many tracts and sermons which sincere men have penned and spoken with the hope of helping such as you! And who will speak of the trouble of glancing over some of these with an eye to getting the help proposed! Moreover, there are always floating about in the community and starting up in your own experience — facts, suggestions, gleams of explanation and truth, which a little wakefulness of mind might turn to great account in the way of resolving your difficulties. And then there is study, properly so-called, the bending of your own solitary investigating thought on your difficulties; a **thing to which** are all degrees, from those painful wrestlings **that** exhaust the **soul down** to that gentle exercise **of the** reason which **hardly whispers of labor.** This being so, what **I** affirm **is, that if** you have a sincere desire to know **the truth it must** be that you are making more or less use **of these natural** means of knowledge. **All** experience shows that **the two** things go together. Do you read or study or inquire or watch in any degree simply for the end of discovering what is true? Is your mind somewhat in an investigating attitude? **The** question **is not** whether you spend time **in thinking,** reading, **arguing on** the dim **sub-** ject; but **whether you** do **it as** a means of bringing out the facts in **the case.** Men talk, hunt up difficulties, **inquire,** and dispute, often to show their ingenuity **or for a** reason still worse. **If** there is no real effort **to properly use** the **means of investigation** lying about you, **you** deceive **yourself if you** suppose you have an **honest** desire **to know the truth.**

4. *If you have a sincere desire* **to know** *the truth, you act according to the law* **of the truth** *you already receive as such.*

Grant that **you wish to** have all the great religious questions settled in **your** mind, **not** as it would suit **your** taste **or present** convenience, but according **to truth. Why do** you wish it? Evidently because **you love truth** for its own sake; or because your better **judgment has** convinced you that to know things as they are and to act accordingly, will, in the long run, be your true wisdom. If you love the truth for its own sake, you love the laws of truth, and, of course, obedience to those laws. That is to say, you govern your conduct by the truth as far as you know it: for he who loves virtue will practice virtue. If you choose the truth because it is wise for your interests to do so, you really intend to walk by it, if discovered: for you know perfectly well that the knowing will be of no service to you, but rather a disadvantage, without the walking. For example, if you wish to know that there is a God, in case there is, you seriously propose to act suitably on the fact should it be discovered. If you wish to know that the Scriptures are His word, in case they are, you mean to treat them as such in reverence and obedience should you find them true. If you wish to know that the day of Divine grace to men is limited, if indeed the stern truth be so, you propose on making discovery of the same to live as becomes a probationer for eternity. Now, with these intentions of conforming to undiscovered truth, it is very certain how you are treating that already discovered. You are obeying it. You are habitually governing your life and heart by it. A true purpose to go by the unknown when found is a true purpose to go by the known now that it is found.

And now let us see what religious truth you do recognize as such. You believe in natural religion, in the law of conscience. Does your conscience in the main govern you, and is it your great question and struggle from day to day to know and do your duty? You believe that a God and a Divine Christianity are possible, at least. And if they may be, it is intuitively your wisdom to act largely as though they certainly are. You surely will come to no harm by acting suitably to the idea of a holy God and a holy religion; but by refusing so to act you will destroy yourself, in case a God and Divine Christianity are facts. The very possibility of their proving to be facts lays you under obligation to your own safety to shape your course and character into forms of virtue. I take the trouble to state this; but you knew it and felt it long ago. Everybody knows that it is perfectly safe to govern himself by the general Christian rules of living; and knows equally well that it is unsafe not to do it. Do you govern yourself by these rules? This great fact of the possibility of a Holy God and His written Word—are you acting according to it? By making fair answer to these questions, you will be able to decide whether there is really within you an honest desire to know the truth, on whichever side of your dark questions it may lie. If you must confess that the tenor of your life treats such truths as you do believe as if they were false, and that you have no purpose of immediately doing otherwise; why, the faithful test is against you. Your heart is yet vacant of that principle which, as a guide to truth in religion, is worth more than any genius and learning that were ever sung and crowned among men.

A man flatters himself that he has a mine of gold on his farm. He goes to a geologist and begs him to make an examination. As soon as the man of science comes to the district where the mine is supposed to lie he begins to inquire into the character of the rocks. What are the strata that crop out to view in the fields? He knows that gold is not found out of certain geologic connections; and if he finds that there is neither primary rock, nor transition, nor the lowest sandstone on that farm, he is obliged to tell the man that his hopes are vain. He need not trouble himself to dig down some hundreds of feet in order to decide whether he is proprietor of a yellow mine. The fact is plain at the surface. The precious metal is not found in connection with that sort of rock. And when a man wants to know whether he has within him that precious thing, worth more than mines of gold, namely, an honest desire to know the truth on dark questions of religion, a bare inspection of the surface will often provide him with an answer. Does he insist on demonstrations as a condition of faith? Is he unwilling to pray to Almighty God for light — to God either as actual or possible? Is he altogether without effort to use the natural means and opportunities of gaining light which fall in his way? Does he neglect to act according to the truth he already receives?

If so, then I pronounce that the treasure he is looking for is not in him. These are not the right scientific connections for it. It goes with quite opposite sorts of conduct. Let him give up all hopes of finding it under such a kind of surface. Still it is worth while for him to consider that in one important respect his situation differs very materially from that of the disappointed gold-seeker. Once satisfied that he has not a mine on his estate, that proprietor knows that he never will have it till his dying day. The soil beneath his feet will always be dull, common earth, let him do what he can. But the man who finds himself vacant of that precious moral element whose worth and tests I have been describing, is under no necessity of having that vacancy continue. There are ways of introducing the absent treasure into his heart. He can have a new interior betokened by a new surface. Will he have it? It is indispensable.

Let me hope that the Tests show that *you* have the indispensable treasure already.

VII.

SECOND CONDITION—
USING PRESENT LIGHT.

VII. SECOND CONDITION — USING PRESENT LIGHT.

1. GENERAL LAW 109
2. REASONABLE 113
3. EXAMPLE 116
4. APPLICATION 118

SECOND CONDITION — USING PRESENT LIGHT.

YOU are wanting in faith. You have concluded to try the reasonable Bible Way for meeting that want; and on examination it seems to you, I will suppose, that you have its first condition of success, namely, a sincere desire to know the truth. Have you also the second condition — *are you using the light you already have?*

Really, each of the three conditions belonging to the Bible plan for getting light, hides in both the others. You cannot truly fulfill one without fulfilling all. But this does not make it undesirable to invite separate attention and action on each condition. It will give to each the benefit of a threefold attempt in its favor. It will, we may hope, triple for each the chances of being clearly understood, strongly felt, and fairly tried.

Our knowledge always begins in a single grain of light. The progress from the crude notion to the wide and sharply defined knowledge is sometimes very rapid — so rapid that the fact of a progress can only be detected by care — but care will generally discover the day to have been preceded by the faintest dawn, and the full corn by the ear and the blade and the single small seed.

The mustard seed gradually ripens, without human care, into the tree in which the birds can lodge. Its growth is merely the result of its own nature and natural circumstances. In the same way, some of our first faint notions of religious truth pass forward into satisfying knowledge. Many come to a firm belief in the Divine existence without any conscious effort of investigation, but by the insensible swayings of the beautiful and skillfully wrought universe which surrounds them from infancy. So at least they think. The landscape must become brighter as the morning wears on; the child cannot help improving in general knowledge as he becomes older; and so, in religious things, time and the incessant shinings of Nature upon us necessarily clear up by degrees many of our views. There is no conscious effort of our own toward the result. The growth of the truth within us is like that of the seed ministered to by the dews and rains and sunshines with which it had nothing to do. But the Bible gives us to understand that when a man has fallen into religious darkness he cannot count on any such way out. He must look to pass from a little light to a greater, by voluntary effort to use duly the light already possessed. He must do business wisely with the first installment of knowledge given him before he can receive another. Only two talents are placed in his hands at first: it is by judicious trading with his small capital that he must come at last to find it doubled and the lordship of cities vested in him. When the son enters on business, does his prudent father set him up at once with the full patrimony? He gives him a little to make his first venture upon. If that little is used with judgment more is intrusted. Thus by degrees the young merchant may become fit to manage, and worthy to receive, the great capital which can whiten the sea with ships and fill stately warehouses with goods.

Once in a while men pass abruptly from want to affluence. An hour is sufficient to change their rags into robes of honor, their crusts into dainties, their cabins into palaces. But this is not the common way of gaining riches. A few dollars are gained, these are made the stepping-stone to others, the double sum is made to roll up another, and so the accumulation goes on at a constantly accelerated pace, until, at the end of years, a fortune is found to be made. Using the little judiciously has made the poor man rich. — I see a man eminent for his learning. Let me question him as to the way in which he has succeeded in collecting such stores of knowledge, and I shall not find that they were imported into his mind in one overwhelming cargo. On the contrary, I shall find that once the simple letters of the alphabet made up the entire sum of his science; that he then traded with this small capital till he had learned the art of reading; that by the diligent use of the art of reading he next helped himself to a knowledge of the common branches; that by putting these together he then slowly mounted into the region of the difficult sciences; and that thus by making every acquisition minister to another he at last reached the proud eminence of a famous philosopher. Using the little diligently has made the ignorant man learned. — It is by precisely the same process that virtue is expanded into its nobler degrees and forms. No one ever knew a good man grow in his goodness save in one way. With the one talent of repentance feebly shining in his heart he goes a-trading and makes it two. He gains new virtue only by using that already possessed. Justice grows by the practice of justice; truthfulness by the practice of truthfulness; love by the practice of love; meekness, temperance, purity, by the practice of these virtues. "Do good and be better, do better and be best." is the law of the spiritual life, of which none are ignorant who have taken their moral science from the Bible or observation.

See the general style of that economy under which we live! Its way is to give a little, and if that is rightly used, to give more. As the man of business swells his estate, the politician his honor, the scholar his science, the talented his various mental faculties, the swift his alacrity, the strong his strength, the good man his virtue, so must the man of defective religious knowledge increase his little into much. Especially the man who has fallen into the leading and abysmal unbeliefs. As he complains of the chill darkness let him heed the

Scriptures as they assure him that one of the most important questions bearing on relief which he can ask himself is, Am I diligently using the light that I have?

It seems but just that if men fail to improve a little light more should be withheld, and that if they make the most of their scanty information they should be rewarded with larger instruction. Do we blame the father who gauges his outlay upon his son's education according to the disposition that son manifests to improve the advantages already in his possession? Do we blame the father who determines not to send to the university the son who never shows any taste for the employments of the common school? It is likely that if we abuse hints and gleams of religious truth, we would abuse also ampler light. He who is unjust in that which is least would be unjust also in much. The man who misuses a hundred dollars would be likely to misuse a thousand. The man who wastes the gleanings of a field cannot be expected to do rightly by the entire harvest. Hence, were God to grant more light on religious subjects to him who does not improve the little he has, it would probably only go to increase the receiver's guilt. For to whomsoever much is given, of him shall much be required, and to whom men have committed much, of him they will ask the more.

Suppose God to do something very strange to the spirit of the Bible; suppose Him to give a man whose views of religious truth are very meager and unsatisfactory to understand that his chances for additional light will in no degree depend on the manner in which he treats the light already in his possession. "Wrap your one talent of truth in a napkin if you will, I shall be just as ready to give you another as if you had put my first gift out at usury. Employ the one torch which I have given to assist you in finding your way upward through this dark world for the purpose of lighting your path downward if you will, it will make no difference with your prospect of receiving from me other torches." What would be the effect on that man of such a word of God? If he could believe that such a message could come from the Author of that Nature to whose whole spirit it is opposed, would it not exert upon him an influence of unmingled perniciousness? But how different the tendency were God to address him in another strain! "See! I have given you a few rays of sacred knowledge. It is not much, but if you honestly try to walk by this you shall have more. Observe that I do not require you to walk according to the sunlight which others have; only according to the starlight which you have. If you obey, other stars shall in due time make their appearance; and if you continue to obey, at last you shall see the morning-star and the sun. On the other hand, if your small stewardship is turned to no account or a bad one, do not expect anything further from me. Expect rather that from him who hath not shall be taken away even that which he hath." Would not such words sound altogether reasonable to that hearer, and would they have upon him one tendency other than salutary? The arrangement which it would be well for God to make, the Bible tells us is made actually — that it is a standing condition of progress in religious knowledge that we try to walk in the light of the knowledge we already have.

Grant that you are so unhappy as to have but dim views of the truth of the Christian Religion. You wish a clearer vision. You want to look on the credentials of Christ and the Bible as some men have looked on them — with a faith firmer than the everlasting hills and stronger than death. Is there no way in which your wish can be fulfilled? Says the Bible, There is. A glorious full assurance of faith is possible to you. There are some things which you already clearly know. That the precepts of the Scriptures in the main correctly express your duty you are well satisfied. You have your one talent of light: with this you must trade. You have your twilight: you must do your best to walk by it. The duties of which your conscience assures you, you must labor to fulfill. This will be doing what the Magi are said to have done — following a star toward Jesus Christ. And, as those wise men of the East are said to have done, you will at last come in due course of your star-following into the presence of the Sun.

Nor do I know of a better illustration of this whole process of getting light in religion by using light already gotten, than this same story of the Wise Men as told in the New Testament and held in the Christian traditions. O three kings, nestling in oriental ease and pomp, serenely studying the serener heavens in star-gazing Chaldæa, what is the matter! Why these flushed faces, these eager eyes, these animated conferences! Why this running to and fro of retainers, this culling of treasures, this lading of kneeling camels, this marshaling of the caravan! A strange star has shone in the west, night after night. Plainly it is not a common star — these astronomers have read the sky too long and well to be in doubt here. And then, perhaps, they have had a dream; or some vague tradition of the star that should arise out of Jacob has floated down to them from the times of the Captivity; or some faint echoes of the current Jewish expectation of Messiah have travelled forth and died away in their doubtful ears. They have put this and that together. This is all that they have for supposing that the star they have seen points at the birth and locality of One whom they will do well to find and honor. It is but a mere hint: but then a hint from the sky is not to be neglected. So they set forward. In vain friends beseech, dangers menace, various plans and affairs urge their claims — they say their adieus and set forward with eyes fixed on the star. It is a very small light — a mere grain of gold on the sky. But they soon notice that it moves before them. Clouds sometimes hide it from view; sometimes mountains interpose their opaque bulk; in the day it is never visible. But they gradually become aware that, visible or invisible, it is delicately adjusting its going to their going; and that the faint accents of the Messianic traditions are thickening and strengthening in the air as they advance. So onward, brave kings and kingly souls, with ever brave hearts, though distant Jacob is to you as the ends of the earth are to us! On through parched sand-plains, over rugged steppes, across broad rivers, among robber-hordes; from city to city, from province to province, from country to country! It is a long travel; but as grows the travel so grows the encouragement. At last Judæa is reached. They find everywhere among the people a positive expectation of just such a Personage as they are looking for. Here too they find the still larger encouragement and light of the Old Testament Scriptures with their gradually brightening lines of prophecies converging on this very time and on this very land. Surely they are trading with the light to some purpose! With firm tread and eye elate with confidence, they move swiftly along the beaten and storied highways of the Holy Land. Omens of success, pregnant rumors of a glorious sequel to their pilgrimage thicken on every hand. And now the star rapidly expands. It draws earthward. It hangs motionless. The journey is ended. Lo, this is Bethlehem! Lo, here is a manger, and here the wonderful Child! O infant King, O Star of Jacob, O Sun of righteousness — into what a day has the original starlight of these men opened? The faint gleam; the gleam moving, the gleam moving in sympathy with their progress; the growing voices in the air; the written Scriptures, the climactic BABE! Sublime progress! By patiently using the little, it has become much. By twilight duly improved, the pilgrims have gradually come to the noon of knowledge. Now they are sure of the actual arrival of the king whose character and mission they can more fully spell out at their leisure from the written Word they have found. No wonder they rejoice with exceeding great joy. How pour the costly gifts! How swales that lowly shed with frankincense and myrrh! How lightens it with Orient gold! Fit sign of the joyful light within these wise and royal pilgrims — all gained by steadily acting on the mere glimmer with which their pilgrimage began.

See how you are to do, you whose religious light is now so weak — a mere star shedding pale rays through the wide darkness of your night! You are to begin acting without delay on that starlight. You are to set forward on that little. You are to try going by that little as well as you can. Have you not a conscience that says that certain things are right and certain things wrong? Do those right things and refuse to do those wrong things. Are you not persuaded that the precepts of the Bible, at least in the main, are reasonable and righteous? Reduce them to practice. This will be turning such light as you have to account. It will be following the star. It will be doing over in this nineteenth century what the Magi are said to have done in the first. Follow your star steadily, despite some difficulties. You will find it moving before you. You will find it gradually gaining diameter and suiting itself to your motions. It will gradually attract about your path hints of truth, prophecies, Mosaic economies, new dispensations. At last it will stop over Bethlehem; and you shall go in by open door to find Jesus and God, with the Bible in outstretched hands, offering it to you. Your journey is ended. Thanks to your star-following, with its implications, your journey is ended most successfully. And I assure you, my friends, you will then in the great joy of your hearts keep Epiphany, the feast of the three kings. You will open your treasures and give the goodliest of them all in one great Act of Faith. Your trading with the one talent will have made it ten talents. Had you kept it laid up in a napkin you would have been cast forth into the outer darkness. So greatly promise and threaten the Scriptures.

No one has a right to complain of a little light on religious subjects, if, on duly using that little, he can have more, and so on indefinitely. Men do complain of it. It seems mysteriously hard that on such momentous topics as belong to religion it should be left possible for man to have such dim and partial views as prevail. Say the Scriptures, What is there hard in it? It does not cut you off from any degree of knowledge to which you may choose to aspire. All it does is to condition success on exertion and good behavior. Is there anything to complain of in this? Do not parents, employers, rulers do the same thing every day without censure? It is best for you to eat spiritual bread by the sweat of your faces. It is best that your theology be a moral discipline in the getting as well as in the enjoying. To succeed well in learning the lessons of religion you must work, work with an honest purpose to find the truth, work with the truth already known as your instrument, work after such a mode as is in itself fitted to discipline your degraded and sinful nature back into the noble type which originally belonged to it. You ought to be thankful for such a provision. It bears on its face plain marks of the wisdom and benevolence of its Author.

So the Bible proposes — and surely your reason does as much — that you follow the star. If you embrace the proposal, you are like persons who have lost their way in a cavern of great length. After groping for a while in utter darkness they discover far away a faint gleam of light. They are glad, for they know that there is the spot where their prison opens up into glorious day. All they have to do is to set and keep themselves in motion toward it. It costs them trouble to advance among slippery and broken rocks; but they have it for their encouragement that their condition is improving with every step they take. The light, as they use it, steadily increases; they are every moment acquiring dexterity and hardihood in surmounting the difficulties of their way. At last they stand at the entrance, and look abroad on sky and field and flood all bathed, not indeed in perfect, but in smiling and beautiful day.

Let me hope that you are faithfully trying to walk according to the light you already have!

VIII.
THIRD CONDITION—
PATIENT DIRECT SEEKING.

VIII. THIRD CONDITION — PATIENT DIRECT SEEKING.

1. THE METHOD 125
2. THE METHOD JUSTIFIED 131
3. THE METHOD URGED 141
4. THE METHOD ACCEPTED 143

THIRD CONDITION — PATIENT DIRECT SEEKING.

YOU are wanting in faith. You have concluded to try the reasonable Bible Way for meeting that want. On examination it seems to you, I will suppose, that you have already met the first two conditions of that Way; that you have a sincere wish to know the truth, and are actually using such religious truth as you already have. Then ask finally whether you will meet the remaining condition, whether you will *patiently seek light in the twofold way of prayer and rational inquiry*.

Let me give you the Biblical idea in regard to this whole matter of direct seeking for blessings, as it stands related to the Divine government. I will give it quite from the believer's point of view. This is what one really needs who has it in contemplation to give the pure Bible plan for getting light a fair trial.

See the Idea.

The government of God is such that we are sure to receive many blessings from it even if we do not seek them. Just as the ground drinks in the sunbeams and dews and rains, and yet stretches out no hand to labor and lifts no voice to pray; so do men constantly receive good things from God without the slightest effort to win them. Were we to have no gratitude, and even blaspheme heaven for its gifts, still they would come. The Mysterious One would treat us just as He does the desert. Yonder expanse of sand yields not a blade of grass, not a cup of water; and sometimes its fevered bosom breathes up pestilential airs into heaven. But the dews settle on the thankless and hostile waste even as on Hermon. God waters it abundantly with His showers, even as He does the plain of Sharon and the ridges of the corn-field. The vitalizing sun darts on it the same genial light and warmth which make green the pastures of Bethlehem and purple the vineyards of Engedi.

And what follows? Are seekers and no-seekers on equally good footing with the government of God? Shall we say, What is the Almighty that we should serve Him, and what profit should we have if we pray unto Him? Far from it. Though we shall have many blessings from God without seeking, it is still best to seek. He who seeks not will obtain much, he who seeks will obtain more. Kind to all, the providence of God will be kindest to those who go personally and knock at His treasury for what they need. There are many Sauls to whom it is given to reckon their prizes by thousands; but the Davids who reckon by tens of thousands are those few, who, remembering that all their springs are in God, direct their eyes and steps to the hills whence cometh their help.

THE METHOD. 127

Look at the farmer in his field! Do you see him working toward harvest with one hand? What breadth and brawn and grasp are in that right hand; how peacefully and steadily that single knot of compact and straining muscles could apply itself to the hoe or the plough or the scythe! But still through all the labors of the year the brawny right shall have help from the brawny left; and to both shall be due the success of full barns after harvest. Seeking blessings from God usually consists of two parts — prayer and direct effort to realize the blessings in the line of second causes. These are the two hands, the right and the left, with which the search must be prosecuted. For example, you want the blessing of clear knowledge on the main religious questions. What shall you do but both ask the at least possible God for light, and study to gather light by rational inquiry! Though you can pray powerfully, prayer alone will not answer. Though you can study powerfully, study alone will not answer. The two strong hands must work together toward the desired result; must combine in that searching which issues in the finding.

Sometimes the blessing is reached after an exceedingly brief seeking. We have to lift but one prayer and strike but one blow, and the work is done. While we are yet speaking for the first time, God hears; and while we are yet doing for the first time, lo, God's answer, like Peter, is knocking at the gate! Does the sinner wish to open his heart to Christ? One honest struggle with himself and one upward casting of the eye for help, may suffice to roll back on its rusted hinges the iron gate which for a lifetime Christ has rapped in vain. Does the Christian wish the conversion of his friend? One faithful appeal to that friend's conscience and one humble appeal upward, may suffice to change the sinner into a Christian. Does the man troubled with unbelief wish to have day let in on the Evidences? One earnest cry heavenward and one comprehensive sweep of an alert eye around, may discover at once the magnificent total of God, His Son, and His Word. So brief is that double-handed seeking sometimes required for the finding. As the first cast of the net sometimes fills it with the treasures of the sea; as the first shaft sunk by the adventurous miner sometimes brings him to crystal waters or yellow gold; so the first effort made prayerfully for the Fundamental Light may bring it to you, even before the voice of the prayer has died away on the ear, and the vibration of the stroke has ceased to tremble along the muscle. "Hear me," said Elijah when he had built his altar, "O Lord, hear me!" And, quick as thought, the fire of the Lord flashed response from a blue heaven and consumed the very altar-stones on which the prophet would fain see some sign of Divinity.

Though the seeking is sometimes thus promptly successful, yet immediate success in full measure can seldom or never be counted on with any confidence.

Though the object sought be altogether and mightily desirable, and though it be sought after the most unexceptionable manner — with deep sincerity, earnestness, and free outlay of labor in all appropriate directions — yet we are never justified in concluding that we shall reach it immediately on our first effort. It is true we may; but there is no promise to that effect. We have many and great promises to a proper seeking of proper objects; but as to the moment when success shall come, nothing is said. On this point God holds himself in reserve. The seeking must be patiently followed up. The prayer must be repeated, the direct effort in the line of second causes must be repeated, until such time as infinite wisdom shall see fit to bestow the blessing. That time may be to-day, or next week, or next year. The law of the promise is, Seek till you find; Knock till it is opened; Imitate the importunate widow; Remember that God is the rewarder of them who diligently seek him; Search for wisdom as for silver and dig for it as for hid treasures. In accordance with this is the testimony of David: "I waited patiently for the Lord and He inclined to me and heard my cry." And in accordance with it has been a multitude of more recent experiences. How many beseech and struggle months and years for moral victories for themselves or others ere gaining them! So for light on questions of doctrine — the current experience is that it follows patient seeking, Even as the husbandman waiteth for the precious fruit of the

earth, and has long patience for it, till **he** receive the early and latter rain ; so, very often, men must wait on God in a long course of mingled prayer and labor before they can fill their bosoms with the ripened sheaves **of** the blessing they seek. Indeed, time is found to be an important element in almost all enterprises. Blessings coming as soon as we have lifted hand and voice for them are the rare exceptions. They are uncovenanted. Beginners **in** religion are apt to take a different view. To their slender knowledge of the Scripture, its promises to prayer and seeking seem very unconditioned ; **as if** we have nothing to **do** but to utter one fervent petition and give one hearty wrench on the powers **of** Nature to put the truthfulness of God under obligation to fulfill our desires. But advancing knowledge shows them their mistake. They learn to take account of the very reasonable and usual limitations implied in the nature of the subject, in the connection, and in the general scope of the Scriptures. They find that all the promises are given to persevering seekers. Patient diligence is seen to be the only sure key to Divine treasures. Would they realize the being and government of God ? Would they say with mighty conviction to Jesus, "Rabbi, **we know** that thou art a teacher come from God ?" Would they have a quick, bold faith in the Scriptures as an infallible and complete Divine Message ? Surely there is a promise and a way for them ; but instead of finding **it a** way which a single step will finish, they find it paved with days and weeks ; and instead of unloosing into heaven one strong-winged prayer and so prospering to the top of their bent, they prosper only by dispatching through the sky messenger after messenger in long procession, like files of autumn-birds departing in search of summer.

You see at once that this way of granting blessings will often make men *prize them more highly.* It is not always true that what is cheaply gained is little valued ; and that on the contrary what costs us much comes to hold a high place in our estimation. Yet it cannot be denied that it is often so. In very many minds this is evidently the prevailing law ; and in all minds, at times, it exerts a very important influence. Now this fact may sometimes be sufficient to justify God in requiring patient seeking as the condition of finding. The Searcher of hearts sees that were He to grant the object sought on the first application, or soon, the seeker would never take it so closely to his heart as it deserves and needs. He would look on it with a comparatively indifferent eye. He would neglect and scatter it, somewhat as the young man sometimes does the estate which came to him through no care and toil of his own. But should he reach the blessing on the path of long and arduous prayer, by the strivings of weeks and months with God and himself, then it would be to him a precious thing. He would watch and rejoice over it as the miser does over the jewel which he has traveled half round the world to find. Now, it is very necessary that a man think much of the great and precious religious light for which he asks; very necessary that the clear views of God, of His Son, and of His Word for which he tries be greatly prized and carefully kept; and God, who knows the man and his circumstances thoroughly, may see that there is no way of securing this high esteem and careful cherishing so good as that of making him look upward for the blessing with a persevering eye, and labor for it with a persevering hand. This may be one reason why God puts him under the unpleasant regimen of delay. It is not that the Father above is fond of laying burdens on men. It is not that He has a selfish vanity to gratify in seeing you come humbly knocking at His gate day after day, and in making you wait His good pleasure. But it is that you may have the greater profit in the end — that you may so prize the blessing when it comes as to make the most of it.

You also see at once that the way of patient seeking may itself involve a *very valuable moral discipline and culture.* It learns one patient self-control; it holds him to honesty of purpose and steadiness of religious effort; it keeps him in contact with the idea of God, of His government, and of his own dependence on it, as being at least so many gigantic possibilities. There is wholesome restraint here. There is vast impulse here in wholesome directions. Here are precious and elaborate cultures — more precious and **elaborate** than any **ever insisted on in the schools**, than **any that ever** turned **clown into** philosopher, **than** any **that ever** brought **forward** tropical gardens of **orange and palm in arctic latitudes.** For here is a daily exercise of sincerity of heart, of **religious sensibility, of industry in** religious directions, **of a** sense of the Biblical Religion as being at least an august possible truth with its many implied duties. So **the whole character is** stressed toward virtue. So **the roots of** all goodness are made healthy **and strong.** So by the **continuous** waving of **the** slender sapling it gradually **comes to** strike itself strongly into the soil, and **thickens and** shoots greenly upward night and day into a stately pillar propping **the sky.** Who shall say that such a result may **not** often be cheaply purchased at the expense **of** a little, **or a** great deal, of prayerful waiting! **The very** foundations for virtue **are of** more consequence **than** time. We **can afford to** wait when waiting is itself so great a **blessing.**

Very often no moral self-control **whatever is** required **in** asking God once **to grant a** certain wish, **and in** smiting Horeb once with our rod in search **of water.** The self-control **would lie** in not doing **it.** But to keep **smiting the flint** and appealing to heaven with unflagging diligence till success **may be** pleased to **come,** however long it may tarry — this is really putting the bit into the wild horse's mouth, and breaking him **to** systematic and useful service. **The world says to the new** seeker, Give up your search; it is burdensome, and after all will come to nothing. Invisible tempters say to him at both ears, Give it up; it is burdensome, and after all will come to nothing. His own indolent and perverted and easily discouraged heart is ever crying out to him from within, Yes, give it up; why will you have this long disquiet and all to no purpose? And now, if through all he holds on his patient way of the double-handed seeking, praying with his right hand and working Nature with his left, he is a self-conqueror, a self-conqueror in a sacred direction. He is not only practicing victory, but practicing it toward the right point of the compass. He is learning how holy fields are won. He is learning how to triumph at Ascalons, and scale the walls of Jerusalems. And every day's contest enables him to hold his will toward high and sacred ideas with a firmer rein and a steadier step.

Of all prayer, that dictated by some specific and great want takes us nearest to the idea of God. It is the only sort of prayer which gives us what we may call contact with that supreme idea. So the difference between one prayer and patient prayer for the great boon of light on the fundamentals of religion — and where in all the round of the possible is there a greater, save virtue itself — is the difference between a transient and a lasting contact with the most reforming and exalting of all human conceptions. To see God as He is, would be, in tendency, to be changed into the same image.

To come into His immediate sphere and presence would be to be penetrated by a thousand sweet and exalting influences, overflowing from Him in all directions, as do perfumes from a garden full of all sweetest flowers and spices. And to touch the very hem of His robe — awful and yet blessed privilege — would be to receive mightiest healing virtue against sin; and the oftener we could touch the more we should receive. Patient prayer really takes up abode in the audience chamber, say of this Great Idea — an audience chamber full to overflowing with grace and light, a very tropical land to bring rapidly forward all rich and graceful plants of goodness. The mere transient seeker comes and goes, gains and loses, and has only the privileges of a sojourner where his brother dwells as a citizen. Every time we wakefully press our petition as before God, we earnestly take for granted His possible being and government; and our long seeking is really one long exercise of this potential assumption. How potential it is! What great and practical implications it has! What restraints from the wrong does it impose! What stimulus toward the right does it give! It plainly requires of us very much the same sort of conduct as would complete demonstration of the Divine existence; a sense of which is worth more than all other means put together for improving character. Whoever goes earnestly to God as possible, only once, does by that single going quicken his sense of the Mighty Possibility; but he who goes a hundred times in patient system gives the principle the benefit of a hundred impulses and of a systematic cultivation. On account of these incidental disciplines and cultures involved in a patient seeking, it may be, God would be warranted in often making it the condition of our finding. Do not be stumbled if it is made the condition of your finding that blessing of blessings — light on the fundamental questions of religion.

You also see, almost at once, that a blessing may often *do more good by coming after some delay than by coming immediately;* and that meanwhile to keep up our desire and preparation for the blessing it may be necessary to keep up the seeking. There is a great choice often as to the time of bestowing a given alms on a poor man. Circumstances may make it much more for his advantage to receive the sum to-morrow than to-day. The physicians know many a sick man who had far better receive strength to walk abroad a week hence than now. The parent often delays a year giving his child the advantages of a certain school, and feels sure that the delay will be all for the child's advantage. Many a scholar has felt that the university would have been of double the advantage to him that it has, had he entered it a year later. Now there may be the same choice of times for advantageously receiving many religious blessings — a choice depending more on our circumstances than on our characters. Such may be our circumstances that we had better receive even a spiritual blessing a month hence than now. For example, you wish clear light on certain gravest religious questions — say that mighty trinity of them looking toward God, His Son, and His Word. The clear light you wish may do you more good by coming after some delay than by coming on the instant. How do you know but that your case is altogether like that of the young man whom it is best to keep away from the university a year longer? That delayed privilege will prove a greater blessing to him than if he were having it to-day. Not that knowledge is not good; not that the proposed education is not of the best; not that, if now possessed, that education would not do most admirable service; not that if things were exactly as they should be, it would not be better to have that education now than at some future time; but that, as things are, a greater profit will come from it when circumstances and character have been allowed to ripen somewhat. Who can say that this is not exactly the case of you doubters, seeking the removal of your doubts? It is really an education that you are seeking — the very highest. And think it not strange to hear that there may be a choice of times for graduating this education at the greatest, though least visible, of universities.

A teacher is asked for the answer to a certain problem. He can give it at once. In exceptional cases he will do so. But in most cases he thinks it not best. He gives the child a grain of light, and sends him back with it to his desk to pore over the problem. From time to time he gives additional light-grains, as they are applied for and as the solution advances; until, at last, after many applications and many helpings, mingled with constant effort of his own, the child sees his way clear to the answer. Do we blame the teacher because, as a rule, he chooses to give the answer in this way of patient seeking? We commend him. We know the child prizes the knowledge all the more; it is more truly and familiarly his own; and in gaining it he has gained a most valuable discipline and culture.

A college is asked for its crowning instructions and honors. It can give them at once, and will do so in special cases for cause shown. But its plan for most is to bring them forward by a graduated course in which the college shall spread out its helps, and the student his applications and studies, over years. For years he must renew his application for instruction daily at a recitation room, where he will work and where the teachers will assist. So he will gradually mount by a succession of applications and helps and studies to the highest degrees and privileges of the college. Is the college blamed for having such a plan? By no means. In this way, say we, the seniorities and diplomas of the institution will commonly best come, will be the most prized, will do the student most good and the public most service. The gradual discipline and culture of that long procession of mingled applications and aids and studies will be invaluable to him. It is his education.

A man wants the higher posts and honors of the State. The State can grant them at once — does so in cases of extraordinary merit or public crisis. But its rule is, Present yourself daily at this polytechnic school for aid, apply yourself faithfully to such tasks as may there be given, and take promotion step by step according to the zeal and faithfulness you show. Then do the same at this bureau or in that camp. So by degrees the striving scholar, in this way of daily application and daily help and daily labor, mounts through cadetships and captaincies of many grades to the baton of a marshal or the portfolio of a privy counselor. This prize was in his thought from the first. From the first it was a prize which the empire was willing he should have, if worthy. But he must have it in this way of patient seeking. Is the empire blamed? Not at all. Only praise is heard. It is felt that this is the natural way of bringing forward men to great posts. By it the training keeps pace with the acquisition. The individual is better improved while the country is better served. The final success is all the more highly prized and effectively used on account of its tardy coming. And the nation and the press break forth into eulogy over the liberal views and wise prevision and large-thoughted policy that established such a method. The youth are glad at their splendid opportunities and magnanimous emperor. What could they reasonably ask more? Here are the rungs of the ladder offered to every foot, and there shall be a patient helping for every step of the patient climbing. They are more than satisfied. And then it is possible that any given aspirant may, through some special grace of events, suddenly rise by one grand uplift from the bottom to the topmost round of honor. Has no humble page been unexpectedly knighted on the field of battle? Has no Joseph, fresh from prison, gone forth viceroy of Egypt? Has no Daniel, just out of mortal peril, been made president of princes and ruler over the whole province of Babylon? I salute thee, Dupuy, — this morning plodding in the ranks, and still in the uniform of a common soldier all red and sodden with battle — I salute thee marshal of France! Who knows but such a bright exceptional case may be yours, O young aspirant for glory? But if not, if you are shut up to the current method of advancement by patient seeking, you have only thankful words to say. The emperor is most wise and kind. It is an equal, far sighted, and generous policy. Do we not begin to succeed at once, and go on succeeding in proportion as we do justice to our opportunities? What more utterly reasonable? So ambitious parents feel, so feels all France, and so the whole fair-minded world. Why, here is England to-day soliciting praise and getting it, for doing far less — for having at last concluded to grant her posts of honor, without respect of persons, on a plan of patient seeking without the patient helping. And we begin to hear among ourselves the first outcries for a similar system. Could we learn to-day that such a system has been fairly adopted, and that henceforth no public post will go by mere patronage and party policy and demagogism, but by courses of application and labor in the direction of preparation for those posts, we should feel that a new day has dawned on the land. The golden age of politics has arrived. All sensible friends of the country approve. All worthy aspirants to public honors more than approve. And yet the State provides no instruction, but leaves every one to help himself to qualifications as he best may. What if it should step in with a long succession of positive aids to match and reward your long succession of honest endeavors!

So, men of dim views in religion, do not complain of the Scripture way of turning your twilight into full day. This way is as old as mankind. It is befriended by ages of experience. It has its roots in a profound knowledge of human nature. It is the King's Own of judicious teachers, of the higher education, and of the most advanced government. It is the *beau ideal* of these times in matters secular. Try it in matters religious. Here you are, with little or no faith in God, in Jesus, in the Bible; and that Bible comes to you proposing to give any amount of light in the way of patient praying and inquiring. It guarantees success. The plan is utterly reasonable. It stands strong in the theory and business and history of the world. It is commercially sound. What if you have to persevere a little or much at your labor on so great a matter? The result will more than pay for the outlay, whatever that may be. But you are not to wait long for some light. You may not have to wait at all for even meridian splendors; but the glory may come to you in sudden outburst, as highest honor sometimes comes to lowly soldier or civilian. At the very least, your case is to begin improving from the time you begin the double-handed seeking. And you are to reach a true faith in all fundamental things just as soon as you become truly virtuous persons. It is only the sublimer measures of faith — the assurance, the mountain standing strong, the foundations of the everlasting hills — that may call for the long courses of seeking. But then these sublimer measures are so precious that no price is too great to be paid for them. Pay all the patient seeking that may be necessary. Pay months and years if need be. Chronic doubts may require chronic relieving. But of this be assured — you will not have to go far toward the east before meeting at least the dawn. Ascend to the hill-top and I venture to believe that you can see the morning even now. And Oh, what a beautiful morning it is! So richly toned, so variously and exquisitely painted, so pregnant with the glory of the coming sun! What encouragement to go forward, every step treading in new brightness, every uplift of the face detecting a new whiteness on the landscape! What prophetic eloquence, and almost song, in those magical and now fast-shifting colors! See, the sun appears! And a long time before that sun shall stand directly over your heads, and flood with light every nook and corner of your landscape, it will be plain to you that everything is moving surely on to midday. How steadily the morning grows! How steadily the great orb ascends! The laws of Nature are evidently drawing at that radiant car. Evidently they are drawing along the arc that goes straightest to the zenith. They will surely arrive. And then, amid the glorious noon of faith, you shall shine and rejoice and say with the supreme satisfaction which many have felt before you, and are feeling to-day, all over the world, We speak that we do *know* and testify that we have *seen.*

May I not hope that you are ready for the patient direct seeking; and that, with cordial prayer for light keeping pace with every step of the intellectual effort, you will now join me in cordially examining a few of the many Evidences of the Biblical Religion?

Part Second.

IX.

PRESUMPTIONS.

IX. Presumptions.

1. FIRST ASPECT 147
2. AVOWED PURPOSE 150
3. PROPOSED MEANS 151
4. PRECEPTS 151
5. FACTS AND DOCTRINES 153
6. LITERATURE 160
7. ADAPTATIONS 162
8. EFFECTS 168
9. FRIENDS 174
10. FAITH AND VIRTUE 175
11. OTHER RELIGIONS 177
12. ALTERNATIVE 179

PRESUMPTIONS.

HUME confessed that he had never read the Bible with attention.

An eminent statesman and historian uses the following language. "The Christian Faith has been, and is still, very fiercely and obstinately attacked. How many efforts have been, and are still, made; how many books, serious or frivolous, able or silly, have been, and are, spread incessantly in order to destroy it in men's minds! Where has this redoubtable struggle been supported with the greatest energy and success, and where has the Christian Faith been best defended? There where the reading of the Sacred Books is a general and assiduous part of public worship; there where it takes place in the interior of families, and in solitary meditation. It is the Bible, the Bible itself, which combats and triumphs most efficaciously in the war between incredulity and belief."

These words of M. Guizot are true. The Biblical Religion is the strongest among those who are best acquainted with it. Accordingly, I think it will greatly help you to judge of the claims of this Religion if you will join me in a rapid survey of some of its leading features.

1. *The Biblical Religion is one.*

The same God, the same way of living, the same fundamental doctrines in all directions, are taught, though with different degrees of clearness, in all parts of the Bible. It is true it has different writers. It is true it has an Old Testament and a New, a Mosaic Economy and a Christian. But really these are the same thing in different stages of development. The one is the dawn, the other is the noon. The one is the child, the other is the man. The one is the sapling, the other is the ripe cedar of Lebanon out of which temples are made. This is the Christian account of the matter; and every tolerable reader of the Bible knows it to be just. There is no more appearance of conflict between its different books than there is between the different chapters of the same book. Besides, the New Testament vouches for all the Old. So that one cannot be an intelligent believer in Christ without being also a believer in the earlier records which He indorses. Whatever is said in favor of Christianity is really so much said in favor of the whole Biblical Religion which Christianity professes to fulfill. The two are practically one.

2. *The one Biblical Religion is truthlike in its first aspect.*

As soon as you come into the presence of some men, and look in their faces, and hear them speak, you feel drawn to them. By a subtle understanding which you can hardly explain, but which is very satisfying, you are convinced that they are strong and high and good. You need no laborious trial of them. Their very way of carrying themselves flashes to you a sudden sense of their worth. Well, some of us know something of this feeling when we come into the presence of the Bible. It is so truth-like. It does not look and speak like an impostor. Its face is so frank, its eye so genuine, its whole carriage so ingenuous and sound-hearted. How simple, direct, and circumstantial are its narratives! How full of coincidences which could not have been designed — near a hundred between the epistles and history of Paul alone — and yet how careless of merely verbal and formal inconsistencies which only try the fairness of an interpreter! How unsparingly they tell the weaknesses, sins, and misfortunes of favorite characters, best friends, and own countrymen; and who but honest Jews, to whom truth was a sacred thing, would ever have told such a story as we have in the Bible of the checkered misbehavior and chastisements of the Jewish people, of the patriarchs, of Moses and David and Solomon and Peter! How faithful is the Book to the great and popular crimes of its own times and of all times — sparing neither numbers, nor riches, nor power, nor rank, nor antiquity, nor friendship! How clearly it sees that the heart is the fountain of corruption; and so, most unpopularly and unprecedentedly, directs the brunt of its effort toward inward reform — insisting on a renewal of the heart as being the first step in personal religion! How completely are all castes and classes, save those based on moral differences, ignored by it — so that beggars and kings, sages and simple, publicans and priests, are treated with equal favor, and appear before it on one inexorable level as to the exactions it makes, the rewards it offers, and the penalties it denounces! And then see with what a cordial air it invites examination into its claims — saying in many ways, Prove all things, Seek for wisdom as for silver, O noble Bereans searching daily whether these things are so! See with what easy confidence it gives crucial tests of itself in its promises; especially in its promise of faith to all persons conscientiously living, sincerely praying, and patiently inquiring; or, if you will have it at the shortest, to all persons who will intelligently undertake a thorough reform of heart and life. Then light shall begin to stream in. Then the soul shall begin consciously to move toward the mouth of its cavern. And, if the process which begins to give light is continued, it shall at last bring the lost one out into clear day. Such is the engagement. Who cannot test it? The Bible frankly commits itself to stand or fall by this plan of inquiry. Does not all this look straightforward, honest, consciously truthful?

3. *The Biblical Religion is noble in its avowed purpose.*

It declares man an undone being in character and

prospects; and declares it to be its mission to rescue him, without respect of persons and over all the earth, to pardon and virtue and eternal life. "I came to save the world," said Jesus. "The Son of man is come to seek and save that which was lost," said Jesus. You see that the Religion is not wanting in dignity of professed object. That object, as related to man, could not be loftier. There is nothing worse than sin to be saved from, nothing better than eternal life to be saved to.

4. *The Biblical Religion is suitable in its proposed means.*

It proposes to do its great work of saving men by means of a written revelation whose matter and form are both inspired by Divinity, by means of a vast body of miracles in which Divinity Himself powerfully attests His Word to the senses of men, by means of an atonement in which Divinity Himself dies for human sin, by means of a Holy Spirit in whom Divinity Himself steps forth to renew and sanctify sinful human hearts. Certainly a great system of instrumentalities! Could a greater be imagined, even? It is altogether in keeping with the greatness of the object which the Biblical Religion proposes for itself.

5. *The Biblical Religion is holy in its practical teachings.*

Of course there are particular precepts to which unbelievers sometimes take exception; but I am now speaking of the bearing of the Scriptural precepts as a whole. In regard to this there is no question. Its holy character is admitted by even the worst enemies of the Bible. Of course you freely admit it. You know that were the biddings of this Book fully reduced to practice by any person, it would improve him beyond measure. You know that were any community to obey them perfectly, that community would be almost as fragrant and beautiful as a Paradise. Prisons would be empty. Courts would have nothing to do. Crime and the very seeds of crime would perish. Selfishness and all bosom-wickedness would disappear. Society would be washed clean as by the turning through it of a river. And instead of foulness, outward and inward, would be the dainty whiteness of every positive excellence. Where is the virtue that is not enjoined somewhere in the Bible? I have never heard of it. Where is the amiable trait that ever drew love, or sweetened the air of home, or softened the ways of general society; where the epic goodness that saves states, illustrates centuries, and does honor to human nature, that is not bidden in some form within its comprehensive decalogues? I have never heard of it. Of course I cannot go into details. Nor is it necessary. I appeal to your knowledge of a Book with which you have been familiar from your infancy; and confidently challenge you to point finger at a single vice or fault which the Bible has forgotten to forbid, or at a single virtue or amiability which it has forgotten to enjoin. It cannot be done. The spirit and drift of the Scripture law are holy in the last degree. The way of living it requires would picture with mingled beauty and sublimity the face of the world. The Christian code is the most promising landscape-gardener that has yet offered service to the public. Even unbelieving Bolingbroke confesses it. "No religion," says he, "ever appeared in the world whose natural tendency was so much directed to promote the peace and happiness of mankind. It makes right reason a law in every possible definition of the word. And therefore, even supposing it to be a purely human invention, it had been the most amiable and the most useful invention that was ever imposed on mankind for their good."

6. *The **Biblical Religion**, as to its doctrines and facts, is in striking accord with Nature and **Historical Antiquities**.*

During recent years much research has been made in Bible lands. Ancient languages have been compared, ancient manuscripts discovered, ancient ruins unearthed, ancient inscriptions read. And, altogether, much independent light has been cast on places, customs, and events referred to in the Bible. With what result? At first, some triumphant outcries against the Book, especially against its supposed chronology. Next, an incurable discord among the outcriers. Then, as search and discussion proceeded, trait after trait of verisimilitude brightening out from the venerable pages, as some old Roman buckler of Corinthian brass, dug up on British moor, thickly embossed by artist and darkly bronzed by time, gradually becomes studded with bright points under the patient frictions of the antiquary. At last, thousands of agreements established between the Record and the Antiquities, and not one disagreement on which learned opposers of the Bible can unite. Such has been the history. No thorough scholar in these matters will venture to deny it. One of the most eminent of such scholars, after a careful survey of all the researches, says with representative voice, "The monumental records of past ages — Assyrian, Babylonian, Egyptian, Persian, Phœnician — the writings of historians who have based their histories on contemporary annals, as Manetho, Berosus, Dius, Menander, Nicolas of Damascus; the descriptions given by eye-witnesses of the Oriental manners and customs; the proofs obtained by modern research of the condition of art in the time and country — all combine to confirm, illustrate, and establish the veracity of the writers who have delivered to us the history of the chosen people." Even unbelieving Renan feels it necessary to confess, "The striking accord between the texts and the places, the marvelous harmony of the Bible ideas with the country which serves them for a frame, was to me like a revelation." Strong as is such testimony it is not too strong. Nor Egypt, nor Phœnicia, nor Judæa, nor the plains of Shinar; nor Young, nor Hamilton, nor Lewis, nor Layard, nor Rawlinson, **nor** Champollion, **nor Botta, nor** Lepsius, nor **Bunsen — nor** private explorers with their freedom and numbers, nor public commissions going forth with **public resources at command —** none **nor all of these have** furnished **a** single **well established fact** against **the Bible history.** On the contrary they have furnished immense corroboration. Startling corroboration in **many instances.** For example, a comparison of the leading languages **of** the world points to a common origin **of** mankind, and that in the part of Asia where the Bible **places it.** Scarcely a **great fact which** the Book affirms of **the** race — **such as** the original **paradise,** the **sabbath,** the fall, the **worship by** sacrifices, the flood — **which is not echoed** all round the world in immemorial traditions. The tombs of Egypt, the giant **cities of Bashan, the Moabite stone,** great Nineveh **again** brought **to the** surface after a burial **of near three** thousand years, say Aye **to** the **Scripture Record with** voice still more imposing. **But all** the intelligible monuments and antiquities say it, so far as they speak toward the Bible at **all. Would** you say it for yourselves? Read **Thomson's " The Land and the Book."** Read Hengstenberg's " **Egypt and the Books of Moses."** Read **Rawlinson's** " Historical Evidences."

So **much for Scripture as harmonizing with Historical Antiquities. It also** harmonizes **quite as** well with the observed constitution and **course of** Nature.

On the one hand we have the Book coming to us through different channels and at different times; on the other hand we see all our arts and sciences and civilizations coming to us in the same detached way. On the one hand we have the Book becoming more clear and high in its forms of truth as it advances; on the other hand we find the order of Nature with its gradually advancing day, and gradually advancing man whose narrow notions as a child pass by degrees into the broad knowledge of mature life. On the one hand is the Book, obscure in parts and sometimes for the present impossible to be understood; on the other hand is the mysterious universe of matter and mind over whose parables we are obliged to ponder long and often ponder in vain. On the one hand is the Book, largely capable of different interpretations and evidently largely needing care and honesty to draw out its true sense; on the other hand is the book of Nature with its seeming self-contradictions; with its variously interpreted laws of health, laws of husbandry, laws of political economy; even with its variously interpreted laws of the most famous natural sciences, especially in the earlier stages of such sciences. On the one hand is the Book in regard to whose sense sad mistakes have actually been made; on the other hand is the book of Nature encumbered worse than any attic with the rubbish of exploded scientific theories, or of theories that ought to be exploded — astronomical, geological, mathematical even. On the one hand we have the Book giving us what in certain places and at certain times ought not to be read; on the other hand we have the book of Nature giving us what in certain places and at certain times ought not to be spoken of. And so on. I am confident that, however far you may proceed, you will find that no objection can be brought against the general aspects and implications of the Bible which does not lie equally against the known scheme of Nature. Still more confident, if possible, am I that you will find no objections greater than many which can be started against the existence of actual things.

Or look at the direct teaching of the Bible. We find it teaching the boundless wisdom and power of an Author of Nature; and, looking around, we find a universe which, in the vastness of its extent and in the variety and wonderfulness of its contents, accords with such an authorship. We find it teaching a Divine Providence that condescends to the smallest conceivable particulars; and, looking about through the microscope, we find a world whose smallest details are wrought and adjusted with an exquisiteness as wonderful as the economy of yonder solar system. We find it teaching a God who at the same time sustains and operates in all directions and at all distances from His throne; and, looking away to the sky, we find it occupied by spheres of whose shining majesty almost the same things can be said — spheres which not only act where they are not, but which are able to fill every point of surrounding space, as far as thought can travel, with unceasing power and control. We find it teaching a God who has a severe, as well as a tender, side to His character; and, casting about, we find dislocated strata, destroyed races, and a current world furrowed with famines, pestilences, and death. We find it teaching a certain order in the appearance of the various great forms of life on the globe; and, looking down into the bowels of the earth, we find the stony records of just such a succession. We find it teaching a profound depravity in all men, and this depravity passing over from parent to child; and, looking about us, we find actual society profoundly corrupt throughout, and the physical and mental and even moral traits of children tending to take shape after the parental pattern. We find it teaching a God who in a sovereign way chooses some individuals and nations to privileges and honors not allowed to others; and, looking up and down the actual world, we find it checkered with endless cases of the same unexplainable discrimination. We find it teaching a Divine Incarnation; and, looking about us, we find the world filled, not only with seeming traditions and anticipations of it, but with actual incarnated human beings. We find it teaching the Atonement and Mediatorship of Jesus Christ; and, looking around, we find no end to cases of successful and righteous mediation between contending parties, no end to cases of successful and righteous self-sacrifice for the good of others. We find it teaching the fall, the probation, the regeneration and sanctification by a Divine power, the resurrection, the day of judgment, the two after-worlds; and, looking around, we find the world with its visible ruin, visible probations, visible moral revolutions and victories as in answer to prayer, visible wonderful vegetable and animal transformations, visible courts and prisons and palaces wherever wise governments are strongly maintained. We find it teaching sorceries and demoniacal possessions; and, looking about us, we find at least strong suggestions of such things in many of the phenomena of lunacy and spiritualism. We find it teaching us to believe in miracles of great number and variety; and, looking about us, we find the world stocked with wonders which no philosophy can fathom, venerable with the miracles of geology, and even proving to us great events in the future which will be totally aside from all previous human experience. And so the analogy proceeds. I know of no point of Scripture-teaching which it does not reach. From the day when it was discovered that the Bible, contrary to all other books of its time, hung the earth "upon nothing," down to this day when we find it calling the Pleiades, that center of revolution to our whole firmament of stars, by a name which means *the pivot*, the light has been growing; and now the Bible with all its difficulties is just as credible a work of God as is the difficult Nature which it so strikingly resembles. And as to God Himself, how powerfully does this great resemblance between the Word and the Deed suggest a common Divine Author!

7. *The Biblical Religion is splendid in its literature.*

Of course I do not pretend that some men do not claim that the Bible is a very childish sort of book in matter and manner. Ignorant men sometimes say it. Men of culture sometimes say it, under the impulse of a recklessly speaking dislike. But no candid, well-informed man will say it, be he friend or foe. You are able to see for yourselves that there are many beautiful things, many sublime things, many pathetic things in the Bible; that somehow many of its narratives are wonderfully fresh and effective, many of its poems very sweet and rich, many of its doctrines and persuasions most aptly and strongly put. Still, perhaps, you distrust somewhat your own literary judgment. Then take testimony. So you do on other matters. On mathematical matters you consult mathematicians; on matters of commerce, commercial men; on matters of farming, farmers. So do in regard to the literary merit of the Bible. Refer the question to literary experts of the first class. Consult the great masters of thought and expression — the men who *are* literature; the Miltons, Goethes, Scotts, Carlyles; the men whose characters or attitudes toward religion guarantee their testimony to be honest as well as competent. What say such men? Sir Isaac Newton says, We account the Scriptures to be the most sublime philosophy. Sir William Jones says, I have regularly and attentively read the Holy Scriptures, and am of the opinion that this volume, independently of its Divine origin, contains more true sublimity, more exquisite beauty, more important history, and finer strains both of poetry and eloquence than could be collected from all other books. Milton says, There are no songs comparable to the songs of Zion, no orations equal to those of the prophets, and no politics like those which the Scriptures teach. Says Carlyle, speaking of the book of Job, " I call that, apart from all theories about it, one of the grandest things ever written by man. A noble book! All men's book! Such living likenesses were never since drawn. Sublime sorrow, sublime reconciliation; oldest choral melody, as of the heart of mankind; so soft and great, as the summer midnight, as the world with its seas and stars. There is nothing written, I think, of equal literary merit."

So speak Scott, Goethe, Dickens, and others. Surely such men, if any, are reliable critics. Who are entitled to speak in the name of literature if not these immortal authors? By their mouths she approves and crowns the Bible as one of her greatest monuments. As a mere book it will never die. Such hight of thought, such breadth of expression, such aptness in speaking to the great heart of the race — surely it will live and be read in the world's latest afternoon; and when the last ray is fading out of the eye of humanity it will not be toward Homer or Plato that the straining orb will be found directing itself, but rather toward the various glory of that one book which deserves to be called the Book of Mankind.

8. *The Biblical Religion is strikingly adapted to the nature, condition, and leading wants of man.*

In their silent libraries philosophers have set themselves down to draw up systems of government. In some instances they have succeeded in producing what has reflected great credit on their ingenuity. The paper constitution shows admirably. Here is learning, here is skill, here are just views, here is great judgment in selecting particular laws — in a word, a very fair looking theory. But, on attempting to carry it out into the real world, it is found to be nothing. It is infirm. It lacks adaptation to actual life. Somehow it cannot work among men, as men are. And so it is sent back to the obscurity of the shelf — perhaps to be again drawn forth in distant years to show the talent of its author, and to remind men that something more is needed to give practical success to a theory than great ingenuity in devising it.

Quite another character and fate belong to some political systems. They have passed from paper to practice. They have gone from the study into actual sovereignty over men. Perhaps they never took paper or study in their way to sovereignty. And yet what prodigious daily effects! Here are none of your philosophical essays, quietly reposing in their embalmment for other ages; but actual engines working away most effectively on actual society. Most effective are they — but not much can be said for the character of the effects. Like wild beasts they are strong chiefly to devour. They lift the few and lower the many. They swell the palace of the ruler and narrow the cabins of the people. And, if we turn from these effects to examine the nature of the systems from which they come, we find a medley of ancient customs and prejudices, of ancient truths and errors, of ancient rights and wrongs, of which the chief thing to be said is that it is well adapted to give greatness to the imperial families of Caliph and Grand Mogul.

Widely different from each of these is the Biblical system. It is no mere paper constitution. As said Napoleon, "The Gospel is more than a book; it is a living thing; active, powerful, overcoming every obstacle in its way." Nor is it a one-sided, sectional force. It is both a plausible theory and a great generic power. And the power is one that looks and strives toward the needs and cravings of all mankind. This might be suspected by one knowing only its history. In the early Christian times it spread with immense rapidity. It came, and saw, and conquered in many a land. Before the first century was through it had overrun the great **Roman empire. No brute force was** used. Nay, **the success was** against **force and** prestige **and all influence and** passions **of an** exceedingly **corrupt age.** Ten general persecutions **came up against it and fell.** Philosophies, acute and powerful, Grecian and Roman and Oriental, marched out to give it battle and became its vassals. Institutions and vices, strong in the ripeness **of** centuries, **frowned on** its progress **and** were shattered. Over learning and riches, over numbers and station, over depravity and antiquity, over armies and emperors, **over the combination** of **the highest and all** human **forces, that great** Christian **Force went forward in** steady triumph till **the Roman world was** covered with its temples, till the masses **were** leavened with its spirit, and till **senators and** Cæsars acknowledged it Divine.

What was the **secret?** Nothing but poor and despised men talking and **preaching their** system — **what** was the **secret of its swift advance?** One **not prepared** to admit that **it was befriended** by **a Divine power, will at** least admit **that it must have had** some strong points of **adaptation to the** people **of the** age; and, when **he reflects on the** great variety of peoples included in the all-devouring Roman empire **of those** days, strong **points of** adaptation **to the nature and condition of** mankind. **And since those** old times, **what vitality** it has always **shown under the** attacks **of open enemies,** what **vitality even under the skillful stabs of false** friends!

What numbers of the worst of men in all the walks of life has it suddenly revolutionized! How it has grown and triumphed in general revivals, often changing permanently the whole face of large communities in a few days! Surely, I say again, there must be large elements in this human soil adapted to the Christian tree — else it could not have grown so fast; nor have withstood the droughts and storms and axes of the woodmen so well.

What are these elements? On examining the Biblical Religion you find that it is popular in form, various in manner, profoundly in harmony with the elementary conscience of the world, flexible in its circumstantials while most inflexible in its essence; full of strength for the weak, of consolation for the sorrowful, of hope for the discouraged, of stimulus for the sluggish, of support for just authority, of defense for the defenseless, of action for the practical, of the seeds of philosophy for the speculative, of authority for the many, of terror for the bad, of reward for the good, of pardon for the penitent, of life for the dying. These are great points. Most men are not philosophers — far from it. So a religion in the form of a philosophy would not be suited to them. It must express itself after the manner of the common people; it must put its ideas into living forms, and connect them by the more plain and easy principles of association. This the Biblical Religion does. It knows how to tell its story effectively to the humblest classes. Men are very various in their turns of mind. One takes most kindly to narrative, another to proverb, another to poetry, another to epistle, another to the lofty oration. The same person in various moods is most apt, now to this and now to that form of writing. The Bible provides for this variety. Its histories describe, its poems sing, its apothegms curtly speak, its arguments enchain, its prophecies proclaim in mingled prose and song. Man everywhere is profoundly possessed by a sense of guilt and danger and insufficiency — often covered up from view by occupation and other causes, but on special occasions breaking forth at the surface, like some subterranean river, into wide lakes and streams; and always giving sign of itself to careful observers in all the religions of the world, and in all the leading civil economies and traditions. The Bible echoes to these elementary convictions as no other book does, and goes further with its offers of relief. Men are weak and need strength; the Bible offers strength to any extent. Men are ignorant toward religion and the future after death; the Bible offers to meet this need more fully than any other teacher. Men are timid of the Great Unknown before them and crave a sense of absolute safety in regard to it; the Bible offers such a sense, and constrains poor Byron to say, "Indisputably, the firm believers of the Gospel have a great advantage over all others; for this simple reason, that if true they will have their reward hereafter; and if there be no hereafter, they can but be with the infidel in his eternal sleep, having had the assistance of an exalted hope through life, without subsequent disappointment; since, at the worst for them, out of nothing, nothing can arise, not even sorrow." Men are everywhere tempted, often very sorely, and need victory; the Bible offers protection and victory in the greatest straits and against the greatest odds. Men are born to trouble — ah, what fights of afflictions sometimes — and need comforting; the Bible offers almost any degree of comfort, and points to cases almost without number in which it has made its offers good. Men get dull and discouraged, and need stimulus and hope; the Bible offers the inspiration of unlimited motive and royal expectations. Men are guilty and need peace and reform; the Bible offers pardon, regeneration, and sanctification. There are bad men who can only be restrained by fears; there are good men to whom a heaven is appropriate and who long for heaven; the Bible spares neither threats nor promises, but holds up in one hand the blackness of heavenly wrath and in the other the whiteness of heavenly crowns. Men come to be aged, sick, suffering, dying, and need a joyful immortality to look forward to; the Bible offers to all an immortality ruddy and athlete with the glory of perpetual youth.

I came to a young man who for some time had been painfully nearing his grave. Yesterday he was a skeptic. It seemed as if he would never be otherwise; his face was set like a flint. To-day I found him a believer. How came the swift change? He explained. "I find," said he, "that the Christian Religion is adapted to the wants of man, especially at such a time as this." He had made a great discovery.

9. *The Biblical Religion is most salutary in its observed effects.*

I have called your attention already to the fact that Christianity, unlike many beautiful speculations, has a faculty for going into actual effect in the world of men. Not all the effect one could wish, most certainly; but still effect of the most delightful and suggestive character. What careful observer will dispute Lord Bacon, when he says, There never was found, in any age of the world, either philosopher or sect or law or discipline which did so highly exalt the public good as the Christian Faith!

Yonder community smiling with order, thrifty with industry, wise with culture, delightful with amiable intercourse, and rich with Christian virtues and institutions — what was it once but the worst of western hamlets! Intemperance reeled. Profanity buffeted the name of God. Daily and nightly gambling shuffled its cards and bred its quarrels. The orgies of the dram-shop made midnight hideous with sounds that wrung the waking hearts of wives and mothers and sisters. Children grew up without instruction and without restraint, without principle and without shame. In a word, the place was Sodom — a smoke in the nostrils of morality and decency. But a stranger came, bringing with him the spoken Bible. He labored, now encouraged and now discouraged, until a good measure of the fundamental Gospel had been put into firm contact with the public mind. Then came a rushing, mighty wind. Christianity fought with the abominations of that abominable place, like some great Captain, and conquered. Sodom was born again. And the laborer, looking forth on the well-watered garden where just now was the waste, howling wilderness, sung in his heart the song of Miriam over a mightier than Miriam's deliverance.

A great change has come over yonder household. Once its heads were children of Belial. Brutal drunkenness consumed the avails and faculty of labor. Rose ever the shrill voices of strife, and not seldom the din of blows and cursing. Through the livelong day were heard such words and seen such practices as made common respectability shut its eyes and ears. The children bade fair to outdo even the shocking example set them. It was ignorance and idleness, it was want and filth, it was insubordination and tumult, it was hatred of man and defiance of God, it was lying and stealing and worse. Heaven, if there be a heaven, have mercy on the wretches! *Can* anything be done for them? Even the good man, who knew by experience something of the might hidden in the right arm of Christianity, asked himself, in momentary forgetfulness, as he passed that vile tenement, whether aught could cleanse the Augean stables. Yet the Gospel of Jesus did that great feat. It came to those hard, corrupt hearts, and melted and reformed them. It turned that den into a cheerful home in which dwelt order, peace, purity, thrift, happiness, usefulness, and noblest virtues — into a monument more royal than sculptured pyramid, not only of its own wondrous conquering faculty, but also of its faculty to crown all families with the highest forms of blessing.

Such effects come from a great change in individuals. Christianity swept the house and the village because it had first swept the individual heart. I summon up to my thought a man as unworthy as ever trod the earth. I ask myself whether there is any power abroad among men which is able to make new that body of death. Rejoicingly, I find myself bidden by a thousand facts to answer, Yes. Yes, Heaven be praised, there is a power at work in the world which can reach even such an encyclopedia of sin! It is the Word of Faith which we preach. This can cleanse that cage of unclean birds. This can sweep and garnish that house, after having cast out of it seven devils. See, while I speak the work is begun. See, while I speak the work is finished. The wretch is already a new man in Christ Jesus. The unprincipled heart is made conscientious, the hating heart is made loving, the sensual heart is made pure, the heart filled with low and groveling aims and affections is made to dwell on high even while living below. Surely, O Religion of Jesus, thou are not a dead letter of books, but a thresher of mountains with an iron flail, a breaker up of the world's fallow with unequaled plow-share, a stalwart sower and reaper of heavenly grain on earthly soil!

Has Christianity ever been known to lead a man into bad courses? Did any intelligent father ever imagine that his family was made less pure and upright by its means? Was ever a community suspected of being made more wicked by the faithful preaching of the Gospel in it? Never. All the effects are in the opposite direction. Not in vain do we gather millions of children into our Sabbath-schools, and persuade them toward early virtue. Statistics show that the ranks of criminals are not fed from such children. Not in vain do we gather millions of adults weekly before our pulpits, and urge them to that "holiness without which no man can see the Lord." Statistics show that gallows and prisons are not fed by such men. Not in vain do we send the vernacular Bible to search out every mansion and cottage in the land. It is to-day visibly consoling thousands of sorrowful hearts. Thousands of weak and tempted men are to-day visibly restrained by it from evil. It is visibly reforming great numbers of the worst of men, and as visibly sanctifying great numbers of the best. It is converting multitudes of dens, most dreary and wicked, into pure and delightful homes. Indeed, the Bible is father and mother of homes. Every now and then it gathers up its forces into a spring tide, or overflowing Nile; and entire communities that were black with foulness, are suddenly cleansed and made green as the most emerald spring. So many of these oases has it created from the world's great desert, that one is strongly drawn to believe that the whole dreadful Sahara may at last be recovered to verdure by the steady use of the same means. Indeed, whole countries are already largely recovered. Great Britain and the United States of to-day have been made what they are out of such unpromising stuff as the wild Norsemen of a thousand years ago — made by the Gospel. The Gospel has filled these lands with schools and colleges, with humane and charitable institutions, with public economies and private good, to be found nowhere else. Historically it is so. And what the Biblical Religion has done for these countries it is visibly doing for other nominal Christian countries, just in proportion as the Bible has faith and currency among them. Even heathen lands are beginning to shine under the same transforming power. Christianity is evidently beginning to do over for them what, ages agone, she did for the old Roman world. She found that world a cancer. Its gods were personified vices, its temples were brothels, its women were almost slaves, its slaves were ill-used cattle, and its very amusements were brutal cruelties. The young Christianity came abroad and speedily changed all this. She renewed to its center the standard of morals. Woman rose. Slavery disappeared. Disappeared the vile deities and viler worship. Common people were discovered to have souls. By degrees vice became the exceeding shame that it is. Virtue ceased to be valor. The weak and oppressed found a friend able and willing to shield them from the rapacious and powerful. Instead of gladiatorial shows and Eleusinian mysteries and temples polluted with Bacchus and Venus, came pure sanctuaries and a society bottomed on the Decalogue and the Sermon on the Mount. And from that time to this, just in proportion as the people have been kept in believing contact with the Bible, have all vices faded and all virtues freshened; just in proportion as it has been withheld from such contact has society grown corrupt. I appeal to history. Such results are not only to be presumed from the nature of the Biblical Religion, but they are historical. It belongs to such a religion to do such things, it is adequate to do them, they are found to vary directly as it varies, and there is no other assignable cause of which so much can be said. What more in our philosophy proves the relation of cause and effect? And if less good has as yet been done than could be desired, let it be remembered that men are very depraved, that the habits of an ancient apostasy are terribly strong, that the Religion proposes to deal with free moral agents, and that the world is on a long path which may **gradually** brighten and ascend till it becomes a Milky **Way in** the skies.

10. *The Biblical Religion is widely accepted by great and good men.*

It has met with success in high quarters. **It** has commended itself to men of the widest understandings, the most accurate and extensive culture, the **most** careful and exhaustive investigation, and, withal, the most pure and exalted character. I see Pascal sitting at its feet. I hear Newton and Locke calling themselves after its name. I find Milton, **and** Boyle, **and** Grotius, **and** Hale, and Brewster, gladly enlisting in its service. **Nay, I** find an army **of** poets, philosophers, orators, statesmen, **men of** science, **men of** affairs — men of the **greatest faculties** and attainments, and as good as great — moving with elastic step behind its standards. A glorious following! Not of mere geniuses, you perceive — **else it were a** much smaller matter — but of men whose characters were unspeakably more lofty than **their** intelligence. The body-guard is composed of kings. **They are** the world's greatest **and** best. **Their** brows are hidden with laurels. **We uncover** before them. To **their** homes and haunts we go on pilgrimage. Their very **names** are an inspiration. **From** age to **age,** down to the latest, their words and deeds shall drop sweetly from the lips **of** men.

Such are **the** men. Unlike Hume and many others **of** his **class,** who confess that they have never read **the Bible** with **attention but yet** presume to **pro-**

nounce against it, they thoroughly examined the Book, and then accepted it with all their hearts. And yet, forsooth, some affect to think scorn of the Gospel. They venture to speak of its patent inconsistencies and absurdities. They venture to ridicule it as fit only for dotards and children — as I have known men to do, whose narrow faculties and narrower knowledge, if enlarged a thousand fold, could have been insphered in the great soul of believing Newton. What more unlikely? The likelihood is, that a religion which triumphantly carries the verdict of such great and principled judges, has merit of the highest order, and is able to show evidences of the most solid and convincing aspect. When your specimen has come back to you from the most faithful and illustrious chemists of the age, with their formal certificate that it is genuine gold — who shall blame you if you begin, at least, to take high encouragement?

11. *The Biblical Religion is acceptable everywhere, just in proportion as men are well disposed to virtue.*

Every believer will find that as his virtue varies in degree, so varies the degree of his faith. Every unbeliever will find that in his worst moods as a sinner, he is always the most emphatic in his unbelief. Perhaps you have not yet noticed this. But do you watch yourselves. You will find I am right. I have observed myself and others too narrowly to be deceived in this matter. I am willing to carry my assertion to your inmost consciousness and future experience, and there leave it. Not many weeks will elapse before your watching thought will become convinced of the close sympathy between your state as to virtue and your state as to faith. No delicate barometer sympathizes more closely with the weight of the air, no well-poised vane more closely with the direction of the wind. Faith and goodness are in the same scale of the balance. As one rises the other rises; as one sinks the other sinks. The experience is as uniform as the laws of Nature. So uniform is it that one is bound to conclude, on principles of experimental science, that were his character to sink to the bottom, to the bottom also would sink his faith; that were his character to rise to the summits of sainthood, his faith would rise to as lofty assurance. And history accords. Think of Rousseau, and Voltaire, and Paine, and Vogt, and Stirner, and Heine, and La Mettrie, and Enfantin, and many another — those abandoned men on the one hand, and those fire-spitting adversaries of Christ on the other. "Crush the wretch," said Voltaire; and crept into the sty of the sensualist. "Crush the wretch," said Paine; and grew purple with drunkenness and worse. "Crush the wretch," said Max Stirner; and wrote, "All which I can be and have, entirely careless whether it be human or inhuman, I will be and will have." "Crush the wretch," said La Mettrie; and wrote, "Virtue and vice are empty words; the chief care of a reasonable man should be to satisfy his desires."

This on the one hand. On the other, if you find a man of splendid and surpassing goodness, you are sure to find a believer in that Christ whom all the vices hate and persecute. Even if you find a devout Theist, you are sure to find him as devout a Christian. Even if you find an habitually praying person, you are sure to find him kneeling by the side of a Bible. All this is very suggestive.

12. *The Biblical Religion, in main respects, is vastly superior to the times from which it sprang, and to all other religions.*

We have a very tolerable account of the religious condition of Gentile nations, from an early period down to the time when the Bible was a completed book. And this account shows a wonderful contrast between the Book and its contemporaries. It is plain, not only that they were grossly corrupt in their living, but that their religious theories were of a sort to match their living. Turning from the general run of them to the Book is like turning from night to day. Even if one makes selections, and puts the choicest of those old times and countries and schools of philosophy, as to religious views and practice, by the side of the Scriptures, the contrast is still wonderful. It is still the difference between night and day. I say only what is universally admitted by scholars of respectable habits.

How came the Biblical Religion to stand so high above the general level and all special levels of its time? How came so pure a system to grow out of so corrupt a soil, a soil whose other products were all so corrupt? How came so rational and correct a system to issue from times so crude and childish, as well as abominable, in all their other religious theories! And yet the Bible rose from a nation remarkably bare of literature. The most advanced part of it is not from the hands of cultivated and trained thinkers, but from those of illiterate peasants; for the most part, from the illiterate peasantry of one of the least speculative countries on the globe. And yet scholars shall go hunting through Vedas and Zendavestas and Hesiods, and even through Platos and Senecas and Ciceros; and, so far from finding in any one book or school of books a religious system at all comparable with the Biblical, they shall not be able to cull such a system from all others put together, much less from writings tolerably consistent with each other.

And to-day — though eighteen centuries have gone by since the last chapter was added to the Bible, and though the world since then has made great advances in some things — there is not a scheme of doctrine and practice, in any part of the world, that would so well commend itself to your common sense and common conscience as does that of the Bible. Our own time has been largely leavened with Biblical ideas. They are at large in the common atmosphere, and are breathed by everybody. So, when you take the teachings of some exceptionally correct infidel and compare them with the Bible, you **really to a greater or less extent compare the Bible with itself.** That you may see what the Book is in comparison with other systems, you really need to go to countries or times that have been wholly aside from its influence. But waiving this, and **allowing comparison** to be made between the old Bible **and the fairest** specimen of unbelieving religious speculation now abroad in Christendom, I know that your sober English **judgment** would say that a great gulf yawns between them — to the **very** great advantage **of the Bible.** Take the very best book of young Germany, **and this** would be **your** feeling. **I only** assume that **you** hold fast common sense and a **tolerable system of morals.** You would feel that, if **the Bible** has difficulties, not **a rival but** has greater. **You would feel** that, if there are **vexatious differences** among the interpreters of the Bible, they **are less** many and serious than those between the adherents of **any known school of philosophy.** You would feel that the **best of them all is very** far from being so noble in **its purpose ; so** great **in its means ;** so holy in **its practical teachings ;** in **such striking** accord, as to its doctrines and facts, with Nature and history ; **so** strikingly adapted to the **nature, condition, and leading** wants of mankind ; and so salutary in its observed **effects, as the** old Biblical Religion **under whose** fruitful boughs our fathers lived **and died.**

13. *It is really the Biblical Religion or* **none ;** *and no-religion is the overthrow of* **society.**

Confessedly, no other of the so-called Revealed Religions can compete with the Biblical in general credibility. If we are shut up to choose between this and the best of the others, current or classical — say the Brahminical, the Buddhist, the Mohammedan, the Greek and Roman — the choice is soon made. In purity, in reasonableness, in sublimity, in self-consistency, in superiority to its age, in intrinsic power, in conformity to facts and Nature, in adaptation to the wants of mankind, in usefulness, — not one of them but falls wonderfully behind Christianity. If this is not Divine, how much less those! So feels every intelligent infidel in Christendom. Not a man among us would, on giving up his Bible, for one moment think of supplying its place with the Hindoo or Persian or Arabian or any other Scriptures. But might he not supply it with Natural Religion? Might he not by mere light of Nature hold fast to God, to His government, to our responsibility to Him, and to the reality of moral distinctions? Nay. The same principles of criticism and modes of reasoning which he has allowed to destroy his confidence in the Bible are equally good against the most elementary doctrines of the religion of Nature. It has long been seen that the leading objections against the Bible apply with equal force against the constitution and course of Nature, as the work of God. And it is easy to see that the whole way of dealing that puts away the Bible is just as pertinent against even the common principles of morality. With it one could as well disprove to you the guilt of lying and stealing and murder. That axe will cut down anything you please. Had I space I could give you some convincing examples. But they are unnecessary. None know better than you, from the effect produced on your own minds, whither that sort of objecting and caviling, with which you are familiar as used against the Scriptures, tends. It strikes at the roots of all religious faith. And no one who allows it to destroy his Christianity can logically save from its devouring edge the simplest teaching of Natural Religion.

A subtle sense of this awakes in most minds as soon as they have given up faith in the Bible. They feel unsettled universally. And, after a while, they are found drifting, drifting downward toward complete religious skepticism. Of course men do not often feel like giving up all faith at once. They are terrified at the hugeness of such a lapse. So they commonly feel their way very gradually to the bottom. But the bottom is where, if spared, most of them arrive sooner or later. The noted leaders are there already, and the disciples will evidently all arrive in due time. Their children in most cases move faster than themselves — but they are all moving. The drift is as sensible as was ever that of any straws to the heart of a whirlpool, or of western stars to their setting. After a few years of infidelity very few distinctly recognize to their own hearts either a God or the reality of moral distinctions.

They may be unwilling to confess it. They may hardly be aware of the state of their own minds. But a critical observer will have little trouble in discovering, from many tokens, that they are really just as unsettled on Theism and the whole theory of morals as they are on Christianity. For now many years I have stood and looked in at the clear windows of such men's lives and language — pressing searching face against the panes — and I think I know all about the process going on within. Everything is steadily drifting toward the complete annihilation of faith. And now I can boldly affirm to the inmost consciousness of almost every reflecting man among them, that he is just as far from the elementary Natural Religion as he is from Christianity.

Neither in theory nor in fact, is there any stopping-place for most persons between Christianity and total religious skepticism. They will not and cannot stop at Mohammedanism, or any such system. They will not and cannot stop at Natural Religion. According to experience, and according to consistent logic, they are bound to go on to total Night — not taking harbor with even the most simple elements of moral and religious truth. For even the doom of these elements is spoken when Christianity dies. From that moment they pale and weaken; and at last gaspingly ask to be buried by the side of the dear dead Biblical Religion — the mother whose bosom nourished them and without whom they cannot live. Come to the burial, ye Heavens and Earth — put on all your sables and come to weep at the dreadful funeral of the last of Religions! Woe worth the day! It is the blackest yet seen by a world that has seen many dark days.

Who does not know it? The entire absence of religious belief is repugnant to nature, at war with all interests, and utterly dissolving to society. This has been the feeling from time immemorial with those who have governed mankind. And it has even been the feeling of mankind itself. From the beginning, men have shrunk from a faithless world with the mighty instinct of self-preservation. And such a world *is* the world's destruction. Any reasonable man may know it sufficiently well from the nature of things; and any observing man may know it still more impressively from the course of human experience. We do not need to see the world actually voided of the last atom of faith, and then incontinently falling to pieces. Experience has a less terrible way of teaching us. Do we not know what would be the effect of losing all heat from our globe, though such a disaster has never happened? Our experience of the effect of partial loss abundantly informs us. It would be universal death. In the same way experience informs us that the entire removal of religious faith from the world would result in mortal catastrophe. We have had countless partial losses of faith. We have had countless persons, families, communities, with as many different degrees of it, and not a few with little or none. And, altogether, the tendency of things is as clear as the sun. We know what would be the effect of abating faith to nothing among men, as clearly as we know what would be the effect of taking away the sun from the world. We know it by an induction as broad and conclusive as ever underlaid a science. It means disorder. It means wickedness. It means the decay of homes and governments. It means the French Revolution; and such men as Robespierre, and Mirabeau, and Proudhon, and Cabot, and Fourier, and Comtè. It means alternate revolutions and iron-fisted despotisms in swift succession. It means a horrible carnival of vice and violence and misery all over the world. In short, it means the *last ditch* for humanity, and immeasurable mire at that. The earth would be a blot, and mankind a nuisance that ought to be abated.

Ye who would lead secure lives; who care to enjoy the fruits of your labor; who want your children to do well; who have not lost all regard to your country; who are not yet become misanthropes, and would be sorry to have the planet become an intolerable cess-pool fuming black clouds against the sun till all light and sweetness disappear — stand up for *some* Religion. Nay, stand up for some *revealed* Religion; for the majority of men, to say the least, must have an authoritative system with truths and sanctions which do not need to be reasoned out after the manner of philosophers. And this is the same thing as saying, Stand up for the Biblical Religion. It is this or none.

Thomas Paine sent the manuscript of his "Age of Reason" to Benjamin Franklin for his judgment. That sagacious philosopher returned it with these words: "I advise you against attempting to unchain the tiger. Burn your piece before it is seen by any other person. If the world is so wicked with religion, what would it be without?"

X.
THREE PROPHECIES.

X. Three Prophecies.

1. THEIR AGE 189
2. TYRE 192
3. BABYLON 195
4. MESSIAH 199
5. SUMMING UP 203

THREE PROPHECIES.

I PROPOSE to give an account of the fulfillment of certain prophecies contained in the Scriptures. The better to secure my object, I will begin with a few words on the age of those parts of the Scriptures to which I shall have occasion to appeal.

Once in a while some one ventures to suggest that the so-called prophecies were written after the events which they describe took place. Of course this is easily enough said. If my ignorance is sufficiently great, or my conscience sufficiently small, I can affirm very gravely that there is nothing reliable in the common and accepted histories of the day; that the American Revolution is a fable; that there never were such men as Napoleon and Charlemagne; that Julius Cæsar flourished two centuries ago instead of nineteen; that Sallust and Virgil and Horace, Xenophon and Thucydides and Herodotus either were not real persons, or were Italian and Greek monks of the time of the Crusades. 'Tis true men would lift their eyebrows in derision; 'tis true they might decline to waste argument on so unreasonable a person; still I can say the absurd things and even attempt to offer reasons in support of them. So, if one chooses, he can say that the Epistles of Paul and John were written after the Papacy was matured; that the books of Isaiah and Daniel were composed after Christ's time; that Ezekiel and Zechariah were never known till after the date of Alexander the Great. Nothing is easier than such assertions — nothing. The clumsiest man can speak and print them to any extent. All he needs in order to do it consistently is a readiness to cast away the foundation on which all received history stands, and to admit that nothing whatever is worthy of credit by a man save what some one or more of his own five senses has tested.

There is no national history in the world that has so many marks of literal and conscientious truthfulness about it as the Jewish. It is no flattering eulogy, as we well know. On the contrary, it is a grave account of a course of misconduct and disaster on the part of the Jews, to read which must have been to them mortifying in the extreme. Nothing but honesty would have thought of constructing such records; nothing but their indisputable truthfulness could have compelled so proud a race as the Jews to acknowledge them as genuine history. The man who needs to be told that nations do not feign of themselves such histories as the Old Testament contains, from Judges onward, is not likely to receive any benefit from argument. Now, these candid, severe, and searching annals inform us — not directly, but still more impressively by the manner in which events and persons are linked together — that Isaiah wrote about one hundred years before the first destruction of Tyre, one hundred and sixty years before the destruction of Babylon, and seven hundred years before Christ; that Ezekiel, Amos, and Zechariah wrote about three hundred years before the second fall of Tyre, and all the prophets at least four hundred years before Christ. We are certified of these dates in precisely the same manner in which we are certified that Hume wrote a history about one century ago, Tacitus seventeen centuries, Xenophon twenty-two centuries, Herodotus twenty-three centuries. And the works of these Pagan authors we are confident we have now. Why? Because we have books bearing their names, attributed to them by universal tradition, internally consistent with such an authorship. This is the sufficient reason. Just the reason, too, we are confident that we have the writings of those ancient Scriptural Jews. Certain books are inscribed with the names of Isaiah, Ezekiel, Daniel; they are such as those men would naturally write; it is the overwhelming and uncounteracted tradition that they were the authors. Let the man to whom this is not enough quit his hold of historical facts altogether. The whole great Past is vanished — dead. The scenes which genius has pictured, schools have studied, cabinets and senates walked by, and all people quoted as incontestable verities, are a mere novel; which let him who has infinite leisure read.

Setting it down, then, as among the best established of facts that the book of Isaiah was written about one hundred years before the first destruction of the city of Tyre, and the books of Ezekiel, Amos, and Zechariah about three hundred years before the second fall of that city, let us examine their predictions of these events. These may be found chiefly in the twenty-third chapter of Isaiah, the twenty-sixth of Ezekiel, the first of Amos, and the ninth of Zechariah. The following particulars are given. Tyre would be destroyed by the Chaldæans; the citizens would extensively escape; they would have no rest in their places of sojourn; the city would be restored after the lapse of a period equal to the life of the king who should destroy it; this period would be seventy years; after a while the city would be destroyed the second time; it would be burned; its remains would be cast into the sea; it would never again recover its original importance; still there would be a time when it would be devoted to the service of the true God; at last it would become a mere fisher's rock.

Such were the predictions. How have they agreed with facts? About one hundred years after Isaiah wrote, Tyre was destroyed by the Chaldæans. The citizens did largely escape; history informing us that they and most of their effects were removed by sea before Nebuchadnezzar entered the city. They literally had no rest in the places of their sojourn; history informing us that the conqueror marched immediately to the sack of Egypt, and spread the terror of his name through all the coasts and islands of the Mediterranean where they had taken refuge, keeping them in constant fear and uncertainty. The city was restored in seventy years, and this was the age to which Nebuchadnezzar lived; history informing us that he reigned forty-four years, and was mature enough to take charge of an army when he began to reign. Rebuilt Tyre was destroyed the second time by Alexander the Great, who cast the remains of the old city into the sea to form a causeway for his troops to assail and burn the new. It has never recovered its old consequence; was however at one time the seat of flourishing Christian churches; but is now a mere fisher's rock, and every day becoming more bare and scraped. For a long course of years the harbor has been becoming shallow, and now only small boats can enter it; so that an engineer would say that Tyre must remain a perpetual desolation. Not a ruin, nor fragment of a ruin, can be found to mark the site of her ancient greatness — as says the Scripture, Though thou be sought for, yet shalt thou never be found again.

At the time when Isaiah wrote, Tyre was in all her strength and glory, and for the thousand years of her history had never once been subject to a foreign state. At the same time, too, the Chaldæans were a weak and obscure people, little likely in human judgment to perform the feat predicted of them. Observe how clear and circumstantial are the predictions! What a number of particulars specified! Were these merely fortunate conjectures, these merely accidental coincidences? Of the hundreds of cities which have fallen, what one besides Tyre would all these predictions suit — the Chaldæan conqueror, the escape, the restoration, the seventy years, the age of the conqueror, the second fall, the burning, the casting of all the ruins into the sea, the partial restoration, the Christianizing, the perpetual desolation? Even the single particular that every trace of the city should vanish, has never been realized in the case of any other historical city. Tadmor, Palmyra, Baalbec, Babylon, Thebes, Nineveh — all have their mounds of rubbish, their broken columns, or their quarried foundations. But not a fragment of Tyre remains. The few wretched hovels in the vicinity of its site, and to which its name has been given, have not a stone of the famous city in them; and the few fishermen who now dry their nets on the scraped rock of new Tyre, with the Bedouins who pitch their tents for a night on the opposite sands of the earlier city, see nothing whatever to remind them that here once shone the mother and queen of the world's commerce.

Outside of the religious field I do not think men ever ascribe such coincidences as these to hap-hazard contingency. At least I do not remember to have seen it done. But I do remember that it has been suggested that predictions may sometimes work their own fulfillment. So I ask myself whether the enemies of Tyre, hearing of the predictions against her, might not have been prompted by them to assail her and shape events into the predicted forms. Did Nebuchadnezzar, after besieging the city for thirteen years, allow the citizens to escape with their property in order to save the credit of a Jewish prophecy, or, for the same reason, live till he was seventy years old? Did the Medes and Persians break down the Babylonian empire just at the end of seventy years in order to give Tyre a chance to be rebuilt and fulfill Isaiah? Did Alexander the Great build his causeway that the words of Ezekiel might stand good, They shall lay thy stones and thy timber and thy dust in the midst of the waters, and though thou be sought for, yet shalt thou never be found again? There is but one explanation: Those Jews were real prophets. They spake by inspiration of Him who sees the end from the beginning, and from ancient times the things that are not yet done.

Again, setting it down as among the best established of facts that the book of Isaiah was written at least one hundred and sixty years before the fall of Babylon, and the book of Jeremiah at least sixty years before that event, let us examine their predictions in relation to it. These predictions may be found in the thirteenth, fourteenth, and forty-fourth chapters of the first-named prophet; and in the fiftieth and fifty-first of the second. The following particulars are given. Babylon should be shut up by the Medes and Persians; their leader should bear the name of Cyrus; the river Euphrates should be dried up; two gates should be left open; the city should be taken during a feast when all her rulers and mighty men were drunken; the king and his family should be slain; the sacked city should cease to be inhabited; the shepherd should not even make his fold, nor the Arabian pitch tent there; it should even become pools of water, a possession for bitterns, a den of wild beasts and dragons and other doleful creatures.

Such were the predictions. How do they compare with facts? Years pass away and the Medes and Persians are actually blockading Babylon; and, strange to say, their chief is Cyrus. After the siege has lasted two years, he changes the course of the river that flows through the city, enters by the dry bed at dead of night, finds the gates that guard the passage up from the river neglected in the disorder of a feast, marches direct to the palace where he finds all the principal men already overcome with wine — and Babylon is fallen. Still the city, unlike Tyre, is preserved. In a short time, however, Ctesiphon and Seleucia are built, and the citizens gradually forsake their old dwellings for the new cities. The obstructed Euphrates overflows, and makes pools along the forsaken streets and markets. The irrigation of the plain is neglected, and the fervid sun parches it into a desert where no shepherd can feed his sheep nor Arab his camels. At last a Persian king turns the spot into a hunting ground, stocking it with wild beasts. Lions roar to lions in deserted temples, dragons hiss to dragons in vacant palaces, the bitterns from their pools cry to owls and cormorants in ceiled houses. Nothing but ruin to this day — one wide scene of unrelieved and affecting desolation, where sat for nearly two thousand years the Lady of kingdoms and Beauty of the Chaldees' excellency!

Here again observe how circumstantial are the predictions. Of course it is safe enough to predict that any given city will fall at some time: but to tell by what nations, by what prince, whether by day or night, by assault or stratagem, in time of sobriety or of revel — in short, with some fifteen or twenty specifications of circumstances such as should never be connected with the fall of any other historical city — this would be a very different matter. Suppose it were predicted that the city of New York should fall; fall by a coalition of Mexicans and Bolivians led on by Montezuma XIV.; fall in the course of a blockade; fall in the night when the mayor and aldermen were at a feast; fall by being entered on Broadway, where the usual sentinels and guards had not been set; fall with the accompaniment of the death of the mayor and all his family: further, that after a while the city, though left standing, should cease to be inhabited; become marshy; have its mansions become the lairs of fierce and loathsome animals, and never recover from its desolation to the end of time; — I say, suppose all this were predicted of our commercial metropolis, and you could by some wonderful clairvoyance look down the stream of the next thousand years and find facts answering to the prophecy in every particular, would you hesitate to say, This is a real prophecy. The men who make it are counseled by Him who dwells in the remote Future as in the Present? What would it signify though some should shrug their shoulders, and say that it is indeed a very happy conjecture, one of the most remarkable of accidental coincidences? Would you not know better? What would it signify though some one should begin to descant to you on the power of a clear prediction to verify itself? Do you not know that such a thing would be likely to do quite as much to defend the city as to destroy it; that where it would lead assailants to make special attack it would lead defenders to post special vigilance; that the same hint which would fix an attack on the night of a feast would prevent any such feast from being held, the same hint that would lead men to take advantage of a certain neglected post would prevent that post from being neglected? This argument has special force in the case of the Babylonians. They were more likely than their assailants to have been aware of the Jewish prophecies respecting the fall of their capital. The Jews, with Daniel at their head, had been living among them for many years. Certainly the fall of Babylon and its subsequent condition are a monument to the reality of a Divine inspiration hard to be gainsayed! Put the book by the facts — Isaiah and Jeremiah by Xenophon and Siculus and Strabo and Pliny — and the mind says solemn amen to all civilized ages and nations who have well heard the facts, as with one voice they say, Holy men of God spake as they were moved by the Holy Ghost.

Setting it down as among the best established of facts that the Old Testament prophecies were written several centuries before the time of Jesus, let us examine what they say respecting the Messiah. The following particulars are given. Shiloh, always understood by the Jews to be the Messiah, should come before the scepter should depart from Judah; should come while the temple was yet standing; should come at the end of four hundred and eighty-three years from the issue of an edict to rebuild Jerusalem; should have a forerunner strongly resembling Elijah; should be of the tribe of Judah, the family of David, and city of Bethlehem; should do His first preaching in Galilee; should announce Himself the Messiah; should be a man of sorrows, despised, rejected, put to death, put to death with the wicked and entombed with the rich.

Now look at the fulfillment. Twelve years after the birth of Jesus, Judæa was reduced to a Roman province, and has never since had a ruler of her own. The temple was yet standing, though had He appeared a few years later it would not have been.

From the twentieth year of Artaxerxes, who gave the edict to rebuild Jerusalem, to the crucifixion, are, in round numbers, threescore and nine weeks — four hundred and eighty-three years. John the Baptist prepared the way of Jesus in the spirit and power, the rough strength and energy of Elijah; His lineage and place of birth were according to prediction; according to prediction the first preaching, the scorn, the persecution, the rejection, the death, the burial — facts which were never denied by the early Jews.

No room here for the supposition of happy conjectures and accidental coincidences! Save Jesus, there was no person who claimed to be the Messiah, or suffered as such, till long after the departure of the scepter from Judah, the destruction of the temple, and the threescore and nine weeks of Daniel. Of all mankind Jesus is the only person whom all these predictions suit. Even less than the cases of Tyre and Babylon can this of Jesus be explained on the basis of fortunate guessing and chance agreement. But Thomas Paine rises in his place and says, " This is no solution of ours; we have a better one, most natural and satisfactory. How easy for some Jew who happened to find himself a native of Bethlehem, and a descendant of David, and living about the time to which the Old Testament had ventured to point, to conceive the idea of passing himself off as the person predicted and get put to death for his pains!" But will Paine tell us whether an impostor is likely to set out to personate such a spiritual and sorrowful Messiah as the prophets predicted? Will he tell us whether the Jews would have despised and rejected Him had He come in the guise of a secular and conquering prince? He knows history; he knows the Jews; he knows also that Jesus of Nazareth always claimed to be only the meek and suffering Head of a kingdom not of this world. Let him answer these questions to the Reason whose Age he celebrates and whose honor he drowns in his cups. And when he is about it, will he not tell us further, how it happened that the passing away of the scepter, and the destruction of the temple, and the completion of the four hundred and eighty-three years managed to occur in the life of one man? Will he tell us how many ambitious impostors have lived and died like Jesus Christ? Will he tell us what Jesus would have gained, that a wicked man cares for, had he gained all He asked? Ah, let this man Paine stand up and protest by Collins and Voltaire, that, of all pretenders he ever met with, this same Jesus is the most anomalous and unaccountable! Let him go further. In a sudden flash of clear honest conviction let him declare that Jesus was no pretender, that the laws of human nature and the teachings of history and the instincts of conscience all pronounce the thing incredible. I declare it in his stead. Jesus was the veritable Christ. Those were real prophecies which spake of him so circumstantially centuries before His birth. Isaiah, Daniel, Malachi, and one far more ancient than these, patriarchal Jacob, were the inspired men that all learned and civilized nations that ever fairly considered them have always supposed them to be. From Tyre, from Babylon, from the Son of Mary, we accept the testimony. The one plunges headlong from her sea-throne into nihility; and her last word is, Thus spake the prophets. Another lies putrescent and vulture-flapped and outcast of all nations; and the giant corpse ceases not to repeat from age to age, in mute thunder, Thus spake the prophets. And Thou, Son of man, as born, living, dying — passing beautiful in thy human relationships and heavenly works, in thy crowns of goodness and crosses of trial — Thou reachest our ears with a yet more majestic volume of sound, while still repeating, Thus spake the prophets! Even so, for the holy men spake as they were moved by the Holy Ghost.

There are other prophecies nearly or quite as striking as those which have been examined — particularly those relating to the Jews, to Egypt, and to Papal Rome. I have given three as specimens of the whole. Examine the whole at your leisure, and see how worthy of faith is that great Biblical Religion, which, compacted into a unit, offers in behalf of itself such a broad seal of authentication in fulfilled prophecy. Such a seal validates at once both Theism and Christianity. It affirms in the same breath a God, a written message from Him, and that message centering in Jesus Christ. I hope there are none here who need this witness in order to faith; but I know there are some here whose faith needs to be pushed by it into affecting vividness and busy practice. And full surely do I know that in view of the one argument from prophecy, when carefully weighed, all present in this assembly ought to be able to lay their hands on their hearts and devoutly say with me this Apostles' Creed: —

I believe in God, the Father Almighty, Maker of heaven and earth: and in Jesus Christ His only son our Lord; who was conceived by the Holy Ghost, born of the Virgin Mary, suffered under Pontius Pilate, was crucified, dead, and buried; the third day He rose from the dead; He ascended into Heaven and sitteth on the right hand of God the Father Almighty; from thence He shall come to judge the quick and the dead.

I believe in the Holy Ghost; the Holy General Church; the Communion of saints; the forgiveness of sins; the resurrection of the body; and the life everlasting. *Amen.*

XI.

AN
INCREDIBLE IMPOSTURE.

XI. AN INCREDIBLE IMPOSTURE.

1. THE MEN 207
2. WHAT TO CHOOSE 209
3. THE MOST IRKSOME? 210
4. THE MOST DANGEROUS? 212
5. THE LEAST LIKELY TO SUCCEED? 215
6. THE LEAST GAINFUL IF SUCCESSFUL? . . . 217
7. WELL? 219

AN INCREDIBLE IMPOSTURE.

IF the Christian Religion is a mere fable, it certainly is a very cunningly devised one. There is so much coherence about the system, it includes so many great moral discoveries, it is so incomparably superior both as a theory and as a practice to everything else of the kind that has come down to us from antiquity, that no reasonable person can for a moment suppose it to have had its origin in a shallow mind, or even one of average capacity and intelligence. The contrivers of the Christian Religion, whatever else they may have lacked, certainly did not lack great sense and genius. Theirs is no ordinary fable, but one of the world's masterpieces.

Further, if the Christian Religion is a fable, its contrivers were not only very intelligent men but also very wicked men. Having laboriously fabricated the system themselves, from beginning to end, they were perfectly sure it was not Divine. Having never wrought a single miracle in support of it, they knew perfectly that they had never wrought any. And yet these men passed their lives in pretending to work miracles, and in trying to persuade men that the man-devised religion was God's own. They called God to witness that it was so. They staked their souls on it. Still worse, they called their leader in the imposture God, and paid him Divine honor, and required all others to do the same. They lived and died and went to possible judgment, still clinging to these crimes. Not satisfied with this wholesale attempt to swindle their own times into falsehood and idolatry, they committed their story and system to writing, and sent it down to do what it might toward cheating all times to come. All this they did while having great religious light, and while denouncing damnation against whomsoever loveth and maketh a lie. That they did all this is proved by uniform tradition, and by the New Testament — a book which they as plainly indorsed, prompted, or wrote, as Tacitus did his history, and which confessedly gives with substantial correctness the teachings and claims of the founders of Christianity. Scarcely any language is too severe to characterize such men. They were unblushing and unrelenting hypocrites; they were gross, systematic, life-long liars; they were deliberate, daily perjurers; they were conscious, heaven-daring idolaters. Their lives and deaths were one enormous falsehood and blasphemy. If it is true that Christianity is a fable, then we are sure that its contrivers must be classed, not only among the craftiest, but also among the worst of men.

Now I have a question to ask. I would like to know what sort of a religious system such persons would be likely to frame. They have concluded, say, to turn religious impostors. They are now sitting down to determine what particular shape their imposture shall take; what particular system they shall try to put off on the world as Divine. They can think of a great many systems — hundreds of them. Now, of these conceivable systems, which will they be most likely to take? Remember they are crafty and bad men, very crafty and very bad — men governed wholly by passion and policy. I ask, What sort of a religious scheme will persons of this stamp choose for their imposture? Will it be the one most of all opposed to their governing principles? Will it be the system which is at once the most irksome to their feelings; the most dangerous to their persons; the least likely to succeed; and the least rewarding, if successful, in such things as bad men desire? Your quick reply is, Of course not. You do not wish a moment to consider what answer to give. You know at once that for them to make such a choice as that would be as much against the laws of Nature, would be as much of a miracle, as it would be for a stone to move up instead of down when left free in the air. Instead of such a system they would certainly choose just the reverse — the one that seemed to them likely to minister most largely to their passions and selfish policy with the least risk, delay, and inconvenience to themselves — the one whose propagation promised to be the least irksome to their feelings, the least threatening to their safety, the most likely to succeed, and the **most** rewarding if successful **in** such things as unprincipled men desire most. There have been several scores of religious impostors, among them some twenty false Christs; and in the **whole** number there cannot **be** found one whose scheme of imposture plainly took no counsel of **his passions** or his policy, but was at the outset, evidently to himself, the most opposed of all possible schemes to his gratifications and selfish interests.

And now, my hearers, with the aid of these premises am I not able to construct for you an unanswerable argument for the truth of the Christian Religion? **It is** altogether incredible that shrewd and wicked men, setting out to propagate a religion, and having an indefinite number of religious systems to choose from, should have chosen that given in the New Testament. **It** is impossible, as human **nature is, that** such men should have chosen such a **system** to propagate. For, it must have been plain **to them** at the outset that of all conceivable religious **systems** this was the least fitted to meet the **demands** of their policy or their passions: from the outset it must **have been** as plain to them as day that of all schemes of religious imposture possible to them this would be the most irksome and dangerous to **them in the** propagation, the least likely to succeed, **and the** least rewarding **to** them if successful. **Let me** now proceed to show this.

1. It must have been perfectly plain to those men, **from the beginning, that** they could not adopt a religious scheme whose propagation would be so *irksome* to their feelings as Christianity.

The Christian Religion gives no countenance to sin in any shape or in any person. It curbs all passions and denounces all vices. A life regulated strictly according to its rules would be gloriously pure and bright. This cannot be denied. Now the propagators of such a system would of course be under the necessity of appearing to conform to it very rigidly themselves. They must seem models of pure and noble conduct. Otherwise men would be sure to discredit them, and could plead as authority for doing so the teachings of the system itself. All their lives long, with the watchful eyes of multitudes on them, they must walk with the most shining outward propriety. They must seem pure and meek and disinterested; temperate, unrevengeful, unambitious, uncovetous, devout; must seem to be what Jesus and His apostles are claimed to have been. Now, to lead such lives would not, indeed, be very irksome to really righteous men — men whose hearts are rich as any placer with holy principles. But far otherwise with grossly wicked men, such as the founders of Christianity were, if they were impostors. To such it would be a perpetual crucifixion. To such it would be constant vigilance, constant self-restraint, constant spurring up of themselves to what is essentially and intensely disagreeable. And these Jews must have plainly seen at the outset that it would be so; and that among all the schemes they **could devise not** one would place them under such galling restraints, as long as they should live, as this same Christianity. A system like that of the Pagans around would allow their lives to match freely with their wicked hearts; one like that of Mohammed would leave their passions and their policy large liberty; one such as the Jews had framed out of Moses by glosses and Rabbinical traditions would allow at least their pride and ambition and avarice and re**venge to** walk **abroad** in open day; but this strict Christianity would grant them no license whatever, and even refuse **to** be propagated unless they would cut off all spotted indulgences and live the lives of saints.

2. It must also have been perfectly plain to these men, from the beginning, that they could not adopt **a religious** scheme whose propagation would be so *dangerous* **to** them as that of Christianity.

The Jews have always been intolerant, exclusive, and expectant of a political Messiah. **At** the time when Christianity came, **it was** their cherished idea **that** the predicted Christ would reign in outward glory as their king, defeat all their enemies, and raise them to a preëminence among the nations more **proud** than they had ever attained in their palmiest **days.** They were wedded to the traditions which contradicted and suppressed Moses more than they were to Moses himself. But Christianity set itself stoutly against all these cherished faiths and prejudices. It gave no quarter to the unscriptural traditions. It acknowledged in the Messiah only a spiritual and suffering Deliverer. It offered its blessings as freely to Gentile as to Jew, and called on the children of Abraham to recognize the substantial equality of the circumcision and of the uncircumcision before God. Such a scheme as this, it was easy to see, would awaken intense opposition in the Jewish mind, especially as it included no bait of worldly advantage whatever. And as to the Gentile world, still worse was to be anticipated from it. The nations were broken up into castes; those who held the power and the riches and the honor would naturally shrink from the Christian doctrine of the universal brotherhood of men. The nations were filled with the lust and habit of revenge, rapine, and war; they would loathe the Christian precepts of meekness, contentment, justice, and peace. The nations were idolaters; they would find in Christianity an unsparing breaker of all their choice and worshipped images — a grinder to powder of the whole mythology that came down from the fathers, and sung in poets, and reigned in priesthoods, and breathed grateful perfume from altars, and shone in the marbles and gold of temples, and satisfied every man with a god after his own heart. The nations were formalists and ritualists; devoted to the external; men of processions, and robes, and sacrifices, and postures; they would find in Christianity the severe simplicity of a spiritual worship, very bare of forms, and barer still of permissions to trust in them. The nations were gross and sensual, steeped to the lips in all manner of vice, wallowing like swine in the worst forms of corruption and debauchery; they would find in Christianity the stern censor, the unsparing denouncer, the bitter and tormenting threatener of their indulgences. "Filled with all unrighteousness, fornication, wickedness, covetousness, maliciousness; full of envy, murder, deceit, malignity; whisperers, backbiters, despiteful, proud, covenant-breakers, without natural affection, implacable, unmerciful," as they were — such a religious system as that of the New Testament would chafe and smite them at every turn, would be as distasteful to them as gall and wormwood. In a word, no scheme which could be devised would run so strongly counter to the spirit, wishes, and habits of the age as this. An attempt to propagate it would be really an attempt to tear down all that men most clung to in the views and practices and institutions of the times. Such an attempt was certain to rouse against those who should make it a storm of feeling and persecution of the severest kind. It required no extraordinary sagacity to foresee for them exiles, dungeons, stakes, scaffolds, crucifixions. What actually occurred might have been anticipated by any sensible man — an Israel howling around their tribunals, Crucify him, crucify him; a Gentiledom reeking with ten general persecutions, and with the life of almost every Christian leader. One could not contrive a system better suited to rasp and exasperate both the besotted many and the arrogant, powerful few than this very Christianity. One could not put forth a scheme of religion which all classes of those scandalous times would be so unwilling to have prevail as this same rigid, humbling Christianity. And, I repeat it, intelligent impostors must have seen this; must have foreseen the intense danger to which they would expose themselves by trying to establish such a system in an intolerant age; while at the same time they were conscious of being able to contrive a hundred systems less repugnant to the spirit of the age, and therefore more safe.

3. It must also have been plain to these men, at the outset, that of all systems of religion which they could devise, Christianity was the one least likely to succeed in *getting establishment.*

It had nothing whatever of a worldly nature to tempt people to its acceptance. We have seen that it was fiercely at war with the prevailing tastes, opinions, and practice of the age when it appeared. Specially distasteful must it have been to the more influential classes; for their interests and privileges were most intimately wrought into the old order of things, and must suffer the most from its disturbance. The rich and noble fattened on the general corruption, and rose the higher the lower the people sunk. All the passions and policies of the time went to fortify it against such a religion; and what had the time besides **passions and policy?** There **was no element of power** which Christianity **could press into its service for** proselyting, save the poor, **beggared,** stupid remains of **a** Pharisaic conscience. **And** if, perchance, a few under its feeble **promptings** should **be** disposed **to** accept the new and purer system, what had they to expect but the sternest treatment from the host of their less impressible companions? The first converts to the imposture, like the impostors themselves, must lay their **account** with disgrace and troubles of all kinds —**nay,** with fire and sword. With **no miracles** to indorse it, **with no sword** to enforce it, with human nature **against it, w**ith society and institutions against it, with interest and education and passi**on** against **it,** the imposture could not reasonably be **expected** to make any progress. If the ship **were launched** it could not sail. There was no wind from **any point** of the compass, and no canvas to catch **it** if there **was.** Some **form of** polytheism, with a **plenty of shows and a** plenty of indulgences, might **win its way;** a Mohammedanism, with **a** naked scimeter in one hand **and** a sensual Paradise **in** the other, might come to flourish; even a modified Judaism, appealing to the pride of one people and accommodating somewhat the prejudices and passions of others, might stand a chance of considerable success; but this Christianity, without prestige, without robes, without force, without indulgences, without miracles, and even without truth as a revelation — what success could be hoped for it? A system less likely to succeed could not have been contrived. It was doomed, to begin with. And, to begin with, sagacious impostors must have seen it so. In thinking over the various schemes of deceit they might adopt, it must at once have occurred to them that, of them all, not one had so unprosperous and impracticable an air as this same prickly Christianity.

4. It must also have been plain to the founders of Christianity, from the beginning, that, of all possible religious systems which they might try to establish, the Christian, if established, would prove the *least rewarding in such things as bad men most desire.*

What is the controlling desire of such men? Is it to see truth triumphant? Is it to do good? On the contrary it is to promote selfish ends, to gratify evil passion in some form. Could they succeed in establishing Christianity, how much would it do for them in this direction? Would it give them any facilities for sinful pleasures? Would it gratify their avarice with silver and gold? Would it give them outward pomp and political power? A successful Mohammedanism would do this: not so a successful Christianity. This system gives a virtual prohibition of selfish ambition, of carnal indulgences, of secular rule, to its founders. They could not be Epicureans or generals or princes, without defying their own teachings. "But they might have great notoriety, great respect, and great influence: and undoubtedly bad men are often fond of these."

Yes, but these they would have as the successful founders of any religion. What bad men most desire is not notoriety and influence, but notoriety and influence which they can turn to a selfish and carnal account. And here such a religion as the Christian would hamper and thwart its successful propagators as no other would. It would compel them to use their fame and influence apparently for pure and benevolent ends: the moment they did otherwise their own teachings would proclaim them impostors. Shrewd, capable men as they were, they must have foreseen this. No thunders out of heaven were needed to tell them. As worldly, selfish, unprincipled men, they must instinctively have felt that they could not establish any scheme of religion which would prove so unprofitable to them as this as yet hypothetical Christianity. In considering what delusion, among the many delusions conceivable, they should select to propagate for their selfish and wicked ends, a single glance would settle that no system if successfully carried out was likely to net them so little that they cared for as the system that now bears the name of Christ.

My argument is now complete. I have shown that the founders of the Christian religion, if impostors, were exceedingly bad as well as capable men. I have shown that to such men no religious system would be at once so irksome in the working, so dangerous in the propagation, so little likely to succeed, and so little rewarding if successful, as that which is found in the New Testament. It is plain also that they must have abundantly known this from the very commencement of their enterprise. Did those men act, not only without motive, but against all motive? Did they laboriously palm off upon the world a system which they knew to be false, and as clearly knew to be more squarely opposed than any other both to the tastes of the age and to the objects they had in view in undertaking it? Let those believe this who can. Of incredible things what is more incredible? Believe me, there would have been no Christian Religion in the world had it been left with impostors to announce and establish it. They would never have taken the trouble to do it. With so many more easy, congenial, popular, and profitable systems at hand, they would have cast this aside, after a single glance, as out of the question. Christianity, therefore, is no contrivance of man. It is no cunningly devised fable. Its God is real, and it is really from God. He framed and established it; and we on these Sabbath days speak and hear a Gospel that was born in heaven, and brought to us by heavenly hands.

My hearers, you have now listened to an argument in behalf of as important a statement as has ever been made in your hearing. No matter how many years you have lived, nor where you have been, nor how carefully you have sought to catch wise and weighty words. Never did you hear a sentence that was heavier with importance than this brief one, The Christian Religion **is true.** These few words outweigh all the arts and sciences. In one breath they affirm both Theism and Christianity. If we deny them and keep to the denial, if we doubt them and keep to the doubt, we shall be castaways from God. If we accept them with a working faith we shall inherit an eternal kingdom. Is such faith involuntary? Nay, it comes surely to every one who will candidly and patiently inquire after the truth: not in full stature at first, not at once **in all cases, not** all at once often, but after a **while and by degrees,** according to the honesty and earnestness of **the search.** On this fact rests the justice **of** making **such** great issues depend on **an** intellectual reception of Christianity.

The **Christian** *Religion is true.* Then it deserves to be enthroned as a king in this community. **Every person** should be willing to take the law from **it;** nay, more than willing. It should preside over **all** business and over all pleasure. It should nullify **all** faiths, customs, **and** laws which conflict with it. Old and young should ponder it diligently and reverently. **It should** be everybody's text-book. **Every** home should be its sanctuary, and every heart **its royal** pavilion. After its words none should speak again, and its speech should drop upon us.

Ah, **how far** is it from being so! In how many of our **families does it** bear no rule! How many enterprises **make** no account of it — how many hearts are careless or averse to it! And yet, if there is anything great, valuable, and authoritative in the world, it is this same system of faith and practice which reveals Infinite God and which Infinite God has revealed to us. None will trifle with it or neglect it with impunity. None will forsake it and disobey it without seeing cause to regret their misconduct ere long. None will love it and cleave to it without soon seeing reason to rejoice in their discretion. God will stand by His religion. In due time He will make demonstration of His regard for it in every man's experience. The communities, the individuals, who honor it He will honor. They who submit to it shall rule; they who enthrone it shall be enthroned. The patient hearers of the Word, and brave doers of it, shall find that Christianity is not cast upon the world by its Father as a foundling. He will acknowledge His paternity. His eye watches, His hand guards His child; and blessed the man who shelters and nourishes in his home on earth this true child of Heaven!

XII.
ANCIENT WONDERS.

XII. Ancient Wonders.

1. CREDIBLE 225
2. MOSAIC 229
3. CHRISTIAN 233
4. JOINT IMPORT 247

ANCIENT WONDERS.

AMONG natural events some rise greatly above others in intrinsic greatness and in the greatness of the causes producing them. Are there not some events much greater still?

I think so. The air of all times and countries is filled with rumors of supernatural occurrences. We meet everywhere echoes which might well have been born of the most wonderful voices; everywhere odors which might well have come from the distant swaying of the most royal and perfumed of queenly robes.

Nay, there are events taking place even now, which, to say the least, it is very hard to bring clearly within the class of the purely natural. Is no one of you ever at a loss to see how mere animal parentage can account for the bodies and souls that are constantly being born; to see how it is possible for anything in a way of mere Nature to produce its equal, much more its superior? Nay, do we not know of a science which, at the lips of the great majority of its most gifted and trusted students, declares that the long stretch of organic life on this globe has been many times totally broken and as many times renewed by that greatest of all marvels, a sudden creation?

And then what a fitting preface would miracles be to such a system of religion as the Biblical! A grand palace should have a grand vestibule. A great monarch should be preceded by no common herald. Whatever else may be denied of the religion of the Bible it cannot be denied that it is great. It seeks the greatest objects, works by the greatest means, and claims some of the greatest ideas and literature and effects the world ever saw. Its purpose is the virtue and salvation of mankind. It offers to secure this purpose by a Divine atonement, and by a constant miracle of renewal and sanctification in the hearts of men through the Holy Spirit. Yes, it would be a fitness — such a fitness as we see that Nature loves, and such as we intuitively recognize as belonging to truth — were this great temple fronted by a porch of signs and wonders. Yes, it would be but a graceful harmony — like the accords in music, or the symmetries of physical beauty — were this pure and lofty faith of Christendom found poising itself, in part at least, on such a foundation of elect and precious stones as the marvels which transcend Nature.

But some are disposed to object. They tell me that miracles have never been needed and so have never occurred; that an Infinite Being could have so made Nature as to secure all His ends by natural laws alone; that He who actually secured by these means the greater part of His ends, could, with omniscience and omnipotence to help Him, have managed to secure by them the small remainder. I happen, however, to know that not even an Infinite Being can work impossibilities in the nature of things; and that among these impossibles may well be that of securing from mere Nature as complete results as from Nature and the Supernatural, together.

They tell me that miracles, in their very nature, are amendments — mere supplements and patches to eke out a faulty system — attempts to correct what is too long or too short, too fast or too slow, too weak or too strong; in short, such a thing as could never have come from a perfect Being. I happen, however, to know that great deeds are not necessarily after-thoughts. They may enter into the original plan of their author, with all smallest matters. And why may not miracles have entered into a great primal plan of creation which was never for a moment supposed to be complete without them? In their nature, they are no more amendments than a pendulum is an amendment to a clock, or a roof to a house, or the Winter Palace to St. Petersburg. Did not the builder from the first propose the whole?

Above all, they tell me that miracles are contrary to experience. I happen, however, to know some things in the way of science that make light of such an objection. Grant that miracles are contrary, not only to our personal experience, but also to that of all our predecessors for some thousands of years.

What then? Does it follow that they have never occurred, or even that they cannot be known with scientific sureness to have occurred? Nothing of the sort. We certainly know of real geological wonders which have never once been observed actually occurring during the entire history of our race, thus far; we certainly know of real astronomical wonders, sure to occur after many ages, but of which all previous human history will not have seen a solitary instance, but rather constant facts of directly the opposite bearing. For example. Many ages hence the moon will begin to recede from the earth. That will be an event totally unprecedented in the history of mankind. Nay, it will be an event directly the opposite of what has always been occurring. From long before man, down to that remote future, the moon, instead of retreating from the earth, will have been steadily approaching it; and were the race on that distant day to reason merely from what has been within its time to what will be on the morrow, it would confidently say that the satellite will be still approaching. But it would be a mistake. On that very morrow the lunar orbit will begin to expand, — will do a thing which it has never yet done in all the human annals. And, what is more, it will be a thing which, with the help of a little astronomy, might have been known with supreme certainty. We know it with supreme certainty to-day — thanks to the great observations of Halley, and the greater mathematics of La Place. And many other things of the same sort we know — geological and astronomical — absolutely sure to occur, though contrary to the whole previous human experience.

When, then, I find the Scriptures telling profusely of great events which owed their origin directly to Divine will and power, I am by no means stumbled. If there is a God, I see no reason why He, any more than myself, should confine Himself to indirect action. And I think I do see how He might draw Himself far nearer to the thoughts and sensibilities of mankind were He to insert His own hand occasionally in the scheme of Nature and visibly overrule its ordinary goings, even as we ourselves do in our small way for our small occasions. In view of the traditions of the world, in view of the marvels of science and of daily experience, and in view of the essential fitness of things, I see no reason why a broad highway is not open on which faith in miracles may call about it abundant evidence, and freely travel into all the high places of reason in this reasoning age.

The Bible miracles chiefly belong to two great groups: the Mosaic and the Christian. Let us consider these groups separately.

I. The Mosaic Miracles.

It is granted by all — save the most fantastic of skeptics, whom your English common sense would not tolerate for a moment — that the Hebrews were once slaves in Egypt; that they came out under the leadership of one Moses; that this Moses established what is known as the Mosaic Economy, and of course was believed in as to his sayings and writings by the Hebrews of his time; that the Pentateuch with its account of the exodus is in the main his sayings and writings. I say, this is universally conceded by those whom you would consider sane men. The monuments and traditions require it. The grounds on which our best history rests require it. We have no history at all if the particulars I have mentioned are not history. Your Washington may be a fable. Your Mayflower may be a dream. Your Columbus may be a legend. Why not?

Now the books of Moses give us the following account. They say that the Hebrews witnessed ten general plagues sent on Egypt by means of Moses. They say that, at the stretching forth of his rod, a way was opened through the Red Sea; and that a whole nation actually marched by that strange way, till, from the further bank, they saw the crystal walls fall and drown the pursuing army of the Egyptians. They say that a pillar of cloud by day and a pillar of fire by night visibly led the pilgrim host for forty years. They say that, during this long period, their clothing waxed not old and their daily bread came daily from heaven. They say that, on their coming to Sinai, God came down on the mount in foretold majesty of lightnings and thunders and earthquakes, and spake His law in awful proclamation that sounded through all the marshaled millions and carried dismay to all their hearts. They say many other things of a like character.

What I would have you notice is that the entire Israel of that day must have known whether this account was true or not. They could not have passed forty years in such a wonderful experience without knowing it. And they could not have been without such a forty years' experience without knowing that too, to a perfect certainty. If no such plagues were ever wrought for their deliverance, they knew they were never wrought. If they never went through the Red Sea as on dry land, every soul of them knew that they never did. If they had not been led by that intelligent Pillar for nearly half a century, they all to a man knew that they had not been. If they had never bowed and quaked before a quaking and bowing and speaking Sinai, not a Hebrew of them all but knew it like noonday. Do you suppose the Governor of Connecticut could persuade us that by raising his hand he had made a dry way for us across Long Island Sound, had actually led all our citizens by that way, and had afterward fed us all by miracle for many years, if he had not done so? The events alleged by Moses were of such a nature that the senses of every man, woman, and child among the Hebrews could infallibly judge of them. A common man could judge of them just as well as a philosopher — the least among the thousands of Israel as well as he who was learned in all the wisdom of the Egyptians. So it is a clear case: Nothing could be clearer. No single Hebrew could have been deceived, much less the whole nation. No single one of those events could have happened without their knowing it, much less such a long course and great system of such events. If no such constellation of miracles ever rained its glories about them, the Hebrew public of the time could never by any possibility have been convinced that it did. None but a madman would have tried to convince them. In claiming such an astounding history for them Moses would have made faith in himself forever impossible; and have convicted himself in face of heaven and earth as being equally unsupplied with principle and with common sense.

But Moses did claim such a history for them. What is more, he told them to their faces that they all believed his story. He made this bold assertion over and over again. He everywhere averred their full knowledge of its truth. He staked his whole credit with them on the correctness of these assertions and assumptions. He averred that the people had accepted at his hands a religious system because they believed in him and his miracles. Of course it was so. It would be irrational in the last degree to suppose the contrary. All the monuments and traditions are against it. All the history we have is against it. As sure as there is any reliable history in the world, Israel profoundly believed in their leader and in his miraculous narrative. As a sane man, he never would have dared to put such a narrative before them had he not already known them to believe the substance of it. So all sane critics — believers and unbelievers — feel and always have felt. What more could we have?

' Hence it is plain that the Mosaic miracles were genuine. They were fully believed in by millions, every one of whom must have known whether they were real or not. And if they were real, it is certain that the righteous and beneficent religion to which they testify, with its God and revelation, is true. No one at the present day who admits the reality of such events as the cleaving of the Red Sea into a national highway by the rod of Moses, but will also admit that those events carry with them the entire religion of the Old Testament.

II. The Christian Miracles.

We find in the New Testament a cluster of miraculous accounts not inferior to the Mosaic in the greatness of their claims.

Notice at the outset that it is granted by all — save the most fantastic and impracticable of skeptics whom you and I would not for a moment think of heeding — that there was such a person as Jesus of Nazareth; that He had twelve special disciples called apostles; and that these apostles either wrote or indorsed the various books of the New Testament. These are historic facts. Otherwise we have no history at all. We may throw away our Bancrofts, and Macaulays, and all other famous and much trusted books which offer to return the Past for the instruction of mankind. "I find," says Sir Isaac Newton, "more sure marks of authenticity in the Bible than in any profane history whatever."

Now see the account of miracles given by this apostolic New Testament. It tells us that a host of angels appeared to the shepherds of Bethlehem and sang in their hearing of the Nativity; that a star, moving as if instinct with intelligence, guided a caravan from the distant east to the infant Jesus; that as Jesus was being baptized a voice fell from heaven on the ears of thousands gathered from all parts of the country, saying, This is my Beloved Son. It tells us that, promptly at the speaking of a word or the lifting of a finger or some other sign equally insufficient as cause, the blind received sight, the lame walked, the deaf heard, the dumb spake, the leapers were cleansed, the paralytics took up their beds and walked, the madmen became sane, the sick were cured of whatever disease they had, the very dead were raised. It tells us that at the crucifixion the whole land was darkened and shaken; that a terrible angel flashed down from heaven in sight of the Roman guard about the sepulcher; that Jesus rose from the dead, and was seen forty days among the apostles, and, on one occasion, by more than five hundred brethren; that

He rose to heaven through broad day in **view of the** Twelve; that these men themselves **received** the gift of tongues and **the power of working miracles,** and wrought **them for a great many years** in a great number **of** specified cases, over **a** wide extent of country.

Many scores of such wonders are distinctly recorded; and we are told that these are mere sam**ples of** a much larger number. **See what** breadth **of** statement! " And His fame **went** throughout all Syria; and they brought to Him all sick people that were taken with divers diseases and torments, and those that were possessed with devils, and those that were lunatic, **and** those that had the **palsy;** and He healed them." Similar statements **are several** times made in **regard to** the miracles **of both Jesus** and His apostles. The representation **is that the** whole land was filled with marvels. They overflowed into surrounding countries. They lasted for the best **part of a** century. They counted **by** thousands and **tens** of thousands. They ligh**tened** in city and on country-side. They flashed on the eyes of nobles and commoners, **of** learned and **simple.** Scarcely a hamlet into which they did not go. Scarcely a man who did not have opportunity, over and over again, of examining them personally with all his senses. Their heavy footfall was heard near every door; the family had but to open and look and listen. It would, of **course, have** paid a Jew to **push a** pil**grimage** to Gaul and Britain to come into the presence of such superb events; but they came to greet him in his own streets, and he had but to follow the crowd or to climb the sycamore or to ask the eye-witness of yonder dwelling in order to have evidence of them as triumphant as the mathematics.

Such is the representation. And we are assured that these wonderful things were far from being done in a corner. In general Jesus allowed the whole world to look on while He wrought. He challenged the broadest day to help them. Shine your brightest, O Sun! Gather the wise and the learned; gather the men of theory and the men of affairs; gather the unsophisticated and the prejudiced, the devout and the worldly, the populace and the counselors; let them all come and sift this whole matter to the bottom! So they came — the scholarly Rabbi in all the pride of learning; the honorable ruler in all the pride of place; the bitter enemy with his sharp outlook for imposture; the proud Pharisee drawing his robes more closely about him lest they should touch the shamefaced publican at his side; the Sadducee with his free-thinking; the Essene with his dreamy intuitions; in a word, the great public in all its grades and opinions and habits. And there on the thronged thoroughfare they looked and listened as blind Bartimeus regained his sight. There at the city-gate they looked and listened as the dead man sat up and began to speak. There at the crowded city-house they looked and listened while the roof was broken up and the palsied man was let down before Jesus and cured. And there at Calvary, with its martyrdom and surging sea of people, they looked and listened and felt as night came up at midday, and the ground shook beneath them at the majestic tread of the earthquake.

We are so familiar with this story that we are apt to miss the sense of its exceeding greatness. It is easy for you to read without emotion the oft-read account of the Nain widow's child, or of Lazarus bewailed of sisters; but could you actually stand by the bier which a word is shaking with the throes of resurrection, or by a cave whence swaddled death comes promptly forth at the word of command, you would hardly be able to keep back your exclamations of wonder and awe. Depend upon it, these are wondrous accounts. You must try to transfer yourself to those distant times. You should gather about you in idea the living circumstances under which almightiness is said to have stepped forth to its work. You should, as it were, hear with your own ears the inadequate utterance and the hot tramp of the mighty result. Then would your dull conceptions be roused and empowered as was that ancient Lake of Gennesaret by the descent of the storm upon it. Looking as through your own eyes, you would better take in the huge pretensions of the Scripture narrative — as it tells of lame men leaping as the hart; dumb tongues singing; deaf ears waking up to a gospel of sweet sounds and the voices of kindred; blind eyes that had rolled sightless from birth drinking in with passionate joy the bright aspects of Nature and the loving looks of parents and children; dead bodies in which decay had already proclaimed itself, quickened anew with the mystery of life and soul, and going forth among men with the old potential step of manhood in its prime — as it tells of such events forthspringing with glorious promptitude at the feeblest natural signal, and with a profusion and overtness that spoke to the whole land and age.

Now what I have to say is — and I say it with supreme confidence — that such an account of such events as these could not by any possibility have been believed, either by the Jewish public of that day or by the apostles, much less by both, had it been altogether false.

Just think of it. A boat holding Jesus and his twelve disciples was crossing the Sea of Galilee. The sky darkened, the winds rushed, the waters were lashed into great billows and raged about the little company with terrible outcry. The skiff reeled. It sprang madly aloft, and plunged — as if never to rise again. The water came pouring in. The reverence of the disciples for their sleeping master could hold them back no longer. They awoke Him with, Lord, save us, we perish. Then stood up Jesus and looked calmly forth. At His feet clung the quaking disciples, around Him sky and sea were mingling in stunning uproar, beneath

Him the boat was gradually settling under the wave. Then rose His voice clear and imperative above the storm, Peace, be still. At once all was quiet. The shouting voices of the elements ceased. Ceased the perilous uplift of the sea; ceased the swift march of the tornado. But a murmur, a ripple, a zephyr, survived the utterance of that mastering sentence. The saved boat again moved serenely on its way; while the saved disciples whispered to each other in amazement and awe. What manner of man is this that even the wind and sea obey him?

Such is the account given by these disciples. Are the facts alleged such as it was possible for them to be deceived in? Could they help knowing whether they were out in a violent storm on the Sea of Galilee? Could they help knowing whether Jesus used the words attributed to Him; and whether, immediately on their being spoken, all embroiled Nature sunk into complete hush? Might a single man of them, by any possibility, mistake in such matters as these, with at least three senses brought to bear on them? If not a single man, how much less the whole Twelve? Let a sailor tell you that lately he met a terrible storm and came near being wrecked, but was saved by a sudden lull of the gale just as he had given himself up for lost — would you ever think of suspecting that his senses had deceived him? And should a friend hint, This is an honest man; he doubtless thinks he was tossed by a storm, and that the storm suddenly lulled; but he may be mistaken after all, and have had nothing but a bright sky all his voyage through — would you not think him very unreasonable? And should the entire crew come forward to confirm the story, would it even occur to you that the senses of the whole number had played them false? "No," you would say, "if these statements are not true, these men are flagrant impostors. The things they allege are of such a nature that no one sound man could mistake in respect to their reality. Much less could such mistake happen to a whole crew." I say as much of the facts alleged in that apostolic story. Those many apostles could not have been deceived by some jugglery of their senses into a belief that a furious tempest instantaneously slept at the command of Jesus when it did not.

So of other cases even more striking. Did not the Twelve know by at least three senses whether midnights and earthquakes poured their testifying pomp about the noon of the crucifixion? Did they not know by every sense they had whether a living Jesus was among them for forty days after He had been pronounced dead by the Grand Coroners of Judæa and Rome? Did they not know whether they saw Jesus rising through the day into heaven, and whether thereupon they saw an angel standing among them in white robes to tell of His Second Coming? Especially did they not know whether they themselves possessed the power of working miracles, and whether they **actually wrought them** in great number **and splendor for many years? Do not be so unreasonable as to think, No. You** and I understand very well **that some things are perfectly incredible, and that** this **is one** of them. Those **twelve men could not possibly have** been mistaken as **to** the reality of **any one of these** miracles: **much less as to** the **reality of thousands of them** occurring under every variety **of form** and illuminating a whole lifetime. **The idea that many** able-minded men could lead such **a** marvelous life through so long a period and yet not know whether it was real, is not to be considered for a **moment.** Just as ancient **Israel** must have known, to **a dead certainty and at** the merest glance, that **no such** forty years of **miraculous** experience as Moses **wrote** of had happened **to** them in case it had **not**; so **those** twelve apostles knew perfectly that **no** such gorgeous caravan of miraculous years as they wrote **of** had borne them along in triumphal march, in **case it had not.** It is **a sure** matter. **I would** like to see a **surer.** Yes, the apostles **never** could have believed **such a story** had it **been** altogether false.

But they did believe it. **Do not they** write like believers? **Do they not act like** believers? What charming directness, **simplicity,** and general air of good faith in their **narratives!** What faithfulness in recording **their own** crudities, mistakes, and sins! Truly they were consummate performers if they were merely feigning faith. Never did stage-player, though his name be Roscius or Garrick, so admirably personate reality. And then see how they lived and died! It is agreed on all hands by the traditions and histories that the primitive Twelve who lost their Master by crucifixion passed their own lives in labors, dangers, and sufferings in attestation of the same miraculous story; and at last endured, most of them, martyrdom for the same; and all with no possibility of any such result to themselves (such was the spiritual and pure nature of the system of religion which they taught) as alone could beckon on selfish and unprincipled men to undertake such sacrifices. They had been with Jesus through all His troublous career. They had seen Him crucified. He had predicted just such a general life and fate for themselves; and they tell us that from the beginning of their separate mission they had expected the fulfillment of that prediction. Indeed, the very circumstances and temper of the time — only too well shown in that howling intolerance that beset like wild beasts the tribunal of Pilate, crying, Away with him! Away with him! — must have given to the dullest observer assurance of the utmost trouble to all missionaries of the new faith. And yet the apostles went forward. They went forward with steady foot, and unsparing tongue, and hands bearing aloft a blazon of miracles which themselves had seen and had done and were still doing, and which were known to almost everybody — to meet the scowling populace; the infuriated rulers; the bigotry of the Jew, the scorn of the Greek; want, stonings, scourgings, chains, prisons, wild beasts, crucifixions, infamy; in short to receive in their faces the fiercest wind and sleet and volleys of ill-will, outrage, and death. And when they actually met and were enveloped by the storm, did their courage fail them? Did they shrink and retreat and finally disappear from the too stormy scene? Nay, nay. Nothing overcame those witnesses. Nothing seemed to daunt them. They went on witnessing to the end. Their wonderful testimony was resolutely held up before all faces; until at last they freely anointed and sealed it with their blood. Would you or I have done that for a known imposture? Would any man we ever knew have done it for the merest chance of a success so unrewarding to a wicked man, if attained? Say anything you please of these men; only do not say that they did not believe their own story. That is too incredible. By all the laws of evidence, and by all the light of experience and history, they must have believed it full cordially. Give up all faith in appearances and history, unless, with hand on heart, you are prepared to say, These men were fully persuaded of the miracles for which they so resolutely suffered and died.

But this is not all. The Christian story of miracles was believed by the whole land as well as by the apostles. It was the universal confession, This man doeth many miracles. It was the universal confession, **That a** notable miracle **has been done by them is manifest to all** that dwell at Jerusalem and we **cannot** deny **it.** After **the** Christian age was fairly begun, it does not seem **to** have occurred **to the Jews** to question the reality of the miracles of Jesus and His disciples. They **only** questioned their proceeding from **God.** They ascribed them to Beelzebub, **the** prince **of** devils. They said it **was** magic that did them. So say, not only our Scriptures, but **the** Talmud and all **the** literature assailing Christianity that has come down to us from the earlier centuries. **No** assailant in those times — **neither Celsus, nor** Porphyry, **nor Hierocles, nor** Julian — ever **denied the** miracles; they **only** denied the Divine origin of **them. No** defender **of** Christianity in **the** earlier times ever tried **to** prove the miracles; he always took them for granted and de**voted** himself to showing that they **were** the finger of **God.** The belief in their reality **was** universal. This **is conceded by all save the most** fantastic of objectors whose **principles would** annihilate all history.

What then? **Why,** this general belief was the belief of a public which from the circumstances of **the** case must have **known** whether the Christian **miracles** were genuine **or not.** The nature of these **alleged miracles was such, they** were so openly done, **they were done in such** prodigious numbers all over **the land and for so** many years, that everybody had easy **opportunity** of surely judging them, either by personal observation or by myriad-tongued testimony. City and country shone with them. The whole air was quick with their sublime electricity. It rained miracles. As magnificent princes on some high festival stand and scatter gold among the people from a full hand, so Jesus and His apostles magnificently stood and sowed their shining largess on the land as out of the fullness of a heavenly treasury. It was a nebula that fell, compacted almost beyond counting, till star touched star in one blaze of white mystery. Such is the representation. "And there are also many other things which Jesus did, the which, if they should be written every one, I suppose that the world could not contain (endure) the books that should be written." See what strength of statement! The imposture, if imposture it was, was on so huge and audacious a scale that almost everybody had repeated opportunity of bringing all his senses to bear leisurely upon it. And the alleged miracles were in general events of such a nature that common people could judge of them quite as well as philosophers — I think a little better. Pray, could Gamaliel himself have judged better as to the reality of that quaking earth and darkened heaven which are said to have waited on the crucifixion of Jesus than almost any elbowed man of that great crowd which then went surging through the streets of Jerusalem? And so of many another marvel. It is incredible that a single sound man, however plain, should mistake in regard to such cases; still more incredible that twelve such men should do it; more incredible still that the general population of the land, including millions on millions of bitter enemies well conditioned for detecting an imposture, should join them in the mistake, and fully admit the Christian miracles when really not a single one of them was genuine. If the whole thing had been a fabrication, the apostles would never have been madmen enough to publish it; if it had been a fabrication, the whole people would have known it to be so. Just as the Hebrews of the Exodus must have known that they never journeyed for forty years under such a heavenly canopy of miracles as Moses describes, if they did not; so the Jews of the Christian epoch must have known that their time for more than forty years did not blaze with such an outpour of the supernatural upon it as the New Testament tells of, in case it did not. There are some things that we know. And among them is this, that a hostile nation, a nation fiercely bitter against Christianity and seeking every possible weapon against it, would never have confessed the Christian miracles genuine, as they did, unless they had been compelled by the astounding majesty and abundance of the evidence.

And now, to sum up, this is just the state of the case. In regard to the Christian miracles it is incredible that a single sound sense fairly brought to bear on them should be deceived; much more several sound senses; much more still several sound senses of twelve daily companions of Jesus; most of all, the senses and judgments of millions of hostile persons and virtually the whole national population. That apostolic consensus, joined by the magnificent levy *en masse* of auxiliary testimony from all Jewry and contiguous countries, lifts us to the very climax of moral evidence. It is fairly sublime. Never believe more unless you believe now. Say final adieu to all history and to all the accepted rules for conducting the business of life: and let one broad pall of Doubt drop on all the facts of the Past and on most of the facts of the Present — on everything not directly testified to by your own personal senses. Nay, even your own senses are logically untrustworthy, if such is your logic.

So the miracles are real. Not only does the elder world of Geology glitter with them, but glitters with them the Old Testament world; glitters with them the New Testament world as well. '*Tis true* that at the stretching forth of a human hand a way was divided for Israel through the Red Sea; and that at the touch of human feet the river Jordan became a wall to the marching host on the right hand and on the left. '*Tis true* that a storm suddenly slept at the bidding of Jesus; and that at His death Nature mourned with the voice of earthquakes and with the sables of night; and that He rose from the dead and dwindled away into heaven like "some retreating star." Many such things are true, whole hosts of them.

> "What ailed thee, O thou mighty sea,
> And rolled thy waves with dread —
> What bade thy waves, O Jordan, flee,
> And bare their deepest bed?"

What mean the *hosts* of such events? I need not perplex you with learned inquiries into the nature of miracles. I need not insist on your losing yourselves in the dry mysteries of intricate definitions. All I have to do is to ask of your common sense what is the significance of *such events as we have been considering,* if really wrought to attest such a thing as the Biblical Religion. There is but one answer. You and I know there is but one answer. They mean a great invincible Personal Power in sympathy with a righteous religion; and, of course, itself righteous and truth-telling. What it attests is therefore true: and lo! by a mighty voice which no human being ought to suffer to speak in vain, we are called on to believe in God; in His only Son, Jesus Christ our Lord; and in the Scriptures of the Old and New Testament as His inspired message. I say unto you, Have faith. I say unto you, Have faith, broad, ponderous, and sublime as the everlasting hills. It is but fitting. Nothing short of such a faith will duly match the evidence of miracles.

XIII.

MODERN SIGNS.

XIII. Modern Signs.

1. Answers to Prayer 251
2. Answers to Blasphemies 256
3. Import 260

MODERN SIGNS.

WE tell unbelievers of miracles that took place ages ago. There, far back in the past, are the miracles of Moses, of Christ, of Christ's Apostles — the ten plagues of Egypt, the passage of the Red Sea, the manna, the water-pouring rock, the fiery and cloudy pillar that guided Israel for forty years; and then angelic songs and sights in the midnight sky; a voice falling from heaven to say, "This is my Beloved Son;" the healing of the sick, and hushing of the storm, and raising of the dead by a mere word or touch; the earth-shaking death and not less marvelous resurrection and ascension of Jesus; besides like great events through an entire generation afterward. We point to all these as evidences of a God, and a Divine Christianity; and offer to show against all gainsayers that these prodigies rest on better authority than do the universally admitted histories of Alexander the Great and Julius Cæsar.

Perhaps the unbeliever feels it but fair to confess that he can offer no good reply against such an argument. Yet he is not satisfied. He wishes those prodigies were not so ancient and distant. It seems to him that if something of the kind could only take place within the range of his own observation it would be far more satisfactory; in fact, would put prompt and final end to his doubts. "O that some such Divine interpositions could take place within my time and sphere; that I had not to plant myself behind a telescope in order to receive a faded image of their distant glory; but that my own senses and power of judging, or at least those of my contemporaries in whom I have confidence, could be brought to bear directly upon them, shining among our own homes, and lighting up with their fresh splendor our own streets and markets and rivers and fields! Then faith would be easy to me. My whole heart should say, never to recant, "Lo, there is a God and He governs among men!" "Lo, Jesus is His messenger and the Bible is His book!"

Say you so! Then make ready at once to bid final adieu to your unbelief, your half-faith, your occasional misgivings and debilities on the subject of Theism and Christianity. I am able to present to you substantially just such examples of the personal intervention of God among men as you ask. You shall have examples belonging to your own time and sphere. You shall see God putting out His hand among your contemporaries and neighbors, and working close upon your right hand and your left things which the received principles of science forbid us to ascribe to any other cause. For the present I will cease to insist on things antiquarian and telescopic; and allow you to stand solely on what seems to you the solid ground of the world's current observation and experience. All around us are great Divine actions, as truly such as any which under the great name of miracles are attributed to the world's early ages. We do not choose to call them miracles. The title is unfashionable for such modern and common events. But, for all that, they are direct Divine interpositions; always proving a God, and often so circumstanced as to prove in addition both His Son and His Word; and can no more, in accordance with the scientific principles of evidence, be ascribed to any natural source than could a sundering of the Red Sea under the outstretched arm of Moses.

Let me give some examples.

I. ANSWERS TO PRAYER.

A young man of Indiana left home and settled in business in a city of Ohio. After some time a gentleman from his native place, being in that city, took the opportunity to call upon him. The visitor was shocked to find that he had become a profane swearer.

On returning home the gentleman thought it his duty to tell the sad news to the pious parents. They made little or no reply to his statements; and after leaving them he was somewhat doubtful whether they had fairly understood him. So he returned the next day and repeated his statement. Said the father, "We did not misunderstand you last evening. My wife and myself took no rest during the night, but spent it on our knees pleading with God in behalf of our son, and about day-break He graciously listened to our prayer and granted an answer. James will never swear again."

Two weeks from that time James made his appearance at his parents' house — a changed man. "How long since this change happened?" — they asked. He replied that just a fortnight ago he was struck with such an overwhelming sense of guilt that he could not sleep, and spent the night in tears and prayers for forgiveness. The prayers were fulfilling at the very time they were being offered in the name of Christ.

A merchant of Bristol, England, was nearly ruined in property by a sudden disaster at sea. His wife was overwhelmed by the shock, became insane, and had to be confined in order to prevent her doing herself and others harm. Her condition was at once reported to her father, an eminent Christian living a hundred miles distant in Birmingham. This man had great faith in prayer. So one evening he gathered a number of Christians at his house to ask Divine interposition. They prayed with great apparent unanimity and fervor. A few days after, a letter came stating that, at such a time, the lady was suddenly restored to reason and her usual health. That time was found to be the same day, the same evening, and the same hour of the evening when those Christians were praying to God for her in the name of Christ.

In a certain town lived an aged Christian blacksmith. One day while at work in his shop he began thinking of the sad moral state of the population around him. There had been no revival for many years; the young people were all irreligious, the church was almost extinct; in short, all around was desolation. As he mused, his distress became so great that he threw up work, locked his shop, and betook himself to prayer. The next Sabbath he asked his minister to appoint a conference meeting. The minister would do so, but who would attend? The evening for the meeting came, and with it more persons than could be accommodated at the large house to which they had been invited. All was silence for a time. Then a man burst into tears and begged that, if anybody could pray, he would pray for him. Another followed in the same strain, and another, and still another. It proved that persons from all parts of the town were in great religious distress. And the most wonderful thing of all was that all these persons dated their distress back to the very hour when the aged blacksmith was praying for them in Christ's name, in the secrecy of his locked shop.

These instances will answer for illustration. They are well attested. They are three out of multitudes equally striking and well witnessed. If any one will consult religious journals, Sprague's "Annals of the Pulpit," the Works of Sir Henry More, the "Scots Worthies," The Life of Francke,

Professor Gibson's "Year of Grace," and the records of the Fulton Street prayer-meeting, he will get some idea how full the world is of such wonderful answers to prayer. Now and then a great and complex system of answers, as elaborately jointed and proportioned as was ever palace of prince or cathedral of God, rises grandly heavenward to awe reflecting men. Read Müller's "Life of Trust," and judge for yourselves.

II. Answers to Blasphemies.

A few years ago some followers of Fanny Wright were in the habit of meeting in Concert Hall in the city of New York. One of their most intelligent and frequent speakers at this place was a certain deformed man. On a certain occasion, while addressing the meeting, this man took occasion, distinctly and formally, to defy Almighty God and dare Him in the most blasphemous manner to seal his lips. Suddenly the blasphemer became confused, his tongue faltered, his language lost its coherency, and he sat down amid a shower of hisses. Shortly after he died a maniac; and his wife renounced the principles which had brought her husband to so terrible an end.

At a general muster in the town of Lebanon, Ohio, a wicked man was spoken to on the subject of religion. He was filled with rage. He declared that if Jesus of Nazareth were there he would wring his neck. Suddenly a violent spasm seized his own neck, twisted it round, rolled his eyes nearly out of their sockets, and left him in this frightful condition.

At one time Newburg, in the State of New York, was remarkable for its infidelity. A society, called the Druidical Society, was formed for the purpose of opposing and suppressing the Christian Religion. Its members went great lengths. For example, at one of their meetings they burned a Bible, baptized a cat, partook of the Sacrament of the Supper, and finally administered it to a dog. That very day the man who had administered this mock sacrament was attacked by a violent inflammatory disease, his tongue swelled, his eyeballs protruded from their sockets, and he died before the next morning in great agony, bodily and mental. Another of the party was found dead in his bed the next morning. Three days after, still another fell in a fit and died immediately. In short, within five years from the organization of the society, every one of its original thirty-six members died in some unnatural manner. Two were starved to death, seven were drowned, eight were shot, five committed suicide, seven died on the gallows, one was frozen to death, and three died (as people say) accidentally.

A gentleman near Hitchin in the county of Hertford, England, received summons to appear before a magistrate and answer to a charge of attempted robbery. He went. On arriving he found himself confronted with a man who claimed that he had been knocked down and searched by the person at that present **standing before** him. Considering the relative **social** positions of the two parties, **the magistrate** felt justified in hinting to the accuser **that he** feared the charge was only made for **the purpose of** extorting money; and bade him **take** care how he proceeded and incurred the dreadful consequences of perjury. The man however stood to his charge firmly. He insisting **on** proceeding to the oath. The oath was accordingly administered, and the affair fully investigated. The result was that the in**nocence of the** gentleman was established by the best **evidence.** The rogue retired much cast down at the **failure** of his plot; **and,** meeting **one** of his neighbors, he **desperately** renewed the charge, and declared he **had not sworn to** anything **but** the **truth** — calling **in** the most solemn manner God to wit**ness,** and wishing, if it was not as he had said, his **jaws** might be locked and his flesh rot on his **bones.** Suddenly his jaws were fixed, and he became unable to speak. After lingering **a** fortnight **he died in** the greatest agonies; his flesh literally rotting on his bones.

The following **inscription is** to be seen **in the** market-place at Devizes, England. "The mayor **and** corporation of Devizes avail themselves of the **stability** of this building **to** transmit to future times the record **of an** awful event that occurred in this market-place **in** the year 1753; hoping that such **a** record may serve **as a** salutary warning against **the** danger of impiously invoking the Divine vengeance, or of calling on the holy name of God to conceal the devices of falsehood and fraud. On Thursday, the 25th of January, 1753, Ruth Pierce, of Pottern in this county, agreed with three other women to buy a sack of wheat in the market, each paying her due proportion toward the same. One of these women, in collecting the several quotas of money, discovered a deficiency, and demanded of Ruth Pierce the sum which was wanting to make good the amount. Ruth Pierce protested that she had paid her share, and said she wished she might drop down dead if she had not. She rashly repeated this awful wish; when, to the astonishment of the surrounding multitude, she instantly fell down and expired, having the money concealed in her hand."

Now these facts are mere samples. They are only a few out of multitudes equally striking and well attested. The like may be found by thousands in our libraries, and are reported not seldom in our newspapers. They are recorded on gravestones, inscribed on buildings, treasured in printed histories; they traverse the country in oral traditions. And almost every person, if he has had no complete personal knowledge of such facts, has had dim suggestions and experiences looking in their direction which assure him of their credibility and even probability.

What shall we say to them — to these answers to blasphemies and to those answers to prayer! I repeat, the reality of both is indisputable. They are too many and well attested to be called in question by reasonable men. Beyond question, multitudes on multitudes of them are as good as any history that ever was penned. And what is the explanation? Here, an individual or a prayer-meeting offers a prayer through Christ for a person hundreds of miles away; and in due time news comes that on the very day and hour when that prayer was being offered it was fulfilled. There, a person blasphemes God, or Christ, and dares Him to strike him speechless and putrescent; and instantly speechless and putrescent he becomes. I ask again, What is the explanation of such incontrovertible facts? There is but one answer — GOD AND HIS MESSENGER. The principles of science — the principles on which all experience shows us human life must be conducted, and on which all reasonable human life is actually conducted — require us to say that such coincidences are not by chance, are not by a tangled skein of blind forces and laws; they are by the active will and power of the really existent God to whom the pious or the impious appeal is made; thus testifying to Himself, to His Son, and to His Bible. This is the only solution which science, experience, and consistency permit any man to entertain.

But might not such coincidences occasionally happen in due course of mere Nature? I answer, It is of no consequence to say whether they could or not. It is enough to be able to say that the chances are

a million to one against **any given coincidence of
the** sort occurring otherwise than by **a Divine**
agency. And this we **can say.** Suppose you **should**
hear that in the **city of London there is a** bookseller
of the name **of John Murray. You know nothing**
positively about **the matter, but people say that**
there **is such a man, in such a city, and that** he
sends **on** application such **and such books.** You
act on what you hear, and post **a letter to Albemarle**
Street, London, asking to have **a number** of specified books sent you. By return of steamer you get
just the parcel you sent for. Now, though it **is not**
in the nature of things impossible that the parcel
should have come from **some other** quarter — say,
from some **friend who has** just happened **to think**
that those volumes would be acceptable to you **and**
so sent them — yet you would **not for a** single moment have any idea of resorting to such an explanation. You would have no manner **of doubt** that
the parcel came from Mr. Murray ; **that** there is
such **a man,** and that he sent **the** books in answer
to your application. You would **take the** coming
of the books as a decisive proof of as much. Why ?
Because your experience **in life** would assure you
that there is **not one chance in a** million of the
books reaching you **by any** other **means.** Everybody would consider you **a** lunatic **or an imbecile**
were you to judge differently.

I receive a **letter** purporting to be from an intimate acquaintance. It is possibly not from him, may be a forgery. **But still I am** confident **it is** genuine. The post-mark **is** that **of the** place where he lives, the handwriting **is like his,** the style and subject-matter agree with the supposition that he wrote it; **there is** no positive reason that can **be** assigned for believing that anybody else wrote **it;** and, altogether, **I** do not doubt, that he was the author, despite the bare possibility of the contrary. Perhaps **one in** a million of letters with similar marks may **be a forgery,** and there **is a** possibility **that** this letter **may be the ugly** millionth; but the chances are a million **to one** against it — literally overwhelming. I should **be considered** insane were **I** in practice to make any account **of that one chance.** People never do such a thing. **How** many millions **of** letters **are** every day received under similar circumstances, and not a single one of them but is accepted as authentic with unhesitating confidence!

A merchant receives in course **of** business what **purports to be a** five pound note **of** the Bank of **England. Now he** will not affirm that a spurious note of this Bank is impossible; **or that** one such note among a million is even improbable; or that the particular note which he holds in his hands cannot be that not improbable millionth. Still he is abundantly easy in the faith **that the note** is good. He **ought to be.** Why? Because, its whole appearance agrees **with the** supposition that it is genuine, and all experience **shows** that the chances are **a** million to one against such appearing paper proving counterfeit.

It is precisely on the principle of these examples that we are bound to proceed in explaining such wonderful answers to prayers and blasphemies as I have described to you. There is no occasion to prove that these cannot be mere casual coincidences —chance parcels, forged letters, spurious bills; it is sufficient that the chances are a million to one against any given instance proving such. Grant the possibility of casual coincidences of this sort; grant that one such coincidence among a million of prayers and blasphemies is even not improbable; grant that any particular answer to prayer or imprecation may be that not improbable millionth casualty; still we ought to be abundantly easy in the faith that actually it is nothing of the kind, but a direct personal intervention of the God to whom appeal has been made. Its whole appearance agrees strikingly with the idea that it is such an intervention; and our knowledge of life assures us that as a matter of fact such a coincidence between the appeal to God and the event would not occur casually once in a host of such appeals; in which case science teaches that the probabilities are a host to one that any given instance of such a coincidence did not occur casually in mere course of Nature. This is vastly better evidence than most of the most important business of the world is unhesitatingly carried on upon. It is literally overwhelming; and the man who in secular life should reject such would be considered irrational to the last degree.

But why are not these wonderful coincidences more numerous? Why do not more prayers receive such wonderful answers, more blasphemies receive prompt judgments, if it be true that there is a God? In regard to prayers, I answer first, Many prayers are not fit as regards matter or manner to receive such glorious answers; second, not improbably many which are fit cannot in the nature of things be answered, or cannot be answered consistently; third, not improbably many which are fit in themselves, possible, and consistent to be answered, can be best answered after more or less delay, like many of the requests which children make to their parents. In regard to blasphemies, I answer that human sovereigns find it best in general to punish crimes, not the moment after they are committed, but after a while. Once in a while it is not amiss — on the contrary exceedingly useful — that the sword should flash down in the very act of crime. But generally some delay is better. It may be so under God's government.

Be encouraged, all praying persons! Behind the curtain there is One to hear and answer in Christ's great name. He has done it of old, He does it to-day; in many a land, in many a home and history as narrow and obscure as your own. So pray on. There is a God to pray to, and a Mediator to pray by — so pray on. You are not throwing yourselves away; nor could your breath be put to better account. Go on to pray; go on to pray. You will get answers. If you do not get answers equal to miracles, you will at least get such as are worth the having — answers that will ever sweeten and invigorate your faith until you can joyfully say with the voice of a monarch, Lo, I have found God!

Be warned, ye who sometimes venture toward the verge where stand the impious and scoffing profane! God is not a mere notion of priests. He is not a bit of ancient statecraft fast getting obsolete. The curtain has something besides unbounded vacancy behind it. There is an unbounded Person there; One who has often and terribly come out in vindication of Himself, His Son, and His Word on venturesome and tempestuous sinners. That curtain is shaking yet. I see its great folds throbbing and swaying as if freshly let down behind returning God; I see it edged and fringed with gold as if from a Sun within. And the Sun is really there to-day — and the Son. So look reverently in that direction. Put off your shoes as you approach. Bare brow of body and of soul as you begin to deal directly with that palpitating screen. When you have lifted it you will stand face to face with God.

XIV.
NEARING THE CURTAIN.

XIV. NEARING THE CURTAIN.

1. FITTED TO REVEAL 269
2. WHAT IT REVEALS 277
3. ILLUSTRATION 286
4. VERDICT 288

NEARING THE CURTAIN.

THE traveler often becomes aware of his approach to the sea, or to healthy upland, or to sickly marsh, some time before any such object can be seen. His sensations inform him of new scenes at hand, and of their general character; though perhaps he would find it hard to state on what his impressions are based. You know how it is with blind men. In a way often mysterious to themselves they are in the habit of divining their approach to strongly marked objects, and, to a very considerable extent, the nature of those objects. They are vaguely sensible of the presence of the house, the forest, the mountain, or the man which they cannot see. There seem to be certain characteristic influences flowing out from every object, and which gradually weaken with the distance from it — like the light from a lamp, the heat from a fire, and the odor from a flower — tending to announce and manifest it.

Now it may be so with a world just beyond the grave. A gradually weakening outflow of influences from it into all the neighboring region may tend to manifest its true character to those approaching. Is that future world a scene of waste and silent nothingness? Then it may happen to the man treading the border-land of death to receive some chilling impressions of the great Nothing just before him, as the blind man does of the bare desert which he is about to enter. Is that world a scene such as the spiritualist is taught to expect? Then it may happen to the man treading the border-land of death to find his mind filling with faint sensations of spheres and modes of life as commonplace and disjointed and frivolous as any belonging to the present state. Is that world a scene such as the Bible describes? Then it may happen to the man treading the border-land of death to become subtly aware of nearing a land where a personal God is throned, where Jesus shines and mediates, and where men are treated according to the deeds done in the body. No one can reasonably deny the possibility of this — shall I not say the presumption?

In health it is easy to forget the importance of just views in religion. We can occupy our minds with business and pleasure. We can flatter ourselves that religious things will bear some postponement. So that when our attention is called to them — what with our cares and confidence in future opportunities — it is too often but a dull and listless gaze, little fitted to result in satisfactory knowledge, that we give. But when death visibly makes its appearance at our door it is not so easy to forget, or feel listless to, the importance of just answers to the main religious questions. Business is forever done. Pleasures have said their final adieu.

The mind is driven in upon itself, and then forward to explore the dim profound into which it is about to launch. There is no more forgetting the great problems of religion. There is no more viewing of them with a drowsy eye. They have become matters of immediate and pressing concern. Without any effort the soul at once becomes open-eyed and penetrating as never before — even as the body instinctively expands and projects and brightens the material eye in the presence of unexpected danger. At such time you have seen the dull orb suddenly light up as if the soul herself had really mounted to the window of her turret and were looking forth. You have seen that orb swell, and draw back its fringed curtains, and poise itself wakefully and steadily on the axis of its motion, as if it would penetrate every mystery and anticipate every stroke. So the eye of the soul tends to do as it finds itself nearing the grave and the curtain and the mighty possibilities just beyond — perhaps on the eve of settling by a conscious personal experience all the great problems of religion.

Then, too, the soul may be expected to be the most honest and fair-minded, as well as the most wakeful and zealous, in its dealings with the great religious questions. Who of you does not know it? It is here I touch what is by far the most fruitful source of error in all human inquiries. Too often men look at questions with no hearty wish to know the truth; allow their reasonings to be warped by their pride, their prejudices, their passions, their transient interests; really look not so much to find the truth as to find the means of defending the side which their own prejudices have already taken and determined if possible to prove true. The case is really prejudged in the heart before it is brought to the bar of the reason. With such unfairness of mind, and so little honest wish to know facts as they are, men could hardly be in a worse condition for arriving at truth. And it must be confessed that, while they are in the full blast of life and worldly influences, the best and most careful of men are apt to suffer their views to be shaped somewhat by their feelings and convenience, instead of bending them with an iron hand to the sole authority of evidence impartially sought and impartially weighed. But when men are consciously approaching the end of life, the great curtain which hides the great Hereafter, their passions and prejudices are naturally awed into silence, their consciences and all fair and just principles within them receive new liberty, and they are concerned to rightly answer the main questions of religion as they never were before. They are, or may be, about to appear in the presence of God; and in anticipation of that possible interview the mind instinctively puts its thoughts into an attitude of comparative uprightness. It feels that the point has been reached where it will be useless to impose on its reason any longer for any earthly purpose whatever. In a few days all these questions will be questions no longer. Now, if ever, it wants to see things as they are. If God is real, it really wants to know it. If Jesus is His Son, it really wants to know that. If the Bible is His message, it really wants to know that. It is afraid, as it never was before, to shut its eyes on evidence, to twist and strain and mutilate facts and principles into a preferred shape as it did once. Standing face to face with the grave and the solemn possibilities of a future state, it never before was so fully disposed to see the truth just as it is, never before so radically honest with itself and ready to give every consideration its due weight. How immensely favorable this state of mind to just conclusions! Better than all the logics of the schools, with all the philosophers back of them, is this simple, honest, earnest wish to know the truth which is so natural to one consciously approaching the curtain.

It is true that at such a time the mental powers, or at least the manifestations of them, often sympathize with the enfeebled body. But very often, also, they seem stronger than ever. Friends gathered about the sick man are surprised at the prompt clearness and precision with which that plain mind now thinks and judges. Sometimes the feats of memory and intuition are wonderful to see, and almost seem to belong to a new order of being; and astonish the subject of them quite as much as others. A clairvoyance that almost defies the bounds of human nature shows itself. His whole life flashes up in one thought. Cast a man into the water and let him pass through all but the last stage of drowning, and, ten to one, his thought will show a power of perception and review and self-judgment awful to see. The known facts of this kind are so many, and occur under such a wide range of circumstances, that it is open to serious question whether there is not in every case of dying, however dull and unresponsive the outward organs of manifestation may be, a special rallying of the mental forces as if for some great crisis. However this may be, we know that in almost all cases the earlier stages of fatal disease show no appreciable abatement in even the outward signs of mental vigor. The man can perceive and remember and judge and reason as well as ever. And he is then at the hight of his knowledge on religious subjects. Up to that time, whether he has been aiming at it or not, he has constantly been coming into possession of new items of information on all the leading topics of human thought. It is impossible to live in the midst of this teeming and instructive Nature, and on the shore of the seething sea of human discussion, without having constantly cast up at one's feet something valuable out of the endless treasures hidden in that vasty deep. And it is fast coming to be a doctrine of philosophy that the mind seldom or never loses the impression of any knowledge which it has once possessed; at least its life and ethereal essence remaining with the mind firmly, though its form may vanish. So there must be, up to the last or as long as the powers retain any tolerable vigor, a gradual accumulation of facts and principles in the mind which will aid in all religious inquiries. It is true that prejudices and errors may accumulate also — as fast as truth, and perhaps faster — but then, as we have seen, there is something about the conscious death-hours, especially of thoughtful and cultured men, that goes strongly to nullify the influence and even the essence of all views that are hollow and unreal. Bubbles are very apt to be burst by that pressure. Disguises are very apt to be penetrated by the light that sifts through that curtain. One honest hour before its dusky outspread, gazing at it and waiting for its throbbing breadth to rise, is a greater destroyer of shams than all the spears like weavers' beams that ever logic and eloquence wielded.

Now, these various considerations, taken together, mean a great deal. They mean that at the time when men are consciously approaching death, and especially when there is no appreciable decline but perhaps even a great increase of mental vigor, they are in their best state for judging of the claims of the Biblical Religion — with its Theism, its Christianity, and its written Revelation. I do not say for a learned investigation of those claims. That is quite another thing. The collecting of materials for an argument after the manner of professional scholars might, in those painful and confining hours, proceed at serious disadvantage. Not so the **use of** materials already collected, which is really the only **work** absolutely necessary **to** be done **by** most dying men. Christianity professes to be for all men. According **to it, the** means of a just answer **to** the main religious questions are placed as fully within the reach of **the** humbler class **of** minds as of the loftier. **No** laborious and learned researches, such **as** only men **of** leisure and talent **can** make, are necessary, however useful they may be in their place. Honest looking and simple praying are all that is wanted. **And for this** there **is no** time like that when one, **with all his** faculties about him, perhaps in extraordinary force, **is consciously** nearing **the** curtain which hangs before his Hereafter. Then the mind is most retired upon itself, its ear specially **withdrawn** from the distracting din of the world, its **eye most wakeful** to religion, its interest in it most profound, **its sum** of information concerning it most **large, its** honesty and fairness and wish to know the **truth most decided; and** then too, perhaps, sensation itself comes to the **aid** of the intellect, and mysteriously spells out **the** character of **that** near curtained land whose subtle influences fill **all** the air. Then, if ever, we should expect a vision of the truth.

In view of this **fact I** ask your particular attention **to the** following proposition, to the proof and illustration **of** which the rest of this hour will be devoted. The proposition **is this.** At the conscious approach of death, faith in the Biblical Religion, with its God and Christ and written Revelation, never weakens but almost or quite always strengthens, and very often advances to a splendid assurance ; while unbelief under the same circumstances never strengthens, but almost or quite always weakens and falters, and very often falls utterly.

I have seen many persons, both believers and unbelievers, consciously approaching death. I have heard and read the experience of multitudes more in the same condition. And I have yet to learn of the first case where belief in the Biblical Religion has grown weaker, or unbelief in it grown stronger, as the last hour came near. On the contrary, wherever I have been able to compare the views taken at death with earlier ones, I have found that the believer has always become more unquestioning and unembarrassed in his faith, and the unbeliever more hesitating and tremulous in his unbelief. On the one hand difficulties and hesitations have always shown tendency to melt away; on the other they have always gathered new firmness. It is said that Hume professed to die as faithless as he lived ; the contrary is also said. But how many have I heard of, who, like Hume's mother and Paine and Voltaire, have been known to die amid a furious upbreak of their unbelief. Of how many have I heard, who, like Altamont and Rochester, have in their last hours renounced their atheism and infidelity with horror, and from before the quaking Curtain warned others against such errors with terrible eloquence! But when have I heard of a believer renouncing his God and Bible in view of a dying bed, and calling out loud alarms to all whom it may concern to avoid his egregious faith and folly? Never. On the contrary, I have heard of great numbers who under such circumstances have suddenly expanded into such rejoicing giants of faith as were most marvelous to see, and a marvel to themselves.

Take a single example. Let it be that of one of the greatest and most successful philosophers of modern times, one who in his day reaped all the highest academic and other distinctions, both domestic and foreign, which a British subject could possibly win; and who has ineffaceably written his name in capitals in the history of science — I mean Sir David Brewster. This famous man recently passed away. He had been a Christian believer for many years. For many years his profound study of Nature had walked side by side with an equally profound faith in God and Jesus and the Bible. But when he came to his last days his faith took on unwonted majesty of port and mien. The curtain before which he was standing seemed to shimmer upon him with potent and mysterious day. Hear what was said at a meeting of the Royal Society of Edinburgh by his physician, Sir James Simpson, the Queen's physician for Scotland, and a man of European celebrity for science.

"To Mr. Phinn and other clerical friends he freely expressed in these his last days the unbounded and undoubting faith of a very humble and a very happy Christian. No shadow of dubiety ever once seemed to cloud his mind. In his march forward into and through the river of death, it seemed as if Christ were ever whispering in his ear, Fear thou not, for I am with thee; Be of good cheer, for it is I. Like my former dear friend, Prof. John Reid, he seemed to be impressed with the idea that one of the great joys and glories of heaven would consist in the revelation of the marvels and mysteries of creation and science by Him by whom all things were made, and who, as Prof. George Wilson held it, was not only the Head of the Church but the head and source of all science. 'I have,' he remarked to me, 'been very happy here, but I shall soon be infinitely happier with my Saviour and Creator.' As death drew more and more nigh, the one idea of his Saviour and of his being speedily and eternally with Him, grew stronger and more absorbing. On one occasion, when he had been speaking of the different members of his family whom he would meet in heaven, he paused and seemed to gather up his strength to say with a wonderful power and emphasis, 'I will see Jesus; Jesus who created all things, Jesus who made the worlds, I shall see Him as He is!' I said, You will understand everything then; and it seemed to me as if the 'O Yes' of his answer came out of the very fullness of content. Once I said to him, 'I wish all learned men had your simple faith.' Again there was a pause, and each word was dropped out with a never-to-be-forgotten weight of meaning, 'I have had the light for many years, and oh, how bright it is. I feel so safe, so perfectly safe, so perfectly happy.'

"As a physician I have often watched by the dying, but I have never seen a death-bed more full of pure love and faith than was that of our late President. It was indeed a sermon of unapproachable eloquence and pathos. For there lay this grand and gifted old philosopher, this hoary, loving votary and arch-priest of science, passing fearlessly through the valley of death, sustained and gladdened with the all-simple and all-sufficient faith of a very child, and looking forward with unclouded intellect and bright and happy prospects to the mighty change that was about to carry him from time to eternity. 'I feel,' said another witness of the scene, 'I feel that words express very little of that death-bed; for the marvelous triumph of mind over matter, of grace over nature, was shown not so much in words as in the whole spirit of the scene. I never saw a soul actually pass away before, but I thank God I have been present when his passed away. The sight was a cordial from heaven to me. I believed before, but now have I seen that Christ has abolished death."

These words of a scientific witness of the end of

one of the first of scientific men show a glorious culmination of faith in front of the Curtain. Lofty as was the faith of the life, the faith of the death was loftier.

A single example out of many which have fallen under my notice! It is by no means an extreme experience. I have known others still more striking and brilliant in themselves, though not in the illustriousness of the subjects of them. And I am sure, my hearers, that my entire observation in this matter of nearing the Curtain thoroughly accords with your own. You have all had some personal acquaintance with last sicknesses. You have all heard free accounts of many which you did not witness with your eyes. You have read in the course of your lives very many biographies and obituaries telling how men have viewed things in expectation of death. And I confidently appeal to you, to the oldest and most observant among you, whether my observation has not been confirmed by your own. Did any of you ever know of a person renouncing Theism or Christianity as he came to look into the grave? Did you ever know of one who had less faith in the Bible under those circumstances than he had while in health? On the contrary, have you not met with many well-attested cases of believers whose faith seemed almost turned to sight as the outward man perished day by day? And when, I ask, have you met with a case, seen or heard or read, in which unbelief has gathered strength after the same magnificent manner, and swept down into the grave like an eastern conqueror returning to his capital? Your memory answers firmly, Never.

What does this prove? It may seem as if it proved but mere outposts of the broad proposition which I have laid down, leaving unsupported the whole main camp of allegations. But is it so? Not if the principles of that inductive philosophy on which most modern science rests are sound. For the striking facts just mentioned carry with them an immense induction of particulars, all firmly looking one way, that is, toward an invariable increase of truthful aspect on the part of the Biblical Religion at the approach of death. The fact that faith, within our field of observation, is often at that time pushed forward into even triumphant assurance, shows that in a vastly greater number of cases within that field it must be pushed into the various easier stages of increase. The fact that under the same circumstances disbelief of the strongest kind, within our field of observation, is sometimes pushed backward into even energetic self-renunciation, shows that in a multitude of cases within the same field the weaker disbeliefs and unbeliefs must be pushed to the same point; and that in a still greater number of cases, disbeliefs and unbeliefs of all degrees must be pushed into the easier stages of weakness and decrease. Take the sum of these multitudes and multiply it by the number of persons whose fields of observation have been equally extensive with our own and independent of ours ; and what an immense number of instances have we of dying men helped in the direction of faith? On the other hand we know of absolutely no instances of such men drawn in the direction of unbelief. We have an induction of millions on millions of instances to the effect that the credibility of Religion in main doctrines improves to the view of the mind on the approach of death ; and not one instance in which that credibility has seemed to decrease. And so, on the same principle which leads the astronomer to believe that the principle of gravitation extends to all the stars that shine in the profound of space, which leads the farmer to believe that autumn is a season in which certain seeds will surely be sown in vain, which leads the fisherman to believe that in winter certain nets will be drawn to no purpose — in short, the principle on which all practical life and all science not mathematical is founded — on this principle we are to conclude that the season of death is one which never weakens faith in the Religion of the Bible and never strengthens unbelief, but on the contrary almost if not quite always does just the striking reverse.

Every adult whom I address has had some times in which he was attacked by dangerous sickness, or feared he was, or feared he was about to be. He can remember that, at such times, Religion with its Theism, its Christianity, and its Bible, always began to look increasingly worthy, truthful, divine, that somehow objections and difficulties in respect to it seemed to become faint-voiced, and draw back, and melt away of their own accord; that he was never so little disposed to treat them scornfully or neglectfully, never so much disposed to have about him their friends and ordinances. And he has also noticed many signs of its being just so with others. He has seen that the scoffer is apt to be more cautious in what he says, as soon as some sickness shuts him up at home and he begins to suspect that the enemy is groping for his heart. Suddenly the man becomes less ready with his sneers and bravadoes and arguments. It is easy to see that he is less inclined to quote Thomas Paine, less inclined to like the society of Bible-opposers, more accessible to the counsels and prayers and Bible-readings of Christian friends. And similarly with others. You have discovered that almost every person is more respectful and accessible to the Bible under a sense of danger, and that almost every believer then realizes its truth and importance as never before. I say, *almost*. But when you consider how often a pride of consistency would tend to hide real changes of views, and how often you have no fair opportunity of closely watching the behavior of the sick, and what have ever been the workings and tendencies of your own mind under apprehensions of death, you must feel prepared to strike out that limiting word and believe that the experience of all around you accords with your own — that to all your friends and neighbors and acquaintances, as to yourself, the Biblical Religion begins to look increasingly truthful and divine as soon as it is viewed as from the confines of another world. And what is there peculiar in the sphere to which we belong to make this experience local with us? Beyond question it is so in all spheres and parishes in Christendom. There is everywhere and in every person to whom belongs that acquaintance with Christianity which is the common patrimony of those brought up in Christian lands, a quickening of the mind in its behalf as ever the grave seems to be drawing nigh. Only let a man fear himself hard by the Curtain, and then with faculties still sound fasten open eyes on the Religion, and he surely finds his atheism more tremulous, his infidelity less firm, his Christian faith more unquestioning. And this shows how it will always be under the same conditions if the approach to death is actual as well as suspected. Then the believer will go from strength to strength, and the unbeliever retreat from weakness to weakness. Then faith will uniformly brighten and sometimes pass into splendid assurance, as if vision; and then unbelief will as uniformly grow dim and often become totally extinguished. The whole course of experience goes to show that the dying firmness of Hume covered a sinking heart; and that his case was really one of the many in which men attempt to prop up a fainting courage by giving the external appearance of it.

I have now endeavored to establish two points. The first is, that, as men consciously approach death, and while as yet there is no considerable abatement in the strength of their faculties, they are in their best state for judging of the claims of our main Biblical Religion, considered as a Theism, a Christianity, and a written Revelation. The second is, that, at this best time for just views, the credibility of this religion never abates but almost if not quite always seems greater than ever before — faith in it substantially always brightening and often passing into a splendid assurance, while unbelief and disbelief never strengthen, but on the contrary substantially always grow weaker and sometimes fail altogether. Putting these two facts together, have we not a commanding testimony? That when the mind is most withdrawn from disturbing influences, most wakeful to religion, most full of information about it, most honest and earnest in its inquiries, and most subject to whatever of revealing power may gather about the threshold and curtain of the future world; that then its judgment of the whole Biblical Religion should be almost or quite uniformly more favorable than ever before, is a most significant fact. Is it possible to explain it on any supposition short of the truth of that Religion?

Place yourselves back two centuries. It has just been declared that the planet Saturn is a glorious be-ringed and satellited world. Some believe, some doubt, and some disbelieve. To settle the question, your best situation is in a clear night and before the polished mirror of a telescope. And what is that you see yonder, surrounded by a crowd, if not just such an instrument stretching its dusky column up through the starry evening toward the planet! You cannot for yet awhile have close access to the beaming speculum, but you can approach and pass before it at a little distance, and as you pass snatch a glimpse over the shoulders and between the forms of intervening men. You do it. Lo, sure enough, the glimpse you catch does seem to be that of a radiant orb singularly beset with something which may be all that the astronomers say it is. But there are others who are having that perfect access which as yet you have not. You watch them. Here come up first the believers and defenders of the new astronomy and gaze upon the mirror. In a multitude of cases you hear them assert with supremer confidence than ever that the questioned orb is gloriously zoned, and waited upon by several moons; while from none of them comes a retraction of their old assertions, or even any the less firmness of mien and tone. Next come the doubters to gaze. And in a multitude of cases you hear them declare that they have been too skeptical, hear them renounce their doubts, and say with those who have preceded them that it is true that the planet shines fairly with its cincture of light and cortege of satellites; while the others, almost to a unit, pass away either dumb and uninterpretable, or with a less doubting air than they came. The disbelievers, too, come and look; and in many cases you hear even those whose voices have been loudest and longest in the expression of disbelief affirm that at last they are convinced; that, dark and zoneless and moonless as they had thought royal Saturn, the sight of their eyes is too strong for them as they see his blazing image swimming in the mirror, belted like a knight and jeweled like a king: while the rest, almost to a unit, pass away either mute and uninterpretable, or with mien perceptibly downcast. And in absolutely no one of all that crowd, as they successively look, whether believers or doubters or disbelievers, can you see a sign that the cause of astronomical unbelief has gained the least aid and comfort from that telescopic view. What remains but to believe?

And now the approach of death is our highly magnifying reflector, stretching upward through the night. We living men have caught from it distant glimpses of a starry, crowned, beauteous Christianity many a time when we thought the supreme twilight might be gathering about us. And, in the actual night of the last sickness, all men look fairly on it, and, almost or quite without exception, think they find this Christianity looking more and more like the fair and starry queen she is said to be. What remains but to believe the Religion even as we believe the astronomy! We will believe it; and count apostolic Galileos and Newtons to speak high truth as they declare God to be real, the Bible His own message, and the Religion of Jesus sacred and divine. We will believe it; satisfied from the uniform course of experience that unbelief would be found fainting and failing us at the approach of death, and upbraiding us with its dying breath that we did not believe earlier. We will believe it; confident that when we come in our several turns to near the great Curtain, we shall feel as did Patrick Henry when he wrote in his last will and testament these words: "I have now disposed of all my property to my family. There is one thing more I wish I could give them and that is the Christian Religion. If they had that and I had not given them one shilling, they would have been rich; and if they had not that, and I had given all the world, they would be poor."

XV.
THE CURTAIN RISING.

XV. The Curtain Rising.

1. EXAMPLES 293
2. **CREDIBLE TESTIMONY** 298
3. HONEST WITNESSES 301
4. COMPETENT WITNESSES 302
5. VARIOUS EXPLANATIONS 305
6. ASTRONOMICAL VISION 308
7. **VERDICT** 311

THE CURTAIN RISING.

THE following account is given of Stephen, the first Christian martyr. He was standing before the Jewish Council as the prisoner of Jesus Christ. He had just made his brave confession, had rebuked the wickedness of his proud and bloody judges with the boldness and authority of an apostle, had seen them so cut to the heart by his upbraidings that they gnashed on him with their teeth like so many wild beasts. At this moment he looked upward. Perhaps it was to ask of his God the grace of strength and comfort for the crisis which he saw to be just at hand. But, instead of his gaze stopping at the white ceiling of that council chamber, lo, it seemed to penetrate the stone and mortar as if a canopy of crystal; and, passing upward through thick clouds, upward still through fathomless azure, to rest at last on a bright and beautiful land where shone the central throne of God, and by it, in the place of highest honor, the form of Jesus Christ. The man could not contain himself. He felt that it was no optical illusion, no fantasy of unstrung nerves and a disordered imagination, but a solid and glorious reality — the real heaven, which had long been to him an object of faith, now graciously given to his sight. There were none but scoffers about him; telling what he saw would only bring them upon him in a new storm of exasperation and hatred; still he must speak. "Behold," he cried, "I see the heavens opened and the Son of Man standing on the right hand of God."

On just this day of the week and of the month, Sunday, December 12, in the year 1697, a Christian minister lay dying in the city of Boston. Says his biographer, "He seemed to have some such views as the first Christian martyr had of the glory of his enthroned Saviour. He strove to speak to his wife, and at length exclaimed, 'Oh, what shall I say? He is altogether lovely. Oh, all our praises of Him are poor low things! His glorious angels are come for me.' On this he closed his eyes and never opened them again."

John Holland was on his death-bed. He wished to have the eighth chapter of the Epistle to the Romans read to him. While the reading was going on he suddenly spoke, "Oh, stay your reading! What brightness is this I see?" "It is the sunshine," suggested some one. "Sunshine!" said he, "no, it is my Saviour's shine. Now, farewell world, welcome heaven. Oh, speak it when I am gone, and preach it at my funeral: God dealeth familiarly with man. I feel His mercy, I see His majesty; whether in the body or out of the body I cannot tell, God knoweth, but I see things that are unutterable." So he passed away with bright looks and a soft sweet voice.

Another well-known minister of the Gospel, two days before his death, requested his daughter to come to his bedside; when he thus exclaimed: "What wonderful views I have had this day! I have been brought to the borders of the grave. Oh, what views! Wonderful, wonderful, wonderful! I have heard singing. Oh, how wonderful! Glory ineffable!" On the last day of his life, when his final conflict seemed actually to have begun, he suddenly revived and exclaimed with an air of transport, "Oh, what beauties I have seen! Glories of another world! What joys do I feel! I have seen the Saviour." In this state of ecstasy he continued till the last.

The manner in which Payson, of Portland, died is familiar to many of you; still it may be well to remind you of some particulars. "My God is in this room," he said. "I see Him, and oh, how lovely is the sight, how glorious does He appear, worthy of ten thousand hearts had I so many to give!" At another time he exclaimed, "The Celestial City is full in view; its glories beam upon me; its breezes fan me; its odors are wafted to me, its music strikes upon my ear, and its spirit breathes into my heart; nothing separates me from it but the river of death, which now appears as a narrow rill which may be crossed at a single step whenever God shall give permission. The Sun of righteousness has been gradually drawing nearer and nearer, appearing larger and larger as He approached, and now He fills the whole hemisphere, pouring forth a flood of glory in which I seem to float like an insect in the beams of the sun; exulting yet almost trembling while I gaze on this excessive brightness, and wondering with unutterable wonder why God should deign thus to shine upon a sinful worm."

Another and final instance. Let it be the experience of Adams, a missionary on the Gaboon River, Africa.

By temperament he was very unimaginative and practical. Those who were with him in his last sickness saw that feature still; there was no appearance of wandering of mind, no excitement of the imagination. They refused to believe him misled by a fevered brain; and declared that the full reality of the scene could only be felt by those who were present; who heard with their ears and saw with their eyes — seeing his face as it had been the face of an angel.

"About eleven o'clock, Tuesday morning, he sunk into another paroxysm, and we again thought him dying; but after about an hour he revived and lay for some time in a quiet state, during which he seemed to be engaged in silent prayer. Then suddenly starting up, with great animation, he exclaimed, 'I hear music, beautiful music, the sweetest melodies! I see glorious sights;—I see Heaven. Yes, the gates are open; let me go. I want no more of earth; detain me no longer: let me go. Oh, how beautiful! Oh, wonderful, wonderful views I have!

Who would have thought that I should have had these glorious views? Wonderful, wonderful, wonderful things I see! Surely God would not show me all this glory and then send me back to earth again. Oh, wonderful that such a sinner as I have been should be brought to this, and with tongue unloosed and the bonds of sin broken, see and describe such scenes as these! But I am going. Remember what I have told you. I am going. My speech on earth is finished.' Then with both hands raised and gazing upward he became insensible to earth."

Such are a few examples of a class of facts which no doubt might be numbered by hundreds and thousands. I could myself recite to you scores of them as good as any history that ever commanded the homage of mankind. And I know that I have heard or read of very many others, the particulars of which have quite faded from my memory. Some of you can say as much. Doubtless, every year, through the wide extent of evangelical Christendom, a very great number of these speaking visions occur. From the nature of the case, only a few of them find their way into print. Few devoted Christians have biographies, or even obituaries, to preserve their experiences. Could we collect all the published accounts of such trances as those of Stephen and Paul and Bailly and Holland and Payson and Adams and Welch and Boyd and Fulton and Tennent, and then multiply them by thousands, we probably should still fall short of the actual total.

Now let us ask a very interesting question. In this large class of facts, are there any cases of an actual uncovering of another world to the personal knowledge of living men? Do any of these strangely dying men actually see what they profess to see, and hear what they profess to hear?

In endeavoring to answer this question, let us notice the following particulars.

1. *There is nothing intrinsically incredible in an affirmative answer.*

Many do say, confidently, that we have in such dying experiences, cases of an actual insight into the world of the future life; and certainly no well-informed man can deny that it *may* be so. There is nothing in the nature of the statement itself which ought to prevent our receiving it as true. It is not self-contradictory. I am sure it cannot be shown to contradict, in any particular, the known constitution and course of Nature. On the contrary, it can be shown to be consistent perfectly with the known laws and order of the world. That there *may* be a world other than that which strikes our present bodily senses, no intelligent person will deny; for the very good reason, that multitudes of worlds are known to exist which once lay entirely outside of human observation. The worlds the microscope reveals, the worlds the telescope reveals — gloriously real and many as they are — were once as much covered up from the personal knowledge of living men as heaven now is. We know there is a universe of light and color which the man born blind has no personal acquaintance with; a universe of sound with which the man born deaf has no personal acquaintance. The things exist — exist in unspeakable magnitude, variety, and beauty — though these men have never directly known them, nor indeed have been able to form any conception of them. So there may be such a thing as the Christian Heaven, though our present senses are altogether silent concerning it.

Further, it *may* be that the intelligent principle in us has powers, at present generally sealed up, of seeing and hearing this heavenly world without help of bodily organs. There is nothing intrinsically incredible in this. On the contrary, there are facts of the same general nature frequently occurring. Such are those many instances in which the powers of the mind for inward action, are found independent of the condition of the body; the mind thinking, comparing, judging, reasoning, remembering, all the more powerfully often, the more weak and decayed and broken the body becomes. How the trampled and dying flower-bed will billow forth its perfume! To find that the mind's power of outward action — of knowing the world external to itself — is also independent of the condition of the body, would be to find a fact of quite the same sort with the other. If the one is real the other is credible. Think again of the man born blind. He has never seen; he has never known that he possesses the faculty of seeing. Yet some day an expert oculist succeeds in convincing him that he has the faculty, has had it all his life long; only there was wanting some one skillful enough to unlock it for his use. The operator cuts some restraining cord or draws aside some envious film; and lo, the man is in a new world! Now who can venture to say that we are not in just the same position in respect to the world of a future life, as this blind man was in respect to the world of light and color; in possession of a perfect faculty for observing it, and only needing to have the seals taken off from the faculty in order to bring it into full use? Is it any more incredible that there should be some imprisoned faculty of the mind which the touch of God can set at liberty, than that there should be some imprisoned faculty of the body which the instruments of the surgeon can liberate?

Further, there is nothing incredible in the idea of a bound soul-sense beginning to feel itself at liberty at the moment when the bodily ties begin to break. That is just the time when we should naturally look for some signs of beginning activity and freedom in the powers which are so soon to be in full play. That is just the time when, one would think, God would be likely to allow His servants a glimpse of the coming inheritance; for it is then they most need it for their solace — on their beds of pain, with all worldly comforts receding, and the shades of the sepulcher settling around. When then it is asserted that such death-bed visions as I have spoken of include within their great and shining orbit cases of an actual uncovering of another world to the personal knowledge of living men, I feel bound to grant that it may be so. And I ask you to grant, without reserve, that the thing is not intrinsically incredible.

2. *The subjects of these visions firmly declare them to be instances of actual insight into another world.*

These dying men give us a testimony. Not one of them is willing to admit that his wonderful experience is a dream, a fantasy, an hallucination of the senses. They all declare, with all possible directness and explicitness, that they have had revealed to them the wonders of another world and life; that by an interior sense they have perceived actual music, landscapes, and beings not open to the bodily senses.

3. *These men are witnesses of perfect honesty.*

Beyond all question, they profoundly believe what they say. They mean to tell nothing but sacred truth. They have all lived upright lives, and many of them have furnished some of the purest and noblest examples of virtuous living the world has ever seen. And now they are dying; they have reached that most honest of all honest hours; they are, as they suppose, just going to God and judgment. This is the time for a sincere, careful testimony, if ever. We are sure to get from them the facts just as they conceive them to be; without exaggeration, without coloring, without fanciful embellishment of any kind. Whatever else can be said of these dying Christians, with their upturned eyes and radiant faces, as they declare themselves gazing on angels and Jesus Christ and indescribable glories of heavenly landscapes, no one can for a moment think of denying that they believe every word they say, down to the very bottom of their hearts. And that bottom is very deep in many cases; deeper and richer by far than that which deep-sea soundings have just found so rich in healthy life.

4. *These men are competent witnesses.*

They are not ignorant men, men of feeble and narrow minds, men without mental discipline and culture. In the instances I have mentioned, and doubtless in multitudes of others, they are men of unusual natural abilities, educated, and enlightened by extensive information. They are not always men of nervous and enthusiastic temperament. In such cases as that of Adams, we have the phenomena in their most striking forms in connection with a turn of mind cool and equable and unimaginative in a remarkable degree. Nor do they always appear at a time when the mind is enfeebled and unsettled by disease. You shall find these dying seers talking as calmly and rationally on other subjects as they ever did; as practically, judiciously, and full of common sense as the most sober-minded of us could desire. And in some cases their minds appear even more sound and comprehensive and penetrating, more full of quickness and order and healthful strength and vitality, than they ever were in what were called their best days. The visions, too, occur in all sorts of diseases; are not confined to such as are thought more especially liable to give rise to distempered views of things. Whether the end come by gout, or gangrene, or consumption, or fever, apparently makes no difference. The men I have spoken of all died of different disorders, and all died like prophets. And there can be no doubt that the several safeguards now instanced have often been united in the same person; the great talents, the liberal culture, the extensive knowledge, the philosophic temperament, the disease unapt to disorder the mental action, and every appearance of sobriety and healthful vigor in that action as directed toward other topics, side by side with these wonderful visions, introducing them, following them, enveloping them, permeating them, as perfume does the flower.

What shall we say? Are not these competent witnesses? Were there ever any more so? Unless one chooses to deny that men are ever qualified to judge of supernatural facts, he must admit that these persons have qualifications of the very highest order. If such men are not able to judge whether they see angels and a Divine glory and heavenly scenes, there is no such thing among men as being able to do it. And if so, it would be impossible for God to reveal anything to an individual without revealing it to others. And further, no man is able to judge, on the basis of his single personal observation, whether he sees anything — a tree, a house, a man. You say that you see a tree. What proof have you of it? Only this — it seems to you that you see it; and the faculties, bodily and mental, which must be concerned in the act, appear to be in a sound and healthy condition. This is all the proof you can have, apart from comparing your observation with that of other men; and you are accustomed to think it sufficient. Of course you can judge whether you see the object, when you can judge whether the two parts of this proof are realized in your case; that is, whether you seem to yourself to see the tree, and whether the faculties which must be concerned in the seeing, in case it occurs, are sound. And at last it comes to this, that you are a competent judge when these faculties are in a sound condition. This is the qualification; the only one the case admits of; a good and sufficient one; and yet not good and sufficient unless such dying men as Holland and Bailly and Haynes and Adams are qualified to judge whether they see the scenes of another world. For if the soundness of all their faculties concerned does not qualify them to judge whether they see Heaven, neither does the soundness of all your faculties concerned qualify you to judge whether you see earth.

A thing not intrinsically incredible, when testified to by witnesses of indisputable honesty and thorough competency, is to be believed. Deny this and you deny that two thirds of the world's knowledge is of any value: for so much of it depends on just this principle in regard to testimony.

5. *Though these witnesses were not competent, no other hypothesis than that of the truth of their testimony would be consistent with indisputable facts.*

We can suppose those dying visions to be the illusions of disease, or the phantasms of highly nervous and enthusiastic temperaments under very exciting circumstances, or the creed and hopes of men vivified into pictures and almost into realities by a strong faith spurred up by approaching death, or the result of all these causes together. Will any of these explanations agree with such facts as the following?

First, these dying visions of angels and Christ and God and Heaven, are confined to credibly good men. Why do not bad men have such visions? They die of all sorts of diseases; they have nervous and enthusiastic temperaments; they even have creeds and hopes about the future which they cling to with very great tenacity: why do not they rejoice in some such glorious illusions when they go out of the world?

Second, zealous opposers of Christianity never

have dying visions contradicting those of Christians. Why does not disease, or nervousness, or imagination, or violent disbelief of the Bible, set these characters, when dying, to seeing visions of annihilation, or of a paradise without a God and Christ in it? Certainly we have a right to look for such things if the visions described are due to causes which act equally on the friends of Christ and His enemies. We certainly have a right to expect that the fevers and imaginations which so delude the Baillys and Adamses will play off like tricks, only varied to suit the difference of faith, on the Collinses and Herberts, the Bolingbrokes and Owens.

Third, no dying visions, under like circumstances, occur in respect to any other object than the world of the future state. This is very singular, on the supposition that they are mere delusions produced by causes acting with equal force on all classes of persons. Why, here are misers, thinking of gold, gold, gold, all their lives, and with gold still uppermost in their thoughts now that they are dying (for, alas, they are not aware that it is the last sickness) — why does not the cheating distemper, while allowing them to perceive and talk as sensibly as ever on all other subjects, sometimes make them see mines of gold and caskets of precious jewels, and hear the clink of coin to the amount of a king's revenue, and all so clear and life-like that no persuading can convince them that they are deluded? Here are ambitious men, thinking of offices, honors, reputations all their lives, and with these things still uppermost in their thoughts now that they are dying (for, alas, they are not aware that it is the last sickness)—why does not the distempered brain, while allowing them to observe and reason as soundly as ever on all other subjects, make them see themselves seated on presidential chairs and loftier thrones, and hear the *vivats* of admiring throngs, and all so clear and life-like that to convince them of the mistake would be quite impossible? Here are the votaries of pleasure and fashion, thinking of drives, dances, plays, feasts all their lives, and with such things still the ruling passion now that they are dying (for, alas, they do not know that it is the last sickness, and they hope in a few days to be as busy at their pleasures as ever)—why do not the excited nerves and irregular fancy, while allowing them to view and speak of all other things after the old manner, make them see wardrobes fit for royalty, and gay festive-scenes through which they move in triumphant beauty and delight, and all so clear and life-like that no argument can persuade them that they do not actually see what they seem to see? Such questions cannot be answered. Unintelligent causes do not discriminate between the various classes of men after this wonderful fashion. Altogether, the facts cited can only agree with the idea that dying visions of good men are often cases of actual insight into another world. As its hold on the body loosens, the soul begins to acquire the use of faculties hitherto locked up. A real God permits it to look in upon the realities of a future life; among which are a real enthroned Jesus and a real Scriptural Heaven.

Certain men come to us with a scientific testimony. They tell us that they found their way into a temple glorious as a dream of enchantment, where twin altars blazed and twin pontiffs ministered. Each gave a flaming brand. They bore them forth and flared them up under the familiar sky. Lo, miracle of miracles! That silver segment which hangs so sweetly in the west expands into a revolving world. Those islets of light which roam so mazily in the dark deeps resolve themselves into a system of worlds moving in inexorable order about a blazing sun still greater than they all. And those points that twinkle from their eternal stations — AMAZEMENT — can it be that such great realities hide beneath such slender seemings? What seem so near, depart away by incomprehensible ages of travel. What seem so fixed, take on motion and rush along the expanse as if inspired by a thousand whirlwinds. What seem so frail that the wing of the soaring bird might put them in jeopardy, surround themselves with multiple cycles, of which, to our breathless imaginations, eternity itself is but an elder brother. What seem so confused, turn out to be an economy of systems on whose bright circles embracing beauty and order move in perpetual jubilee. What seem so few to our untaught counting, become the outposts of multitudinous armies, up and down whose shining squadrons darts with air of huge bewilderment our human arithmetic. What seem so small, gather to themselves solar stature, and at times a sphered girth within which the system of the world might hide all its membership, welcome to its side ten thousand fellow systems, and still go forth on revolutions of planetary grandeur. Such marshalings of beauty, such confederacies of sublimity, such hegiras of thrones and principalities and powers of heavenly glory never before met even their thought. It was as if new faculties had been born to them. The hearts of some grew faint. Had they not seen the skirt of GOD — the *holding back of the face of His throne!*

Astronomers come to other intelligent men with this great testimony. Do these intelligent men presume to question it? They have never studied the higher mathematics. They have never even looked through a telescope — most of them. As they now are, they cânnot begin to verify for themselves that sublime astronomical vision. And yet they receive it as science, and ask to have it taught to their children. Do they act unreasonably? If one of them should say in self-justification, "There is no counter-testimony; the positive witnesses are many; I have no reason to suspect them of dishonesty; they show themselves quite sound-minded in other things; what they testify to, though sublime and far beyond anything I am able to discover for myself, is not intrinsically unreasonable but is in the line of the general knowledge and faculty of the race," — I say, if a man should justify himself in accepting the astronomy on such grounds, would any of you hesitate to allow that they are sufficient? Not a single soul. And just such are the grounds we have for accepting the testimony of those other witnesses who testify to glimpses of the Next World. They are honest witnesses — as honest as death. They are capable witnesses — capable as ever wrought at the prose of daily affairs, or stood before juries. They are many concurrent witnesses — reckon them by thousands and tens of thousands. What they tell is indeed beyond our present power to discover for ourselves — something very wonderful and sublime; but wonderful and sublime things, and things that must be taken on trust by most men, are by no means unknown in this age. All the sciences are full of them. Signals of strange and startling faculties, as yet generally latent, abound in the psychological phenomena of the times. From earliest date, a certain weird border-land of experience has ever perplexed and awed both people and philosophers. And, then, there is absolutely no counter-testimony. The witnesses are all on one side. Why should not the jury agree? Why should the judge hesitate to decide in favor of the sublime vision? Especially when he has just decided in favor of that sublime astronomy which no more candid and capable men testify to, and which is quite as much out of the line and above the direct personal knowledge of most people as are the great visions of Paul and Stephen and Adams? Yes — let him be consistent, and say that there has really been a rising of the Curtain to give living men glimpses of a world beyond the grave whose whole economy recognizes a Divine Bible.

Men often wish they could have something like a sensible demonstration of the truth or falsity of Theism and Christianity. If an angel could only come and tell them to believe; if they could only for a moment have the invisible world uncovered to them so that they could see that it is all as the Bible represents — see the glorious Heaven the Christian hopes for, the glory of God, and Jesus standing on the right hand of God — they would ask no more. They would embrace the Gospel zealously without any further delay. But, my friends, you have almost the sort of demonstration that you ask in the facts to which your attention has now been called. You have the demonstration only at second hand. Persons whom you have known, or what really amounts to the same thing, persons of your own times as to whose existence and experience as recorded you should have not the least atom of doubt, have actually looked into the invisible for you; have seen the angels, the enthroned Christ, the Scriptural Heaven. Stephen and Holland and Bailly and Payson and Adams, and uncounted more of the same stamp, have looked under the Curtain, and have been permitted to tell you what they have seen. Were you to go the world around, you could not find more credible witnesses than these; honest men, honest as eternity; capable men; cultivated men; men who, though dying, have all their mental faculties in sound, vigorous play. They come and bid you believe on the strength of their sight. "Believe in Heaven," they say, "for we have seen it; we know we have, know it as surely as we know that we are living men." "Believe in Jesus the Messiah," say they, "for we have seen Him arrayed in Divine glories hard by the throne of God; we know we have, know it as surely as we know that we are now speaking." And really, this seems to me about the same thing as seeing these things for myself. If this seeing of theirs goes for nothing with me, doubtless seeing of my own would go for nothing too. There is no reason to suppose I should be persuaded, though one rose from the dead. I protest to you, my hearers — each such death-bed scene as that of the missionary Adams is an independent demonstration of the truth of that Religion which is preached to you; of God, of the Son, of the Bible. You have ten thousand most irrefragable evidences; for unquestionably there have been that number of such gorgeous Christian deaths. They are occurring every year, all over evangelical Christendom. They probably have been occurring ever since the world of men began; more especially since that time when the martyr Stephen looked up rapturously into Heaven from amid the gnashing wild beasts of the Jewish Sanhedrim. This may well suffice for your faith till such time as God shall be lifting before your own death-beds the Curtain that conceals the world of spirits. Only a few are permitted to *tell* of eternity, seen while yet in the body: but it is by no means unlikely that every person, either before or after speech has departed, while the soul is breaking away from the body, gets real glimpses of the spirit-land which he is about entering. Perhaps the Curtain will soon begin to rise for some of us. Let us see to it that our glimpses shall be glimpses of Heaven. And while our friends are watching our attent, though silent, faces, as if seeing things unutterable, let us be renewing Stephen's vision of a Heaven opened, and a Jesus standing on the right hand of God — Paul's vision of a Paradise in the third Heaven, with its *unspeakable things*.

XVI.
CHRISTIAN DYNAMICS.

XVI. Christian Dynamics.

1. EXPERIENCE 319
2. NATURE OF THE SYSTEM 332
3. TOTAL STRENGTH 345
4. IMPERIAL ROME 349
5. A GREATER EMPIRE 352

CHRISTIAN DYNAMICS.

OF course many objections can be brought against the Biblical Religion. They can be brought against anything. The business of fault-finding is proverbially easy. Almost any expert advocate will boldly undertake to befog to common minds the clearest sunshine of law or of fact. There is nothing so pure, nothing so fair, nothing so true — absolutely nothing — but that an ingenious mind can manage to bring some specious accusations against it.

I have already noticed the leading infidel objections; also given briefly what I regard as a conclusive answer to them all. They lie as much against known facts as they do against the Divine origin of the Bible. That whole way of objecting which is commonly used against the Bible is equally good against every principle of morals, against every historical fact, and even against every mathematical demonstration. I have spent years in study of the abstruser mathematics. I have done my best at examining their principles; and I offer to bring quite as plausible objections against their every particular axiom as any Voltaire can bring against the Religion of Jesus.

This is my general answer. In addition, however, almost every leading objection to this Religion can be met with some valuable answers peculiar to itself. Of course it would carry me too far were I to attempt to deal fully with each such objection. The best I can do is to give you an example of such dealing; and to take for my example one of the most specious charges ever made in the interest of unbelief. This I now propose to do. And I do it the more readily from seeing that the discussion to be undertaken is fitted to throw special light on the nature of the Gospel, and on its claims to reverence from the many reverers of splendid power and triumphant success.

It has long been the practice of infidels to assert the *inherent weakness of Christianity.* A century ago it was given out at Ferney that the System could be put down by a single vigorous arm. A little later, the author of the "Decline and Fall" penned a stately sneer which meant that the religion of Mohammed possessed more tough stability than the Religion of Jesus. To-day, a brilliant Quarterly comes into our reading rooms and argues that Christianity is both feeble to conquer and feeble to endure; that it has little influence with its friends, less force against its enemies, and no ability whatever to bide the light of science.

Why these charges? Plainly from the idea that if Christianity is shown intrinsically weak it is thereby shown substantially false. And the idea is correct. A weak system of religion is not suited to human wants, is not suited to the end it proposes to itself, and so cannot be from a wise and almighty God. I therefore proceed to show that the Christian Religion is not weak, that it is really an exceedingly strong system, really a magnificent self-establishing and self-perpetuating Force, not to say the joint wisdom and power of God.

I appeal, first, to the experience of the world.

"Appeal to the experience of the world!" exclaims the objector; "why, it is just here lies my great strength. How slow have been the advances of Christianity in certain quarters, and how quick its retreats in others! What little influence has it had on most of its professed friends; on the measures of Christian governments, on the masses of Christian nations, on even the membership of Christian churches! Into how many mutually contending sects have its followers been divided, from the earliest times! How is it possible to construct an argument for a mighty Christianity out of an experience that bristles with such facts as these!"

It really is of no consequence to dispute the reality of any of these stumbling experiences. Admit them, and it does not follow that Christianity is weak — unless, indeed, it is true that there is no system on earth which is strong. For a like experience belongs to every other historical system, whether of religion or science or government. Perhaps the objector is a deist. Has Deism — any more than Romanism, **Mohammedanism, or** Polytheism — never had times **of gaining** slowly **and losing** swiftly; times when **the** actual **practice of its friends was** but a poor **exponent** of its theories and rules; times when **its** different schools **were** many and mutually **hostile?** Perhaps the objector **is a** politician. **Has the** democracy or the monarchy **or** the aristocracy ever been without its parties, without its courts and **prisons in** full play, **without** times when friends in**creased slowly** or enemies rapidly? Perhaps the **objector is a man of science. Is** there any leading **science which has not had its** slow as well as rapid spread, **its local** defeats, **a large** practice among its nominal friends inconsistent **with** its principles, various schools shaking argumentative spears **at** each other? In short, no system with **a** history can be mentioned which has **not** had just such an experience in these respects as is charged **on** Christianity. **Even sin has** had it. **Is sin, as it exists** among **men, a feeble** thing? **Is there really nothing strong in the world?**

It is, however, not **true** that Christianity exerts **small** influence on **its professed friends.** Hereafter I mean to show its influence to be vastly great, though much less than a Christian could wish. But it is **a fact,** which **there is no** denying, that the System has had **its** times **of** slow advances and quick recessions. **The** primitive church **was soon** corrupted. **The Reformation of the sixteenth** century ebbed **very rapidly in Germany.** Our missionaries have often labored long with apparently small results. But, before weakness can properly be inferred from these facts, two things must be shown; first, that substantially the whole strength of the System was enlisted in the contest, and second, that the strength of opposing influence was not great. Until both of these points are proved nothing is proved. But it may credibly be claimed that what Christianity had to contend against was human wickedness, one of the strongest things known to history, and indeed able from its very nature to resist successfully any degree of force that may be brought against it. And further, it may be claimed that never yet have the full energies of the System been brought into play; that its power is partly that of an instrument committed to human hands, which are always in some degree unskillful and unfaithful, and often vastly so. The strongest lever, the keenest sword, may accomplish but little through the fault of those into whose hands it falls. Friends of Christianity may plausibly enough affirm that, had it always been diligently used according to the laws of its nature, it would long since have subdued the world.

It is also true that nominal Christians have in all ages been divided into many mutually contending sects. So far as this division has given rise to bitterness and strife between true believers it has of course hindered the success of Christianity. But what is this admitting? Merely that its success is capable of being abated in some degree by the mighty weakness and wickedness of human nature; a thing surely consistent with the possession on the part of the System of any amount of power. Division in Christianity is one thing; division among its followers is another. The one would indeed mean weakness in the system; the other may spring merely from the weakness, natural and moral, of man. I claim that it does spring entirely from this source; that so far from being produced or in any way countenanced by Christianity, it is opposed by it at all points; and that so the System is no more responsible for it and its results than is the eagle for the head wind through which, with powerful and overcoming stroke, he forces a somewhat retarded way.

Yonder planet, to a careless examination, is a mere speck, with very inconsiderable and often retrograde motion, and wholly uninfluential on its neighbors and ourselves; but if you look into the case more carefully you will find that Jupiter is a huge world, doubtless filled like our own with an almost incomprehensible sum of chemical and mechanical forces, firmly holding four reluctant worlds in eternal fealty to itself, ever advancing on its path at more than the pace of winds, and so related to us that were itself blotted from the system we ourselves must disappear. Yonder star seems, to a careless examination, less than the planet, equally uninfluential, always quite stationary, and sometimes altogether occulted; and yet if you look more carefully into the case you **will** find **that Alcyone** is equal to twelve thousand **suns** like **ours, is** potent with solar forces, is the center **of our firmament**, and is wheeling about itself **with supreme** ease, not only our own world and solar system, **but** also the whole glorious Milky Way. Who, with such examples of Great Powers that look like mere nothings to **a superficial view,** but **must** admit that the Christianity which at **first,** perhaps, seems very slow, very weak, and often **almost** suppressed by its neighbors, may yet, on **more** careful inquiry, be found instinct with enormous **force,** even with **the** Wisdom and Power of God!

So much for objections. On the positive side **of** the argument **I ask** attention to the following particulars — the single handed successes of Christianity against prodigious opposition ; its greatly **superior** rapidity and frequency of success as **compared** with opposing moral forces when all have equal **field ;** and, finally, the fact **that** on such field it al**ways** conquers all these enemies as long as it remains pure **and entire,** while it maintains its purity and entireness in **a** remarkable manner. All this in view of features in the System adapted to such effects.

Without help from **any quarter,** this Religion of Christ has achieved a thousand **triumphs** over prodigious power. As examples of successes under such conditions, **I** may instance the many radical conversions it has effected among the most difficult **of** men. Men **of iron** will, men scaled in all varieties of wickedness, men who to strength of sin and strength of nature added the strength of hoary habits; how often have such, by some simple tract, some Scripture sentence, some common sermon, been subdued into new men! The Ethiops whitened, the dappled leopards parted with their spots; and beyond a doubt it was the Gospel, pure and simple, that wrought the wonder.

Look also at the great restraints which the System exerts on the masses in Christian lands. Of all lands the Pagan are most corrupt. Next come the Mohammedan, which have some grains of Christianity in their creed. Still better are the countries holding to the Greek and Roman Churches, which include still more of the true Gospel. And best of all, as formal statistics show, is Protestantdom with its still greater leaven of the Religion of Christ. It is here we find, as nowhere else, the kingdom of the ten commandments. Our legislation, the manners of our people — to say nothing of the practice of our churches — dark as they are when projected on a perfect law, shine like Chaldean stars on the inky background of heathen countries. Further, on comparing together different communities of the same Protestant land, we find those most exemplary in every moral respect which are brought most regularly and closely into contact with Christian principles and institutions. The places among ourselves where the Bible is most read and the sanctuary most frequented, are the places where vices and disorders, and all that wise parents would dislike in a home, least flourish. Now what is the explanation of this? I answer, the mighty restraining power of Christianity. The strict, pure System, with its popular cast and grand sanctions, is evidently just fitted to produce such results. It is a plain cause, a sufficient cause, a cause whose variations correspond with the observed variations in the phenomena to be explained. And what other can be assigned? "Liberty," says an objector, "Liberty! The moral differences you speak of are owing to the different degrees of civil freedom enjoyed; for freedom gives industry, enterprise, education, and comfort to the masses; all of which things favor public virtue." But this explanation does not profess to touch the case of communities belonging to the same country. Also, it does not appear that freedom, apart from some measure of Christianity, or under the same low measure of it, has been wont to stand connected with any better state of public morals than absolutism. Were the ancient heathen republics any more correct in their manners than the average of ancient heathen monarchies? Are the papal republics of South America any fairer to look at than the papal kingdoms of Brazil and Spain? The aristocracies of absolute monarchies, always freer than the other classes, have they as a rule been noticeably less loose in morals than the masses under the same religious influences? Indeed, who would suppose that merely diminishing the restraints on corrupt human nature would be likely to improve its behavior? But does not self-government in the people tend to general industry, enterprise, intelligence, thrift; and so to an orderly and decorous social condition? Far from it. Superior liberty alone is never peculiarly connected with these things. There must be at least liberty and order; which latter is one of the things to be accounted for. Mexico has long had as free a constitution as could be desired; but, as there have been but little order and security among the people, they have had little heart for any but the most makeshift mode of living. And so in several neighboring states. Indeed hardly anything is plainer from the course of experience than that order in liberty cannot be maintained except on the basis of a general intelligence, laborious vigor, and sound principle in the people.

As examples of great historic successes pertinent to my purpose, I may instance the triumphs of Christianity in the Primitive Age and at the Reformation. At both these times she entered the field substantially alone. On her side were none of the gods and demigods of worldly circumstance. On the contrary, every power of this kind was bitterly against her. Antiquity was against her; wealth was against her; art, literature, and philosophy were against her; pontiffs and Cesars, old and new, were against her — all bitterly zealous in giving aid and comfort to her enemy. And that enemy, the central enemy itself — what a very monster for intense vitality and power! They err exceedingly who suppose this foe to have been merely the decayed Paganism, the hollow Judaism, or Romanism with its extensive abuses. It was none of these so much as the giant wickedness of the times, only partly expressed in these forms. Never in the history of the Papacy was Europe more corrupt, both in doctrine and practice, than the monk of Erfurt found it. Never, probably, was the core of society, Gentile and Jewish, more eaten out by vice than when Jesus appeared. Of course this great corruption struggled with all its might against the spread of a religion so strict and pure as the Christian. And yet Christianity conquered. In a brief space it steadily forced its way into ascendency throughout that old Roman world. In a few years it won to the Reformation principalities, cantons, kingdoms; and all, despite that unparalleled enemy with its paladin miters, crowns, diets, conscript-fathers, persecutions, prestiges of all sorts. Do such achievements as these come of strength less than gigantic?

Another fact. Christianity has never declined before other moral forces anything like as fast and often as they have before it, when all have been left to their own intrinsic energies. And so they have been left in the United States and Great Britain. In these countries the law and doctrine of Christ have always recovered in months the ground which they were years in losing. Compare the reactions under the Wesleys, under Edwards, under Chalmers, with the corresponding declines. The infidelity, the formalism, the indifferentism, the legal wickedness of all kinds, came in on foot and went away on wings. And those late religious changes in Ireland — how surprisingly many and rapid have they been! Who ever heard of Protestant parishes, under merely moral influences, changing to Romanist so fast or so often? With us it is no uncommon thing for a revival, in the course of a few weeks or even days, to completely break the staff of wickedness in a community and quite abolish prevalent infidelities and heresies. And, pray, where is the instance of these things, one or all, reciprocating conquests on the Gospel after the same magnificent manner? Of all men, Americans, who hear so often the rushing mighty wind of awakenings and see all things in its path abruptly bending and breaking, should be least troubled with misgivings as to the power of Christianity. This superior rapidity of success shows that, at least in its best states, the System has greatly more conquering power than any other opposing moral force whatever, not excepting sin itself; while the superior frequency of its successes shows that it maintains the conquering state greatly better than any opponent.

Consider also a still stronger fact. It is that, on open and equal field, the Gospel *always* conquers whatever moral forces appear against it so long as it remains pure and entire, while it maintains its purity and completeness much better than any of them. No one presumes to judge unfavorably of the energy of a chemical agent from what it does in an impure state. What does it when it is itself and by itself? — this is the test question. If, when freed from all impurities and keeping every element that properly enters into its composition, the pile of Volta makes the dead man leap, decomposes the firmest substances, fires the least inflammable, bursts rocks asunder, and triumphs over space and time in the instantaneous utterance of our thought a thousand miles away, these effects are the proper measures of the battery's power, and not what it does when the acid is absent or the zinc impure. And so, what Christianity does when pure and entire is the only proper expression of its force. Strictly speaking, it is then only that it is Christianity. Now what does it in this state? I answer, Conquer — nothing but Conquer. The world may safely be challenged to show an instance in which the strict System, substantially nothing more and nothing less, has failed to gain ground on its enemies when equal field has been allowed. The Primitive Church, as long as it continued itself, went on spreading. So did the Church of the Reformation, save where the civil power interfered. Never yet was a real Christian mission planted that did not gain perceptibly, as soon as it was fairly at work without molestation. It is true that sometimes missions have been given up on account of civil interference, want of support from home, a change of circumstances apparently making another field more eligible; but never on account of total want of progress after the Gospel had come to walk about familiarly in the vernacular. And look at home. You will see that, there being given in a place a pure Christian doctrine, a living Christian church, and a faithful Christian ministry — that is, real Christianity with all its institutions in a normal state — it is sure to make progress on all opposing influences. None of us ever heard of a place where it was not so.

But what power has the System to maintain its purity and entireness? Eighteen centuries have passed since the Bible was finished. They have been centuries of great changes. In their course the world has been wrought over into newness at almost every point. But, to-day, the text of the Scriptures, after copyings almost innumerable and after having been tossed about through ages of ignorance and tumult, is found by exhaustive criticism to be unaltered in every important particular — there being not a single doctrine, nor duty, nor fact, of any grade, that is brought into question by variations of readings — a fact that stands alone in the history of such ancient literature. And to-day, also, as in all the past, there is not a single great Christian Sect that does not hold as firmly to the most fundamental elements of Christianity as did the Primitive Age itself. God, a divine Christ, an inspired Bible, the immortality of men, their responsibleness in a future state of rewards and punishments, their actual lost estate, their possible recovery by repentance and faith on their part and by an atonement and Holy Ghost on the part of God, an honest walk of the believer according to the rules of Christ — where is there a large Denomination, bearing Christ's name, that does not lift both hands in favor of these Christian First Principles? They stand better than the hills. Time, the great dissolver, makes no impression on them. We confess to sore corruptions in certain quarters; yet it is true that the Christian World as such, in its creeds and actual belief, still maintains the whole gist of the original Christianity. There is not a main timber in the great ship as it was launched which is not in it to-day, and as sound as ever. On parts barnacles have been allowed to gather. At times men have hindered the sailing and the safety by various outlandish equipments. At times they have made our trireme fantastic with ill-judged paint, and even odious with unfit lading. But, despite this, it is the same ship, as to those great skeleton beams whose heart of oak holds all together, that once plowed the blue waves of Galilee and the Ægean with the fishermen apostles for crew and undoubted Jesus for Master.

So much for what is observed outside of the System. Now notice some strong features of the System itself, from which such effects might naturally be expected. I think one has only to look at these in their combination in order to feel that the Religion to which they belong must be powerful in a very high degree.

I appeal to the nature of the System itself.

Look, first, at the great store of clear and important truth which Christianity confessedly contains. To say nothing of what it tells us about God, it gives us very many just and important views of the history, character, and proper culture of man. Its practical code is of the best — very sound, very complete, very valuable — and the Scriptures are starred with thousands of excellent precepts, each of which is based on a truth as valuable as itself. This is confessed by persons of all creeds. Even bitter infidels say it. Of course truths so widely received, and yet so largely distasteful, must be exceedingly clear. They call for no unusual faculty or learning. They ask for no happy moments of even common minds. As soon as fair statement of them is made, they stand forth to view in sharp and pictorial definition, and commend themselves to the public conscience so eloquently as to compel in their favor promptest and unqualified verdict. Is such an element as this without great force? To suppose it is to suppose that there are no strong adaptations in our constitution to leading facts in Nature. It is to suppose that conscience is no power in the world; the instinct of self-interest and self-preservation no power. We have been told from earliest years that truth is mighty; and surely such truth as we find included in Christianity — so important, so voluminous, so easily and vividly recognized by men at large — surely this is not likely to put the proverb to blush. It does not. It is a great unwasting water-head in the mountains — unwasting because having direct communication with the highest Divine and deepest human nature, with the waters above the firmament and the waters beneath — and if one asks why it is that the vale below smiles with plenty, and swift-paced engines fill its warehouses with useful and beautiful fabrics, I point in part-answer to the rivulets that stream down upon it from every quarter, and to the races whose fuller currents shoot steeply down from their perch among the eternal snows and clouds through all the droughty year.

Next, look at the great simplicity of Christianity. There are things attached to the System, and properly attached to it, which are very far from having this quality — witness the folios of Christian philosophies which hardly any besides scholars are expected to understand. There are things often called Christianity which, if possible, still less deserve to be considered simple — witness the trappings of that great Church which covers the best of Europe. See Fathers, Popes, Councils, and Scriptures brought together in one discordant motley as rule of faith — and this passes for Christianity in its foundation.

See dreams, traditions, and Aristotles, dovetailed and patterned into each other with the most intricate ingenuity — and this passes for Christianity in its doctrine. See a vast ecclesiasticism with its thrones, principalities, and powers; with its croziers, miters, vestments, censers, saint-days, ceremonies, in almost endless patterns of tinsel or magnificence — and this passes for Christianity in its order and worship. Heathendom itself could hardly turn out to us a more intricate and ostentatious system than this for which is claimed so lofty a name. And even in the purest form of the Christian System, there are some things hard to be understood — let us not fear to say it — parables and riddles hard as any of Delphos or Theban Sphinx. Yet, after all, it is permitted me to speak of the great simplicity of Christianity. Though its adjuncts are not always simple, though particular features of it are not simple, yet, as a whole, this Religion is the simplest the world has ever seen. Nothing but Scripture enters into its rule of faith and practice. Nothing but honest effort to do all known duty is made necessary to secure faith in this rule. Its fundamentals of doctrine are few and easily understood: its principles of practice still fewer and almost universally approved. It has but one sacred day; but one order of religious; but two ceremonies, and those in merest outline and of the most unpretending kind. There is nothing that can be called machinery — no diplomacy of manner; no sacred etiquette;

no dramatic gild, scenery, costume, upholstery, illuminations, judicious dispositions of lights and shadows. Whether such things may, to a certain extent, be lawfully connected with the System in the responsibility of human liberty, is a point on which Christian people may differ: but it ought to be plain to all, that they are no part of the prescribed System itself. Here the tenor of things is severely simple. We everywhere recognize the manner of one who, strong in birth and position and unmatched beauty, can consciously afford to appear in the simplest drapery, and to leave to less fortunate dames the sheen of jewels and the triumphs of millinery.

Now, to persons not a few, such a severely simple system is every way more attractive than any other. And, to such as form the bulk of mankind, it is one which can be more thoroughly understood, vividly conceived, promptly recollected, and easily worked: and so one more influential with believers and in their hands. A system whose essentials are so few and plain, can be mastered very early in life as well as by the humblest classes; a system so capable of being thoroughly, generally, and easily understood, has special security against corruption; a system so sparing of sacred days and trappings and ceremonials, commends itself to the necessities of the masses; is cheaply received, cheaply supported, cheaply propagated.

Mark, also, the intense centralization of Christianity. It not only vests absolute authority in religious matters in single Scripture, but sends every one to it directly and personally for direction. And not only so; but the system of general government which it represents God as maintaining, is of the same concentrated and direct character. He is shown to us as, in right and fact, the one absolute monarch in the world of events; supervising and managing them all, whether inward or outward, religious or secular, great or small, with irresponsible and infinite power. Further, He does not govern by the spontaneity of accountable deputies, as other absolute monarchs are always compelled to do largely; but with a personal thought and decision, and, where the case demands it, determining action in relation to everything that happens, down to the motion of the lifeless microscopic mote. And as to leading human affairs, what closer personal dealing could there be between subjects and sovereign! We are individually held responsible for all conduct directly to Him. He hears our prayers in person, pardons our offenses in person, renews and sanctifies us in person, will finally judge us in person. Depart from that confessional, O monk Luther! Rise from before that picture of the Virgin, O Bohemian Huss, as yet unread in Wickliff! Ye poor men of Lyons and kingdoms silent with interdicts, tremble not while vicar-Rome refuses viaticums and clanks in your ears the power of the keys! The duties of Deity are not done by curate. None of the great functions of His government are trusted to the discretion, even the accountable discretion, of pontiff or council, laic or cleric, saint or angel. He is His own parliament and judiciary and executive — His own prime minister and cabinet and constituency. Himself is the State. Everywhere He worketh all in all. Never was there centralization to match this.

Such is the Christian theory of the Divine Government. It is evidently well fitted to take strong hold of the human mind. Naturalism, crowding God almost over the horizon by a thousand interposed second-causes; Paganism doing the same by its acolyth gods, greater and less — what are such proxy systems, in respect to impressiveness, compared with one which keeps ever glittering in its foreground and background and everywhere the majesty and terribleness of an infinite Personal Ruler! The idea of being always in direct contact with an almighty and irresponsible sovereignty, with not so much as a gossamer-web between to deaden its heavy pulsations upon us, is fitted to appeal bravely to our imaginations, venerations, and fears. It at once translates all the doctrines of Christ into the imperative — all the laws of Christ into the awfulness of life and death.

This intense centralization of the Christian System makes it to us a system of great liberty, in the direction of our fellow-men. By vesting the sole authority in religious matters in the Bible, and by sending each man directly and personally to it to gather its meaning in the exercise of his own private judgment, it denies to all his fellows, individually and collectively, the right to dictate to him in religion, either as original authority or as expounders of Scripture. If they choose to advise him it is well. If they choose to argue with him it is better. If they are able in any way to give him light, it is their duty to do it and his duty to allow it to be done. And in case their opportunities are great, their talents commanding, and their probity unquestionable, their bare opinions may be entitled to great weight. But as to any right to dictate religious sentiments, to bind the conscience by mere assertion and authority — this right is given by the Christian scheme to no man or body of men, far or near, speaking or writing, living or dead, outside of Scripture. We are not bound to take their mere word for the smallest item of creed or duty, whether they are popes, councils, or fathers; whether Luthers, Calvins, or bluff Henrys; whether Dort Synods, Westminster Assemblies, or ecumenical commentators. All the right the best of them have is merely that of contributing materials for the use of our free and independent judgments. So says the Christianity that puts an open Bible in the sole seat of authority. If a man with a triple crown on his head comes to me and says, "Believe in the immaculate conception," it is my Christian privilege to say to him, "Prove that this is Scripture; else, though supported by the whole world, it can never enter into my creed." If conservative journals and jurisconsults come to me and say, "Use not your pulpit against sins which have become political institutions," it is my Christian privilege to say to them, "Gentlemen, with all due respect, it will be necessary for you to prove that the course you require is Scriptural; else, I must continue to preach against violent perverting of justice in a province." Such responses are indeed bad mediævalism, but they are good Christianity. I am allowed the largest religious liberty in respect to man; though in respect to the Bible I am under an absolute monarchy.

Now this large liberty is very attractive to most persons. But the chief thing about it is its influence in forming the public to an intellectual habit — to that habit of self-poised and enterprising thought which goes to promote all sorts of freedom and advancement, and thus to place Christianity in command of the most powerful and prosperous nations, whose prestige and wealth and science and power shall preach for her. See what has actually happened. What nations are like the Protestant in popular prosperity? What Protestants can vie in this with the English-speaking race which has long been the best stronghold of the right of private judgment? At this moment there is probably more wealth, valuable intelligence, stamina, durable working power among the people of this country and Great Britain, than among many times their number of other men taken together in any part of the world. It is a proverb — this wonderful Anglo-Saxon energy. And the secret of it is the Christian doctrine of the right of private judgment. This is the subtle electricity which vitalizes all parts of our thrift and ascendency, this the strong heart which, from deep within, silently projects the generous blood to the extremities of the system.

The Christian System consists of two parts. One is matter of rigorous prescription, and remains the same for all countries and times. To this belong the doctrines of Scripture, its moral laws, its sacraments, and its ministry. It proposes that these shall be to us just what they were to the apostles, and to the last generation that shall walk the earth what they are to us. This is the constant part of that great formula which we call Christianity. But there is another part made up of variable quantities — quantities fairly belonging to the System and prescribed by it in a general way, but to which no particular values are assigned within the System itself. Some of its general maxims of duty have elements in them which vary with the circumstances and characters of men. It implicitly requires some machinery of evangelization, but gives no direction as to what; leaving the missionary, tract, Bible interests to be cared for by such organizations and methods as the state of the times may seem to make most efficient. Moreover, the System as a whole is not cast into one unalterable shape.

Now it appears as a busy biography, then as an authoritative lesson, next as a logic and philosophy, again as a parable or a proverb, still again as a many colored poem. It is like an angel who at one time stops at the tent of Abraham under the dusty form of a traveler, at another encounters Joshua as a war-captain with a drawn sword in his hand, at another as a man's hand writes startling laconics on the wall, at another shines and sings as a plumed glory in the air over Bethlehem. So flexible is Christianity — and, I may add, so powerful. Instead of being some stiff machine such as man makes, and to which yielding is the same thing as breaking, it is a solar system such as God makes, where, within the embrace of certain great constants, every orbit is continually changing in many ways, and yet all the changes are so summed and adjusted as in themselves to furnish the conditions of a stable and mighty equilibrium. On the tacit condition that the main simplicity of the System shall not be outraged, each man is left to consult his own sense of fitness and beauty as to its equipage, its dress, and largely all that is mere body in it; and thus, the esthetic partialities of each nature being enlisted on the side of the System, it can be embraced more readily, held more firmly, felt more deeply, and propagated more zealously. As to style of worship, each may adopt that which he finds most apt at impressing and spiritualizing his own mind. Whether he can achieve most devotion standing or kneeling;

with liturgy or without; before **surplice** and **bands or a black coat;** under Gothic, Grecian, or Saracenic angles and curves — let him judge and suit himself. He can be governed **by a** church democracy, or a ministerial conference, **or a** general assembly, or a bishop, as **he** shall **find most pleasant** and profitable to his peculiarity. I feel most at home in the modes to which I have been bred; but if any one has a different taste I will not forbid him to follow it, for Christianity has not forbidden him. He may fight the common enemy with such weapons as he can handle the **best.** If he is best master of **the** sword, let him use that; **if his skill** is in **archery,** let him fit sharp arrows to the string; **if his heavy** strength takes most naturally to the battle-axe, let him swing that like crusading Richard; if it suits him to go into battle on foot or on Bucephalus, with Saul's armor or David's sling, why, in the **name** of Christian liberty and the New Testament, let him go after his own fashion and be Godspeeded. **In** this way every man is turned **to the** best account. His idioms become so many special Christian powers. Instead of rousing into opposition the individualities of a large part of mankind **by one** sweeping act **of** uniformity, Christianity gives **them** full play and enlists them into **its** service. **A system** that so adapts itself to the various circumstances, natural traits, and lawful moods of men, never becomes superannuated, has the freedom of all countries as well **as ages,** lays hold of society at all points, and levies support from a wide range of forces.

Another power of Christianity is its preaching ministry. The Pagan priesthood has always been chiefly sacrificial and ritualistic. Islam has no clerical order: the Imaum not being appointed by the Koran, nor devoting himself to religious teaching as a business. But Christianity has set apart an order of men to the sole work of expounding, enforcing, and propagating religion, chiefly in the way of public vocal argument and appeal—'men who shall not be novices, but apt to teach, manifesting the word through preaching, giving themselves wholly to it, that their profiting may appear to all.' I say *sole work;* for the administration of the sacraments which falls to Christian ministers occupies so little time that it may be overlooked in this connection. Accordingly, all Protestant countries are so many sermon-making and sermon-hearing countries. Of a Sunday there are more popular religious discourses pronounced in them, many times over, than in all the world besides, through all the year. And they come, too, chiefly from trained men, to whom this form of teaching is almost their sole business. All proceeds on the principle that it pleases God by the " foolishness of preaching " both to save them that believe, and to make believers.

A powerful peculiarity of Christianity! It secures to it the best possible defenders and propagators. It secures to believers regular, frequent, and ablest instruction and prompting in Christian principles. And it carries forward this instructing and prompting, this defense and propagation, under the most engaging and efficient forms; mainly by that public address which so economizes the time and labor both of audience and speaker — which so rouses his own powers, moves the popular sympathies, and meets the popular taste — mainly by this, supplemented by such occasional private dealing with individuals as may be required to meet important specialties in their condition.

Let me bring into a single view three other powerful features of the Christian Religion which well deserve a fuller consideration. These are its holy precepts, easy test, and mighty sanctions. I have already dwelt on the fact that Christ comes to us with a practical code of the greatest purity, known to all tolerable consciences to be such. Equally plain is it that if this code were universally acted on, we should have universal paradise. Next, each unbeliever is told that if he will in good faith set himself to acting on the code, he "shall know of the doctrine," — certainly a very fair offer; winning in its first aspect, full of an air of candor and ingenuous self-confidence; making faith easy, if faith is justified; giving a crucial test of the Bible quite independent of scholarly accomplishment and leisure, and indeed of everything save an honest wish to know the truth. And then, to rouse him to this wish, he is pressed with motives so vast that no greater can be imagined. Lo Heaven, if you win a practical faith — otherwise, Hell! After faith has been won, the man continues to be plied from that better fulcrum, as long as he lives, with the mightiest leverage of gratitude, hope, and fear. Shall any tell us that a system whose practical side so appeals to universal conscience, whose intellectual side so approaches the masses of society with most easy and decisive test of itself adapted to their laborious and unscholarly state, and which forever follows up all with infinite motives, does not possess sources of power which, were there no other, would make it a world-mover!

But, as we have seen, there are many others. The Biblical Religion is strong in its unity, strong in its simplicity, strong in its splendid literature, strong in its mingled absolutism and liberty, strong in its great stores of confessed truth, strong in the sublimity of its proposed object and means, strong in the accord of its facts and doctrines with Nature and experience, strong in its adaptation to the wants of mankind, strong in its superiority to all other religions, strong in its terrible alternative of no-religion, strong in its prophecies and miracles and other profuse evidences. Putting together these strong features, what a stalwart Whole do they seem to make? Especially in the light of its actual history — showing what great literary attacks it has borne up against, what bloody persecutions it has outlived, what potent enemies it has overthrown, what huge burdens it has lifted from society, what wonderful individual, local, and national transformations it has wrought, what a shining literature it has created, what a crowd of languages it has taught to speak its Bible all over the world, what an array of schools, and colleges, and churches, and philanthropic institutions it has founded, what delightful art and useful science it has nurtured, what vast sums it is annually expending in the various Christian enterprises, what warm love it has won, what high heroism it has inspired, what rich consolations and joys it has given, what a sovereign hold it has had on the judgments and hearts of multitudes of the earth's wisest and best, what saintly living and triumphal dying it has secured among the worst and feeblest of men. Even the prodigious vitality and force of mediæval errors grafted on it show the rich strength of the stock from which they rob a support. Even the noisy and furious assaults made on it tell of its massive strength — as the noise and spume of the sea bespeak the rocky nature of the coast on which it is dashing.

And yet, great as must be the power of a system to which such facts and features belong, I must regard them merely as tokens of a power far greater than is fairly expressed in themselves. To me Christianity includes the whole personal strength of Deity. It is inhabited of the Holy Ghost. It is as mighty as God Himself. And, in virtue of this personal almightiness working in the inherent fitnesses of the System, it will at last carry everything before it and renew the earth into a heaven. So claims the System itself. Who is able to refute this claim? Where are the facts against it? It is, surely, nothing against it that the Christian Forces are at present more or less latent; are capable of being successfully resisted at particular points; appear at times to advance but slowly toward their goal. Is not yonder oak on the whole steadily building itself up, year by year, into the indisputable monarch of the forest — though from time to time it loses many a leaf, and is even stripped into seeming lifelessness by winds and winters? Is not yonder ocean a great power, with a great voice and resistless wave at command; and is it not gradually wearing away the hardest rocks, and even gaining from century to century on the whole continent which it besets — though it sometimes shows neither ripple nor murmur, and always shows a daily ebb? Is not the wind a great power; able on occasion to travel at whirlwind-pace, level dwellings and forests, sweep before it the white fleets of the nations like so many snow-flakes, and insensibly wear down the face of the whole world — though it often breathes gently as a zephyr, or breathes not at all, and during short periods works no sensible effects? Is not the Earth itself, considered as a unit, a still greater power; what with its cogent attractions, its profound caldron preparing volcanoes and earthquakes, its endless outpour of chemical and mechanical energies in aid of vegetable and animal life, its swift double-rush through space — though its motions and attractions are always silent as death, and though it is only now and then that the glowing giants within thunder away at the gates of the senses? Is not Light a great power; moving at such bewildering rate, painting all Nature so exquisitely, inspiring all vegetable and animal life, and forever creating anew on innumerable retinas all the forms and aspects of the material universe — though there are such things as shadows and even nights, and though one may easily darken his eye and room and places without number where light would be a blessing? Is not this general Gravity, of which we hear so much, a great power; this gravity that reaches never so far, that acts universally, that binds its every material thing helplessly to the earth, that swings round the planets and suns and even firmaments on their mighty ways with such supreme ease — though you and I successfully counteract it at particular points whenever we lift a weight, or take a walk, or cast upward a stone? Nay, have I not heard of one endlessly convertible natural power, just now fashionable among unbelievers, which is slowly reducing yonder vague Fire-Mist into an orderly firmament, with its unspeakable momenta of revolving orbs and wide paradises of vegetable, animal, and even spiritual life? What a dynamic will be that ripened firmament with its schemed millions of rushing solar systems! And yet, according to unbelief, all that power really belongs to the tenuous, eddying nebula of to-day — a power largely latent, capable of being successfully resisted at certain points and in certain measures of development (witness our own successful counteractions of heat and gravity), and going forward to its maturest and most wonderful effects on a path of wonderful length. Why may not Christianity be another such power? Why may it not go on working according to its own stately law until it has built up around itself "the New Heavens and New Earth in which shall dwell righteousness?" Why not? No science is against it. Facts are for it. I seem, every now and then, to catch glimpses in the Christian conversions and revivals of a power that is equal to anything — power that amazes and awes me. There are tremblings that predict the earthquake. There are subtle stirrings of the air that show the coming cyclone. And what if, at times, the Christian chariot seems to drive heavily? Is it not moving against the immense depravity of a world of free moral agents whose freedom must not be ruthlessly trampled upon? And may not the clock on the wall of Heaven, by whose golden circle that chariot is driven, be one that measures off very different years from those that figure in our earthly chronologies? Have I not heard that "with the Lord a thousand years are as one day"?

Sextus Calpurnius, proconsular legate for Aquitaine, has just returned from his travels over the

Roman World. What has he seen? Some things, certainly, which he could have wished not to see — many breaches of the law among subjects and rulers, especially in outskirting countries: much misconduct among the best citizens, tending sadly to the disadvantage of the state: everywhere parties, loud-voiced and fiercely gesticulating parties; Grecists disputing with Latinists, the friends of one provincial policy protesting against the friends of another, the partisans of one general warmly accusing the partisans of another, one scheme of military tactics struggling with hard words against another scheme. He has even encountered on the borders of the Hercynian forest some Roman cohorts in full retreat from winter and savages: nay, under his own eyes, not longer ago than the ides of May, one whole legion was fairly swallowed up in Africa through heat, battle, and mismanagement. But what of that? Has he not also seen the eagle of the empire stretching wings from Britain to Mt. Atlas, and from Euphrates to the Pillars of Hercules? Has he not found this wide region profusely sprinkled with public works — highways, bridges, aqueducts, arches, palaces, Colisea — massive, Roman-built? Has he not found the name of Roman citizen better protection to him than spear and shield among twenty different languages? Has he not met the legions in all climates steadily conquering hunger and thirst; cold and heat; man, Nature, and themselves? Has he not seen great commanders faint before the like children, great national coalitions briefly trampled out, some great Carthage sending up from endless rubbish a smoking testimonial to a still greater foe? Has he not seen haughty kings uncovering before the majesty of the Roman People, empires holding place proudly as Roman allies and wards, and the whole Roman World the abode of order and thrift beyond all other lands? At last, coming to The City, Mistress and Mother, has he not stood by the tomb of the Scipios and there studied the victory, the glory, the empire in its sources? Lo, the soundness of her jurisprudence; lo, the patriotism of her citizens; lo, the passion for glory among all her classes; lo, the substantial rewards she gives to feats of public service; lo, the training of her great families to statesmanship and command; lo, her liberty and flexibility as citizens, her discipline and centralization as soldiers! Yes, Rome *is* mighty. Having felt her pulse both at the extremities and at the central heart, in the fresh present and in wrinkled antiquity; having handled her thews and sinews through parallels and centuries — yes, this is no pretender triumphing by grace of almighty chance, but a true giant full of life and brawn, including in herself a full philosophy of her success. So he comes exultingly to his province again. He, too, is a Roman. He is an element, a representative, and a guardian, of this great Political Force. New spirit awakes within him in view of the dignity of his position and of the power which supports him. His arm is strung anew for frontier strifes and upholding of the Roman Majesty. He feels strong with its strength, royal with its sovereignty, rich with its broad domains, illustrious with its achievements, almost immortal with the life of its Eternal City.

What hinders me from feeling after that old Roman manner? I, too, from my frontier have gone forth to a survey — not for my sake, but for yours. I have not found all I could wish. On the contrary I have found it still a day of battle and process; and that Christianity, like many great Natural Powers, has made a covenant with time. But I have also found myself, beyond a doubt, part and parcel of a very strong system. I see that in my place, however obscure, I am representing, not some fraction trembling on the verge of nihility, but a great muscular Integer; and that even more than imperial Rome at her strongest marches with the standard of my honorable legation. Nay, I see that there is nothing to show, neither in its nature nor working, that this Strong Power which I am defending, and which is defending me, is not as strong as Almighty God — nothing to show that a Force strictly unlimited, if dealing with such a being as man and having unlimited duration to work in, would have a different history from Christianity itself. And — what is a great deal better, and far more than Roman was ever permitted to find — I find that my Rome is as true as she is strong. Her claim to a Divine founding is just. Her Romulus is really God. Her Numas are really inspired. Her Delphos and Dodonas really give Divine answers. Her Sibylline Books, and her Law of the Tables really come from above. From the seven hills of her strength, she calls the nations to allegiance with a voice potential with the double royalty of conscious Divine right and conscious Divine prowess.

All this I have found. Shall not my heart be glad at such findings? Shall it not sound as with the voice of exulting psalms — as sounds some cathedral when the jubilee of a nation rises within it? I have not lost my youth. I am not throwing my manhood away. I have given myself to the best, and what shall prove the most victorious, of Causes. It is impossible that such a wise Power and powerful Wisdom — with a voice that almost wins battles of itself, and a sword that throbs towards conquest with the pulse of a Creator — should have but a secondary success. She has succeeded already. She will go on succeeding. She will add province after province, kingdom after kingdom, to her Eternal City. At last she will fill the earth with her superb monuments and superber Self. And, from age to age, transfigured men shall stand on her lofty battlements and look away through the glow of a Golden Age to all the ends of the earth, without being able to see the least occasion for such faithward looking words as I have now finished addressing to you.

PATER MUNDI,

OR,

MODERN SCIENCE TESTIFYING

TO THE

HEAVENLY FATHER.

BY THE AUTHOR OF "ECCE CŒLUM."

The First Series is now ready. Tinted paper. 300 pp. 12mo. Price, $1.50. Sent post-paid on receipt of the price, by

NOYES, HOLMES, & COMPANY,

117 Washington Street, Boston.

The publishers of *Ecce Cœlum* now solicit **the attention of** scholars **and of** the public at large, **to a still more** important work by the same author. P*ater Mundi* is believed to meet a great need of the times. Men **are busy, as never** before, at taking **away** the ancient Jehovah **in the name of** *Science.* In books, in popular lectures, in journals having wide circulation and religious pretensions, and even in colleges whose founders hoped and demanded better things from **them, the** public is being industriously persuaded that it **is** *scientific* as well as natural to be without God **in the** world. **Let all** who would see for themselves how little ground exists for **such claims, read** *Pater Mundi ;* and let all who wish well **to the popular faith, to** our holy religion, and to the safety of society, promote its circulation to the utmost. *It is a book for the* times. Though in the form of college lectures, and claiming scientific thoroughness, it is believed to be easy and luminous reading for **all** classes.

EXTRACTS FROM NOTICES.

From the Rev. W. A. Stearns, D.D., L.L.D., President of Amherst College

I have heard them with the deepest interest. They are so clear, so logical, so rich in illustration, so unexceptionable and beautiful in style, and so conclusive in the argument attempted, that I have profoundly admired them. Those gentlemen who heard them when delivered here, would, I am sure, from the comments which they made upon them, agree with me entirely in the judgment I have expressed. May the Great Being whose existence these lectures so nobly defend from the attacks of the foolish, though calling themselves scientists and philosophers, spare the life of the author and enable him to complete the full course of thinking on which he has so triumphantly entered and advanced.

From Rev. Prof. C. S. Lyman, of Yale College.

All whom I have heard speak of these lectures have expressed for them the highest admiration. In thought and diction they are worthy of Chalmers.

From Prof. Julius H. Seelye, Professor of Mental and Moral Philosophy in Amherst College.

It is with great delight that I have received the new book. I like, especially, its whole attitude respecting the question discussed; that it is so full of faith and so uncompromising. Atheism is as unworthy the intellect, as it is repugnant to the heart; and I am tired of tame apologies from timid believers in a God. I like to see a book that has something of a clarion ring about it, and is not afraid to defy denial, when it speaks of the being and the glory of the Heavenly Father.

I believe that Pater Mundi will do great good, and I thank the Lord for permitting the author to prepare and publish it.

From Rev. A. P. Peabody, D.D. L.L.D, Preacher to Harvard University, and Plummer Professor of Christian Morals.

I thank the author with all my heart for Pater Mundi. It is the most efficient work of its class which the present generation has produced; and as the now existing scepticism is deeper, more [pseudo] scientific, more pretentious, than that of any preceding age; the book which, like Pater Mundi, is adapted to our times, must need be both broader and more profound than previous needs have elicited. Its treatment of the great theme is at once thoroughly philosophical and popular, both in style and in adaptation to the capacity of all readers of average intelligence. It was an unspeakable privilege to the students of Amherst College, to have heard the lectures; I trust that the same privilege will be extended through the press to thousands of our young men. While I find no fault nor deficiency in the treatment of any branch of the argument, I am especially impressed by the Seventh Lecture, as the clearest, strongest, and most eloquent statement of the need of God, and of the demonstration thence resulting of His existence, in the plenitude of His attributes, that has come within the range of my reading.

From Rev. Albert Barnes,

I was so profoundly impressed, or, if I may say so, *oppressed* and overwhelmed with the sublimity and grandeur of the truths presented in Ecce Cœlum, and with the manner in which the author presented these great truths, that I am glad he has followed with another volume on the same general subject. I anticipate in the perusal of it great pleasure and profit. I think the author is doing great service to the cause of truth and I hope that God will spare him to complete his work.

So far as I am able to judge, the greatest enemy which Christianity has to encounter now, is found in the oppositions of science, so-called. In fact, so far as I understand them, the aim and tendency of much of this science, are to blank Atheism; and I think a man can do no better service in this age, than to meet and counteract this tendency. I rejoice that God raises up men who are qualified to do it. I believe that the author of Ecce Cœlum is such a man. He has a noble work before him, and I hope he will be enabled to do it.

From the Independent.

We had not read *Ecce Cœlum*, and imagined that the encomiums which we had seen pronounced upon it must be too high wrought for sober truth. But now that we have read *Pater Mundi*, by the same author, we are ready to believe every word of praise to have been within bounds. The present volume is no dry, didactic treatise. It is warm, alive, eloquent. The author proves himself, in his freshness of thought and in the eloquence of his argument, inferior to no writer of the day. We find no slips in science, nor in his multiplied illustrations from ancient and modern literature. And we do find a grandeur of conception and a striking originality of conception, so audacious that scarcely any other writer we know of would have ventured upon it. We see no reason why our author's writings should not become classics in the language. Nothing can be more invigorating to the thoughtful reader.

From the Congregationalist.

We have read it with keen enjoyment, and are disposed to regard it as the most substantial and serviceable contribution to the natural theology of this generation, as it is the freshest and most popular. No better book none more entertaining, can be placed in the hands of inquisitive readers, especially bright minded young men and women. The author lays out his work with a singularly clear perception of the crepuscular skepticism which needs to be dissipated; and enters upon it with manly and generous **fairness of statement, vigor** of argument, and amplitude of apposite and convincing illustration. His style is in the main so admirable, that it may seem ungenerous to take exceptions. Probably the excess of ornamentation, the overfulness of illustration, the easy affluence of the most highly poetic diction, and the general gorgeousness of rhetoric will secure a hearing for the truth by persons whom it is desirable to influence, who might not be attracted by an ordinary book.

From the Hours at Home.

The decidedly oratorical style will **serve to** make the essays, incisive — eloquent, and eminently philosophical **as** we acknowledge them to be — all the more widely popular and useful.

From the Religious Herald.

Cogent argument is so lighted up with brilliant illustration, as to make **interesting** the profoundest thoughts.

From the Christian Union. Rev. H. W. Beecher.

The author, who, in *Ecce Cœlum*, established **a reputation** for that rare combination of excellencies — fervid **rhetoric, scientific accuracy,** and common sense — has produced another book **designed to defend and illustrate** the doctrine of Theism. It is like breathing **mountain air to feel this** man's earnestness; **it is a true mental tonic.** One sees instantly that he is able-souled, **that he can push and** climb without getting **short of** breath; and it is **almost a foregone** conclusion, after reading the first chapter, that one must either **stride with** him to *his* high conclusion, or part company before starting. **This** unequivocal earnestness and power display themselves at the outset; great heart is warmed up to begin with; **so** that one is almost inclined to distrust a leader who has so much the air **of a partisan.** The face **set** like a flint does not wait to be struck to emit **its** sparks, but glows **with** a fiery zeal which inflames everything it looks upon. Yet, no **candid reader will say** that Dr. Burr is dogmatic; he only **plies error with weapons for which** infidelity has claimed a patent **right.** No one who reads this first volume, will wish that the author had **written less or otherwise than he has.**

From the Advance.

The previous work **entitled** *Ecce Cœlum*, received the highest commendation from **the most competent judges.** The present volume will still further augment the reputation of the author as a **thinker** and writer. He puts the Atheistic hypothesis to severe and annihilating tests; fully meeting its objections and cavils. **The** arguments of this work are not only **cogent,** but are expressed in a lucid, glowing, and eloquent style; and the **book entitles the writer to** a position among our best religious authors.

From Rev. Edwin Hall, D.D., Professor in Auburn Theological Seminary

I have read the work with constantly increasing satisfaction and delight. It is entirely worthy of the author of *Ecce Cœlum* and of its subject. So far as my reading extends—and I have long endeavored to read in that department whatever I could lay my hands on that promised to give me light—I regard it as the most original and valuable contribution to the subject, which the age has produced. I shall wait with longing for the second volume. In the meantime, I hope the work may have a circulation as extensive as its worth deserves. If it were left for me to fix that desert, there should not be a library or a family in the land without it.

From the Watchman and Reflector.

The thousands of readers of "Ecce Cœlum" have not got fairly over the feeling of astonishment and admiration which the perusal of that remarkable book brought to them, before another of equal merit from the same author is announced. "Pater Mundi," we are confident, will lessen nothing of the high character which Dr. Burr has won as an acute and accurate thinker, an accomplished scholar, a brilliant rhetorician, and a humble, childlike believer in God and His revelation. The purpose of the author is to defend and illustrate Theism and Christianity from the side of Modern Science. There is a wonderful candor in the entire process of argumentation. Nothing is assumed beyond what the eyes of man behold and his reason assents to. The conclusion, without being asserted, is irresistibly forced into one's own view, and wins acceptance from the thoughtful, reasonable soul. The eloquence of some of these passages respecting the fatherhood of God is overwhelming in effect. We earnestly commend the book to the careful study of our so-called scientific men who are trying hard to rule a personal God out of the universe. We wish, too, that every young man in the nation would read these pages. We are sure that nothing more fascinating in interest and really healthful and elevating in influence can be found among all the books of the day. The book is handsomely printed by Nichols & Noyes of this city.

From the Sunday School Times.

This volume is an eloquent and unanswerable protest against modern atheism in all its forms. "Modern science testifying to the Heavenly Father," is the author's secondary title, and it describes accurately the course and object of his argument. His methods of presenting the subject, however, are entirely original, and are wonderfully effective. The work is particularly opportune. There are in all our congregations thoughtful, cultivated, quiet men, whose faith has been shaken by the bold assumptions of infidel scientists. Dr. Burr's book is just suited to restore such persons to their equilibrium. It is written in a most attractive style and shows a masculine vigor of thought that cannot fail to command respect.

From the Theological Eclectic. Professors Day, Schaff, etc.

We have already spoken of the able work entitled Ecce Cœlum, in terms of high commendation. The present work by the same author exhibits the same power of comprehensive grouping and vivid presentation, and abounds in great thoughts freshly put.

From Rev. Mark Hopkins, D.D., L.L.D., President of Williams College.

I am greatly indebted to the author of Pater Mundi. It is a fresh and powerful work. If any commendation from me will aid its circulation, it is freely given.

From C. H. Balsbaugh, Pa.

Certainly this is a book to stop the mouth of skeptics. It seems to me that never was atheism in its protean forms more squarely met on its own ground, and never more clearly discomfited with its own weapons. No two links of its argument are left together. The author has triumphantly vindicated the title of his book. Its matter and style appeal to both our innate susceptibility to truth, and our sense of the beautiful. In my view, never did logic and poetry more heartily embrace each other; never did beauty smile more divinely on the face of the sternest facts.

From the New York Evening Post.

The clear and beautiful logic, and the crystal style of Ecce Cœlum, fascinated religious minds everywhere in this country. This book is written by the same perspicuous pen. That it is in the form of lectures, rather improves it than otherwise. The special aim of the author is to wrest from the wild materials of this day the powerful sceptre of science, which they have seemed to wield. All the teachings of science and nature point to the "Father of the World." This book is one calculated to strengthen the faith of professors of religion, and to lead captive young minds straying into error. We ought to mention in closing, the beautiful typography of the book. Published by Nichols & Noyes.

From the Evening Wisconsin, Milwaukee.

The style is clear, and always strong and forcible in an unusual degree while many passages rise to great beauty and eloquence. Seldom have we read anything upon the subject of Christian evidence that was so entertaining, so instructive, and so satisfactory as this book. It is the offspring, of a vigorous intellect, and it is a most valuable addition to religious culture.

From the Christian Recorder, Philadelphia.

So charmed are we with this magnificent production of Dr. Burr's, that really we scarce know where to begin its praise. Its excellence is uniform.

Lecture first and lecture eighth equally demand **admiration. So every part** of each lecture. The chain of gold is not only **complete, but every link is** complete. The Colonnade is not only symmetrical, but its **minute carvings** are perfect. To quote from it to our own satisfaction, **would be to** quote the whole book, but we remember that Messrs. Nichols & **Noyes, the** publishers, have a copyright.

How majestically does the author **of Ecce Cœlum send forth his** thoughts into the world! In majesty do **they stride forth either to conquer, to convince, or to** woo. Now as a mailed warrior are they seen, **fully panoplied from head to foot, and crushing by the strength of his arguments every foe—crushing every atheistic shield, and helmet, and breastplate.** On almost every page of Pater **Mundi**, these all-crushing arguments **are** to be met—on almost **every** page **we see** victims lying mangled and bleeding.

We do not know that the author **of Pater Mundi lays claim to the poetic gift;** and yet has he given us a sublime Didactic Poem. **Not in verse, is it given;** it is neither Dactylic, **Anapæstic, Iambic, nor Trochaic.** But **poetic** imagination shines on every page. **Untrammeled by rule,** and enjoying a freedom that the utmost poetic license could **not allow,** the author has given us a poem infinitely sublimer **than could possibly** have been done in **any** other form. Would that **we could give our readers** the concluding pages of Lecture **VII. Such poetic thought! Such** beauty of expression! Such smoothness! **Such harmony! Words answer to words, and sentence** to sentence, with such sweetness **that one** glides along **to** the conclusion, as smoothly as a New England **sleigh, and** as merrily as its ringing bells.

From the Norwich Bulletin.

It will be a great advantage to the reader of this work **to have** made the acquaintance of Dr. Burr's previous **volume,** "Ecce Cœlum," as thus many of the references in "Pater Mundi" **will be the more** intelligible and vivid. The quality of the new work **is in all** respects admirable. Dr. Burr has a wonderful enthusiasm, always fresh and intense. He is full of his subject. He has **the faculty** of so treating profound and sublime themes, as to bring them **easily to the** comprehension **of all. He has a** fervid style, whose richness **seems** inexhaustible. **He has** great fertility in argument, and presents his suggestions with **rare** simplicity and force. The volume will go far to combat **the sophistries of** Atheism, **both in** uncultured minds and **in** those of strong **logical powers.** We cannot **too** highly commend it, and we predict that it **will find a place in every well** stocked religious library.

From the Standard, Chicago, Ill.

If any one should **infer from the title of this book that it is a heavy and** prosy dissertation, he would be astonished on looking over its pages

Nothing could be further from the truth. The author is **an** enthusiast, one of **those** who have not "discovered that one must be indifferent in order to be fair." The book **is** fresh, earnest, and eloquent, and we felt its strong spell before reading a dozen pages. The statement of arguments is admirably clear, the development **of** them is natural and impressive, and there is displayed a wonderful **power** in massing facts so as to give their full and combined effect.

From the *Chicago Tribune.*

This work in some respects is very remarkable. **It is not** only compact in argument, and forcible and clear in statement, but **it** is also absolutely brilliant and sparkling in manner, and rich and copious in illustration. Judging only from the one volume before us, **we** should pronounce it as one of the most remarkable and fascinating books of the **day.**

From the *Orleans Republican, Albion, N. Y.*

The author's premises are bold, and his line of argument clear, forcible **and** persuasive; shirking nothing, anticipating, and answering objections with equal fairness. The work is calm, liberal, and large thoughted; **full of** admirable logic, and profound reasoning; **and** the last three **lectures,** especially, are grand with beautiful and terrible **imagery, exquisite** poetry, and striking allusions to those mysterious **facts and forces of** nature which startle and awe believer and unbeliever **alike; and his** conclusion is singularly suggestive and powerful.

From *Rev. Austin Phelps, D.D., Professor in Andover Theological Seminary.*

I wish to thank the author for "Pater Mundi." Not that it needs any commendation from me: but I cannot **but** be grateful to any man who helps me to a new depth or vividness of conception of God**; and** this you have done by your book. I am specially impressed **by** the power with which it draws the great alternative, — a God benevolent, or a God **malignant.** The *reductio ad absurdum* is fearfully overwhelming; **and the recoil** with which one springs **back from** it gives **one a** lodgment **and a resting-place in** the Infinite **Love which no gentler discipline could secure so well.** This *vigor* of religious sensibility in your works charms **me. We need it** greatly in our Christian literature, to supplement alike the wiry intellect of which we have enough, and the emotive softness of which, perhaps, we have a little more.

From the *American Baptist.*

The author has **a** strong and vigorous style, and a power of grasping and grouping great truths, which make all that he utters luminous and convincing. **Though** prepared specially for educated **men, they are adapted to all readers,** have no abstruseness of diction, **no intricate, far-fetched or dubious arguments.** The author **will** impart no small measure of the **indignation he feels** towards atheism, concealing itself under the name of **science,** to those who read his book, and **we** trust it may have a very **wide circulation.**

From The New Englander.

The author of Ecce Cœlum could not well be expected to write a dull book on any subject, much less one in which God and nature were the chief topic. But whether he would be able to clothe a skeleton of a two-volume argument for Theism—often so dry and grim in other hands—with the flesh and muscle, the life and beauty, that charm us in Parish Astronomy, could only be shown conclusively by the production of a work like that before us. Pater Mundi, will, by the glow and magnetism of its rhetoric, and the enthusiastic earnestness of its tone, as well as the strength of its argument, be sure to command everywhere, appreciative and admiring readers, and prove, we trust, of special value to those who are inclined to regard science as hostile to religion. Its logic is vitalized and made effective by the force and richness of the illustrations drawn from the various fields of science. It is these all glowing often with poetic fervor, that rivet the attention at once, and carry the reader on insensibly from topic to topic. In some of the lectures, indeed, the argument assumes the elevation and almost the form of a grand poem. The sixth, for example, like a sublime ode, returns, strophe by strophe, with each point made in the argument, to the same exultant chorus, which becomes at once a *quod erat demonstrandum* to the understanding, and an inspiration of faith to the heart.

The second volume promises to be even more attractive than the first; for it is to be still more replete with the marvels and sublimities of the sciences as illustrative of the argument. It is too much forgotten by many that God may be studied in flower and forest, in storm and star, and in the soul of man, as well as in Moses and the prophets. The glowing pages of "Pater Mundi," teach impressively that the God of Revelation is the God of Nature as well.

From the Methodist.

The many gratified readers of "Ecce Cœlum," will welcome this new and important work of Dr. Burr. It is a book for the times. Natural Theology can no longer retain its old form: the progress, not only of Science but of speculative thought, demands a thorough revision, "Pater Mundi" meets this demand with masterly ability.

From the American Presbyterian Review.

A new work by the author of "Ecce Cœlum" is sure to attract unusual attention; nor will expectation be disappointed. Dr. Burr is an original and independent thinker, and he writes in a style of singular freshness and rhetorical beauty. His book is timely. Though popular in its address, it sacrifices nothing to effect, and is wholly free from that superficiality which is usually found in the attempt to reduce the conclusions of science to the level of a popular audience. It discusses with masterly ability the testimonies of Modern Science to the being of a God, and defends Theism from the attacks of skeptical science in a bold and critical spirit worthy of all praise. It is as profoundly religious as it is thoroughly **scientific.** While it freely accepts the results of the freest investigations, it ably argues that there is nothing in one of **these** to shake the christian's faith, but much to confirm it. The work cannot fail to have an important influence on Natural Theology—bringing it into harmony with the progress of **Science and speculative philosophy, and** arming it with a new power **of demonstration.**

From the Princeton Review.

Dr. Burr, known to us in his youth as a modest and studious lad, and since, as the faithful and unpretending pastor of a rural congregation, has sudden'y burst on our vision as an author of the first mark in the highest re'.lms of thought, and as a leading defender of precious truth against the assaults of scientific pretenders and pretentious sciolists. He calls to mind the days when the great New England divines, the Edwardses, Bellamy, **Backus,** Smalley, Emmons, were pastors of agricultural congregations.

The universal approbation of Pater Mundi and the previous volume, by **the** press **and by** christian thinkers of **the** highest reputation, we find borne out by actual **inspection.** Real science is proved **to** be the handmaid of true religion, in a series of discussions **which evince a** masterly comprehension of the issues involved—**a thorough acquaintance** with modern science and its relations **to religion—the whole** in a style clear and simple, vivid and graphic. We think the quiet of a country charge more propitious to thorough study and deep thinking, than the din **and** whirl of metropolitan excitements.

From Prof. **D. C.** *Gilman, Yale College.*

I feel moved to express my hearty appreciation of the service the author of " **Pater Mundi** " is rendering to the world by the publication of these **earnest, brilliant** and impressive discourses.

From Hon. Henry L. Dawes, M. C.

The pleasure with which I read aloud to my family " **Ecce Cœlum"** has **prepared me for an** increased delight and profit in reading " Pater Mundi." **I am very proud of the author,** and rejoice in his growing fame.

From **Our** *Monthly, Cincinnati,* **Ohio.**

We are very glad to welcome and commend this book. **The author does,** with singular ability, what he proposes **to do.** His trumpet utters no uncertain sound. There **is** no **danger of any one** mistaking his meaning. **We** think **it** high time the arrogant assumptions and speculations of some **scientific me**n in the interest of infidelity and atheism were exposed, and **the harmony** of all true science **and** revelation vindicated, made more apparent, **and presented in** some popular form. **This** Dr. Burr is doing, and **the first installment of** his work we **have in** this series **of lectures.** That **they will be found** interesting and convincing we **need not say to** those **who have read '** Ecce Cœlum."

AD FIDEM.

A NEW BOOK,

BY THE AUTHOR OF "ECCE CŒLUM."

The publishers have the pleasure to announce a new and important work, by the distinguished author above named, **which will command attention** from all classes, entitled

AD FIDEM;

OR, PARISH EVIDENCES,

As spoken to the People from **Week to Week by One who Believes.**

The new work proposes to do for **the** Evidences **of the** Christian Religion what "Ecce Cœlum" aims to do for Astronomy. It proposes **to** bring these Evidences, without any sacrifice of scholarly accuracy, luminously and effectively within the reach of ordinary minds. It will show the PEOPLE *how to believe.*

To indicate **the general** scope of the work, a brief synopsis **of the Contents** is given below: —

- I. VARIOUS OPINIONS.
- II. GENERAL ASSENT TO FUNDAMENTALS.
- III. A SAD EXCEPTION.
- IV. A GREAT OFFER.
- V. I WILL ACCEPT.
- VI. THE HONEST PURPOSE.
- VII. USING PRESENT LIGHT.
- VIII. PATIENTLY SEEKING LIGHT, — UPWARD AND AROUND.
- IX. PRESUMPTIONS.
- X. THREE PROPHECIES.
- XI. THREE MARKS OF A FALSE CHRIST.
- XII. AN INCREDIBLE IMPOSTURE.
- XIII. SIGNS AND WONDERS.
- XIV. FROM BEHIND THE CURTAIN.
- XV. NEARING THE CURTAIN.
- XVI. RISING OF THE CURTAIN.
- XVII. PROOF BY EXPERIENCE OF THE HOLY GHOST.
- XVIII. DYNAMICS OF THE RELIGION.
- XIX. WHAT WILL HE DO WITH IT.

Published in **handsome** style, uniform with "Ecce Cœlum" and "Pater Mundi." 300 pp., 12mo. Price, $1.50. (*Ready October 1st.*)

NOYES, HOLMES, & COMPANY,
Publishers, Boston.

www.ingramcontent.com/pod-product-compliance
Lightning Source LLC
Chambersburg PA
CBHW030404230426
43664CB00007BB/735